BLACKS, COLOUREDS AND NATIONAL IDENTITY IN NINETEENTH-CENTURY LATIN AMERICA

Nineteenth-Century Latin America Series
General Editor Eduardo Posada-Carbó

The Institute's Nineteenth-Century Latin America Series results from the annual workshop on nineteenth-century Latin American history held at the Institute, and is aimed at encouraging the study of various aspects of what has largely been a neglected period in the modern historiography of the region.

Publications in the Series

1. *Wars, Parties and Nationalism: Essays on the Politics and Society of Nineteenth-Century Latin America*
Eduardo Posada-Carbó (ed.) – 1995

2. *In Search of a New Order: Essays on the Politics and Society of Nineteenth-Century Latin America*
Eduardo Posada-Carbó (ed.) – 1998

3. *Independence and Revolution in Spanish America: Perspectives and Problems*
Anthony McFarlane and Eduardo Posada-Carbó (eds.) – 1999

4. *Judicial Institutions in Nineteenth-Century Latin America*
Eduardo Zimmermann (ed.) – 1999

5. *The Politics of Religion in an Age of Revival*
Austen Ivereigh (ed.) – 2000

6. *Rumours of Wars: Civil Conflict in Nineteenth-Century Latin America*
Rebecca Earle (ed.) – 2000

7. *The European Revolutions of 1848 and the Americas*
Guy Thomson (ed.) – 2000

8. *The Political Power of the Word: Press and Oratory in Nineteeth Century Latin America*
Iván Jaksić (ed.) – 2002

Institute of Latin American Studies
School of Advanced Study
University of London

Blacks, Coloureds and National Identity in Nineteenth-Century Latin America

Edited by
Nancy Priscilla Naro

Institute of Latin American Studies
31 Tavistock Square, London WC1H 9HA
http://www.sas.ac.uk/ilas/publicat.htm

Institute of Latin American Studies
School of Advanced Study
University of London

British Library Cataloguing-in-Publication Data
A catalogue record for this book is available
from the British Library

ISBN   1 900039 47 8

Institute of Latin American Studies
University of London, 2003

CONTENTS

Introduction   *Nancy Priscilla Naro*   1

CHAPTER 1   **National Identity and the Idea of Value in the Dominican Republic**
Lauren Derby   5

CHAPTER 2   **The Influence of the Haitian Revolution on Blacks in Latin America and the Caribbean**
David Geggus   38

CHAPTER 3   **Entre pueblo y plebe: patriotas, pardos, africanos en Argentina (1790–1852)**
Carmen Bernand   60

CHAPTER 4   **Blacks and the Forging of National Identity in the Caribbean, 1840–1900**
Franklin Knight   81

CHAPTER 5   **Race, Gender and National Identity in Nineteenth Century Cuba. Mariana Grajales and the Revolutionary Free Browns of Cuba**
Jean Stubbs   95

CHAPTER 6   **Catalysts in the Crucible: Kidnapped Caribbeans, Free Black British Subjects and Migrant British Machinists in the Failed Cuba Revolution of 1843**
Jonathan Curry-Machado   123

CHAPTER 7   **Antislavery and Abolitionism: Thinkers and Doers in Imperial Brazil**
Nancy Priscilla Naro   143

Notes on Contributors

Carmen Bernand is an anthropologist with field research in the Andes (Peru, Ecuador) and is also an historian of the colonial period. She is a member of the 'Institut Universitaire de France' and Professor at the University of Paris X (Nanterre). Her publications include: *Pindilig, un village équatorien* (Paris, 1992); *Histoire de Buenos Aires* (Paris, 1997); *La esclavitud urbana en Hispanoamérica* (Madrid, 2001); *Buenos Aires, un mythe des confins* (Paris, 2001); and, with Serge Gruzinski, *Histoire du Nouveau Monde* vol. 1 (Paris, 1991); and *Histoire du Nouveau Monde*, vol. 2 (Paris, 1993).

Jonathan Curry-Machado is research assistant for the Caribbean Studies Centre at the London Metropolitan University, where he has also worked as a visiting lecturer in Cuban history. His principal research interest is British and Irish migration to Cuba, and he is currently working on a PhD thesis on the experience, identity and influence of British and Irish migrant machinists in mid-nineteenth-century Cuba.

Lauren Derby is Associate Director and Senior Lecturer in the Master of Arts Program in the Social Sciences at the University of Chicago. Her research has focused on the relationship between political economy, popular culture and the state in the Dominican Republic, Haiti, Puerto Rico and Cuba; her book on everyday life during the Trujillo regime in the Dominican Republic is forthcoming from Duke University Press. She has written widely on cultural studies in Latin America.

David Geggus is Professor of History at the University of Florida, Gainesville. He is author of *Haitian Revolutionary Studies* (Bloomington, 2002); *Slavery, War and Revolution: The British Occupation of Saint Domingue, 1793–1798* (Oxford, 1982) and numerous scholarly articles. He has edited *The Impact of the Haitian Revolution in the Atlantic World* (Columbia, SC, 2001), and (with D.B. Gaspar) *A Turbulent Time: The French Revolution and the Greater Caribbean* (Bloomington, 1987).

Franklin W. Knight is Leonard and Helen R. Stulman Professor of History at Johns Hopkins University, where he has been a member of the faculty for 30 years. Knight's research interests focus on the social, political, economic and cultural aspects of Latin America and the Caribbean, especially after the eighteenth century. He has written many books and articles. He served as president of the Latin American Studies Association between 1998 and 2000 and on several advisory committees including the

St George's University (Grenada), The Historical Society, the National Research Council and the Handbook of Latin American Studies of the Hispanic Division of the Library of Congress.

Nancy Priscilla Naro, the editor of this volume, is a lecturer in the Department of Portuguese and Brazilian Studies at King's College, University of London, and an Associate Fellow at the Institute of Latin American Studies. Author of *A Slave's Place, a Master's World: Fashioning Dependency in Rural Brazil* (London, 2000), her articles include 'Safeguarding Portugal's Colonial Legacies: Pernambuco's 1848,' *Portuguese Studies* (2001); 'Brazil's 1848: The Praieira Revolt,' *The European Revolutions of 1848 and the Americas* (London: 2002); and 'Fact, Fantasy, and Folklore? A Novel Case of Retribution in Nineteenth Century Brazil,' *Luso-Brazilian Review*, vol. 33, no.1 (1996).

Jean Stubbs is Professor of Caribbean Studies at the London Metropolitan University. She has published widely on Cuba, her specialist interests spanning tobacco, gender and race. Her book-length publications include *Cuba: the Test of Time* (London, 1989) and *Tobacco on the Periphery: A Case Study in Cuban Labour History, 1860–1958* (Cambridge, 1985) [*Tabaco en la periferia: El complejo agro-industrial cubano y su movimiento obrero 1860–1959* (Havana, 1989)]; (with Pedro Pérez Sarduy) *Afro-Cuban Voices: On Race and Identity in Contemporary Cuba* (Gainesville, 2000) and *AFROCUBA: An Anthology of Cuban Writing on Race, Politics and Culture* (London/New York/Melbourne, 1993) [*AFROCUBA: una antología de escritos cubanos sobre la raza, la política y la cultura* (San Juan, 1998)]; and (with Lila Haines and Meic F. Haines) *Cuba* (Oxford, 1996).

Introduction

Nancy Priscilla Naro

Black and coloured identities in the Caribbean and in Latin America during the nineteenth century formed in tandem with the imagined, perceived or real persistence of Africa in those societies. The individualised, collective, pristine and even mutated forms of African tongues, religious beliefs, musical forms and customary rights were manifest in thoughts and practices of daily life and customs. They found expression in patterns of farming, domestic toil, construction of space, mechanical and artisan trades, and through personal relations that contributed to the ways in which the Africans, African-derived peoples and those who mediated on their behalf, formulated, pursued, sometimes failed and sometimes succeeded in claiming a share of the rights, privileges and benefits of freedom and free society.[1]

African-derived peoples articulated collective political, cultural and social agendas, as well as pursuing individual aims within broader local and national conjunctures. The African slaves who combated the British invaders of Buenos Aires in 1806–07 illustrate the complexities involved when the issue of personal liberty was related to the defence of a *patria*, where Spaniards distinguished themselves from Creoles and both considered themselves to be separate from African slaves and freedmen. Carmen Bernand draws attention to the wording in the laws and regulations that government officials, church, military, political, educational and social elites assembled. The changes in word usage over time reflected the way in which social constructions of class and race preserved rigid colonial relations of social exclusion. For Lauren Derby, black and coloured identities that emerge in relation to 'otherness' require a historical contextualisation

---

1   See, for example, Monica Schuler, '*Alas, Alas Kongo': A Social History of Indentured African Immigration into Jamaica, 1840–1865* (Baltimore, 1980) and her essay, 'Liberated Central Africans in Nineteenth-Century Guyana,' in Linda Heywood (ed.), *Central Africans and Cultural Transformations in the American Diaspora* (Cambridge, 2002), pp. 319–52. Also Robert W. Slenes, 'The Great Porpoise-Skull Strike: Central African Water Spirits and Slave Identity in Early-Nineteenth Century Rio de Janeiro,' in the same volume, pp. 183–210. Kristin Mann and Edna G. Bay (eds.) *Rethinking the African Diaspora. The Making of a Black Atlantic World in the Bight of Benin and Brazil* (London, 2001) and María Elena Díaz, *The Virgin, the King, and the Royal Slaves of El Cobre: Negotiating Freedom in Colonial Cuba, 1670–1780* (Stanford: 2000); on Brazil, Kim Butler, *Freedoms Won* (Rutgers: 1999); see also Robert W. Slenes, *Na senzala, uma flor* (Rio de Janeiro 1999); Hebe Maria Mattos, *Das cores do silêncio: os significados da liberdade no sudeste escravista – Brasil, séc XIX* (Rio de Janeiro1995); Nancy Naro, *A Slave's Place, a Master's World: Fashioning Dependency in Rural Brazil* (London, 2000).

of that 'otherness'. Derby focuses on Dominican hatred and fear of Haiti in the nineteenth century but traces the origins of those national sentiments to a much earlier period when trade relations favoured the powerful commercial neighbour, Saint Domingue.

African-derived identities were expressed and given form by many unsung and even anonymous thinkers and doers. Free, conditionally free, freed and unfree peoples of African descent through varying degrees of 'agency' petitioned the courts or other public spheres for entitlements to provision grounds, consent to trade, rest, leisure and family time, ceremonial time and protection from arbitrary and cruel physical and psychological treatment. Historians have delved into traditions and explored de facto customary rights that are now seen to be relevant and important to the dismantling of the institution of slavery in addition to complementing and sometimes even challenging the official and formal versions of the processes that brought about the establishment of free labour markets.

In this collection the authors address central events in the processes of state formation and the ways in which revolutions, invasions and wars — the Saint Domingue Revolution, the Haitian invasion of the Dominican Republic, the British invasion of Argentina, the Wars of Independence in Spanish America and the Paraguayan War in Brazil — contributed to black and coloured identities. From these events, as well as the various struggles for liberty and emancipation in Saint Domingue, Cuba and the British Caribbean, political agendas, heroes and heroines like Mariana Grajales Cuello and her family gained national notoriety and international prominence. In addition to those who fought in national liberation struggles, the African-Brazilian abolitionists, Luiz Gama, José do Patrocínio and André Rebouças campaigned to promote reforms of social, political and cultural importance. As Jonathan Curry-Machado shows in his chapter on 'catalysts', vital relationships that developed among workers of different national origins and backgrounds impacted on the formation of identities and strategies of freedom. In terms of the broader significance of the essays to the forging of citizenship and national identity, the research confirms that the social involvements of black thinkers and doers in politics — in elections, civil wars and revolutions, and in office, as well as in religious and cultural activities, family institutions and civil associations — made compelling contributions to the Black Atlantic World.

The authors depart from traditional emphases on the political elites and the agendas that they espoused during the Independence and post-Independence processes of state formation. Instead, the essays address what Jeremy Adelman has argued to be the 'creation of a people from a disorganised and heterogeneous mass'.[2] Saint Domingue represents a sin-

2   Jeremy Adelman, *Republic of Capital. Buenos Aires and the Legal Transformation of the Atlantic World* (Stanford, 1999).

gular and exceptional conjuncture of circumstances that set the slave revolution and the rupture of the colonial pact apart from other colonial relationships in the Americas. Franklin Knight states that internal and international warfare carried on for a decade, after which 'the colony populated predominantly by plantation slaves overthrew both its colonial status and its economic system and established a new political state of entirely free individuals — with some ex-slaves constituting the new political authority'.[3] David Geggus, in his chapter, evaluates the diverse repercussions of the Haitian Revolution of 1789–1804 on people of African descent in Latin America and the Caribbean. On the basis of the responses of free and enslaved persons, the revolution's economic impact and its influence on slave resistance and abolitionism, and on race relations and decolonisation elsewhere, Geggus concludes that, 'in all these domains, the revolution stimulated contrary tendencies and its impact, although widespread and multifarious, was therefore ambiguous.'[4]

Whether a cause and effect relationship can be established or not, evidence is forthcoming in the essays of the shared attributes that societies held in common with one another.[5] Carmen Bernand, Franklin Knight and Lauren Derby deal with black, creole and national identities separately and contextually through evaluations of the isolated, distinct and sometimes local forms of self-definition and the impact these made on a broader conjuncture. Carmen Bernand contextualises basic concepts — *gente de color, negro, africano, pueblo* and *nación* — in colonial and post-Independence Argentina with a view towards identifying the inclusion and exclusion of castes and blacks inside and outside the society of their masters. In the country's unfolding national identity, she reveals how the 'people' were seen and understood by their observers, masters, rulers, missionaries and 'protectors'.

Franklin Knight disputes a singular notion of colonial identity and highlights the complex and non-linear ways in which identities in the Caribbean and the Americas were constantly created, mediated and negotiated both within local contexts and within the larger political context of the competing European empires. For Knight, the search for respectability and dignity that was always inherent to the struggles of peoples of the Caribbean was

---

3   Franklin Knight, 'The Haitian Revolution,' American Historical Review Forum, *The American Historical Review*, vol. 105 (Feb, 2000), p. 103.
4   David Geggus, 'The Influence of the Haitian Revolution on Blacks in Latin America and the Caribbean,' in this volume.
5   In this regard, black identity is held to be one strand of self-perception. For Anthony Pagden and Nicholas Canny, in reference to the mid-nineteenth century: 'Self-perception had become a question of nationhood and of little else', Anthony Pagden and Nicholas Canny, 'Afterword: From Identity to Independence,' in Nicholas Canny and Anthony Pagden (eds.), *Colonial Identity in the Atlantic World, 1500–1800* (Princeton, 1987), p. 271.

compromised by the duration of the institution of slavery, plantation society and the negative social perceptions associated with race and ethnicity.

Two different approaches to the formation of African-derived identities draw on the complex formation of *cubanidad*. Jonathan Curry-Machado identifies outsiders who were complicit with the leaders and participants in the 1840s liberation and independence movements. Some British officials, who were suspected of supplying arms to Cuban abolitionists, aimed to track down and to free kidnapped slaves from other British islands who were technically British and were therefore free under British law. In so doing, their espousal of freedom set precedents that were also endorsed by free British black subjects and by skilled British workers, among whom were immigrant British machinists hired to work on the large sugar estates. Whereas the legal status of slavery in Cuba impeded British abolitionist efforts, Curry-Machado argues that the working class identity among British subjects engaged in the Cuban labour environment bridged racial divides 'that existed between slaves and free workers; blacks and whites'. For him, their presence contributed to easing the boundaries between slavery and freedom. For Jean Stubbs, the social and political activities of free coloureds that she also terms 'free browns' are vital to the understanding of *cubanidad*. Stubbs focuses on Cuba's Mother of Independence, Mariana Grajales Cuello, who, faced with the deaths of her husband and several sons during the Independence struggles, selflessly rallied women, children and men to pursue the struggles for freedom despite colonial persecution and repression.

Nancy Priscilla Naro's chapter concludes the collection with an evaluation of the arguments and positions that informed the gradual process from slavery to free labour. Early proposals at the time of Brazilian Independence are revisited by abolitionists during the course of the transition process that was finalised with the passage of the Golden Law Decree that ended chattel slavery on 13 May 1888. Naro distinguishes between abolitionist agendas and abolitionism, focusing on the positions of Brazil's out-standing abolitionists, the contributions of civil society and the actions of slaves in bringing about emancipation. She suggests, however, that Brazilian elites discounted educational, technical and social reforms to incorporate the poor and the illiterate and, in so doing, marginalised black cultural, religious and political identities from the mainstream of post-emancipation Brazilian society.

CHAPTER 1

Race, National Identity and the Idea of Value on the Island of Hispaniola

Lauren Derby*

*Ayer español nací
a la tarde fui francés
a la noche etiope fui
hoy dicen que soy inglés
no sé qué será de mí*

Yesterday I was born Spanish,
In the afternoon I was French,
At night I was African,
Today they say I am English,
I don't know what will happen to me.

Juan Vásquez, priest, Santiago
at the turn of the nineteenth century

This chapter explores how the bounds of identity, community and even nationality can be fashioned through exchange. As Marshall Sahlins has said, friends make gifts, but gifts can also make friends. However, it is also true that the exchange of commodities can make foes. Interestingly, in eighteenth century Spanish, '*dar jabón*', or to give soap, was

* Much of the research used in this chapter I found in the David Nicholls Collection at Regent's Park College, Oxford University, in 2000. As such, I wish to dedicate it to a person who inspired all those who work on the history of Hispaniola with his rigorous and careful attention to sources, David Nicholls. I would like to thank Sue Mills, Gillian Nicholls and the Nicholls Collection trustees for entrusting me with free access to this rich collection of Haitian and Dominican historical sources before it had even been properly catalogued. And thanks to Alan Knight for his hospitality while I was a research associate of St Antony's College, Oxford University. This essay was presented at the Conference on Blacks in Nineteenth-Century Latin America at the Institute of Latin American Studies, University of London, 26 May 2000. My thanks to the audience, and most especially Franklin Knight, for very useful critical comments and suggestions that have helped me to refine the essay, as well as to Juan Guisti Cordero and Jason McGraw for indicating to me some key sources on Caribbean piracy, and Raymundo González for his seminal work on the *montero* and its centrality within the colonial economy of Santo Domingo.

a colloquialism for conquer, as if subjection was inextricably tied to accepting prestation and the resultant form of indebtedness this implied.[1] This link between exchange and subjugation is thus silently present in the very boundary defining the two nations of Hispaniola island, since *dar jabón* was the eponymous term for Dajabón, the Spanish town on the bank of the Massacre river that has been the official frontier separation of the two nations since the colonial period.[2]

But what of soap? How and why was soap — a seemingly innocent product — linked with subjection? One of the first commodities, soap in the nineteenth century was a key icon of empire, inextricably linked to the civilising mission, intended to uplift native races through training them in metropolitan habits of hygiene.[3] In the seventeenth century, however, soap was both a necessity and a luxury; a commodity that was frequently a gift by virtue of its utility and convenience. Like money, soap crossed borders, since it was itself a medium of conversion from dirty to clean and from commodity to gift.[4] In the border markets of Dajabón, soap, like sugar, tobacco, and at times slaves and debt servants, may also have served as an occasional medium of currency, given both the ubiquity of barter and the scarcity of specie as Spanish and French, buccaneers and hunters, haggled over hides, tallow, wood, vegetables and meat in this New World frontier zone.[5] But more likely, given the scarcity of manufactured goods on the northern frontier of Hispaniola and thus the exogenous and cosmopolitan value accrued to soap as a result, it may have been a commodity used as a gift to establish alliances and rank in this contraband zone where pirates, not states, ruled.[6] In the words of James Clifford, identity should be seen as constantly in flux, as 'a nexus of relations and transactions actively engaging a subject'.[7] Exchanges of everyday items as common as soap,

1   Daniel Lescallier, 'Itinerario de un viaje por la parte española de la isla de Santo Domingo en 1764,' in Emilio Rodríguez Demorizi (ed.), *Relaciones geográficas de Santo Domingo* (Santo Domingo, 1970), p. 114; Nicholas Thomas, *Entangled Objects: Exchange, Material Culture, and Colonialism in the Pacific* (Cambridge, MA, 1991), p. 15.

2   For other suggestions on the origins of the name Dajabón see http://usuarios.lycos.es/dajabon/historia.htm.

3   Anne McClintock, *Imperial Leather: Race, Gender and Sexuality in the Colonial Context* (New York, 1995), p. 208.

4   Michael O'Malley, 'Specie and Species: Race and the Money Question in Nineteenth Century America,' *American Historical Review*, vol. 99, no. 2 (April 1994), p. 392.

5   John Esquemeling, *The Buccaneers of America: A True Account of the Most Remarkable Assaults Committed of Late Years Upon the Coast of the West Indies by the Buccaneers of Jamaica and Tortuga, Both English and French* (London [1684–5], 1924), p. 48, on the planting of tobacco for trading purposes.

6   See chapter 1 of Thomas, *Entangled Objects*, for a discussion of when commodities become gifts. In Thomas' terms, one could say that the exchange of soap may have thus exemplified a kind of 'gift situation' (p. 28).

7   James Clifford, *The Predicament of Culture: Twentieth Century Ethnography, Literature, and Art* (Cambridge, MA, 1988), p. 344.

then, clearly played a part in establishing emergent notions of difference and deference along the Haitian–Dominican frontier.

This chapter considers the relationship between race and national identity in the Dominican Republic. The Dominican literature situates the Haitian Occupation of the Dominican Republic (1822–44) at the centre of any explanation of how race and national identity came to be defined as one and the same, an event which was the climax of a series of nineteenth-century interventions, just after the Haitian Revolution by Toussaint Louverture and Jean-Jacques Dessalines, and in 1856 under Faustin Soulouque. In this view, after two decades of domination Haiti quite naturally became national enemy and *ur*-alter ego. The period of Haitian domination thus serves to explain how anti-Haitianism became the key idiom of official nationalist discourse and popular alibi for blackness in a country in which the majority is black or mulatto. After this event, Dominicans defined themselves in contraposition to Haiti; as Spanish and not French, as Creole or *indio*, and patently not Black. Slavery belonged to Haiti, not the Dominican Republic, where colonial poverty minimised slave purchase, slave imports were terminated exceptionally early, and slave relations were benign and paternalistic, which enabled the formation of a 'racial democracy'.[8] Certainly, any discussion of nineteenth-century Dominican history must account for the change wrought by the Haitian Occupation since it is the key feature making the Dominican path to republicanism unique in the Latin American context. While the rest of South and Central America gained independence in the 1820s from Spain, only the Dominican Republic gained independence from Haiti. Moreover, it was the resultant feeling of vulnerability of having been successfully conquered by this more militarily powerful neighbour that made almost all successive Dominican regimes court annexation to a stronger power — Spain or the United States — so as to protect the eastern portion of Hispaniola from further Haitian or other imperial designs.[9]

Clearly the Haitian occupation was one factor in forging a racialised sense of national identity and what Silvio Torres Saillant has termed

8   While there are any number of twentieth-century Dominican exponents of this idea, such as the politician and sociologist Juan Bosch, it was not an uncommon position among nineteenth-century liberals, such as Pedro Bonó, who described the Dominican Republic as having produced a new race or 'raza nueva'; see his essay, 'Congreso extra-parlamentario,' in Emilio Rodríguez Demorizi (ed.), *Papeles de Pedro F. Bonó. Para la historia de ideas políticas en Santo Domingo* (Santo Domingo, 1964), pp. 352–99. For more on Bonó, see Raymundo González, *Bonó, un intelectual de los pobres* (Santo Domingo, 1994).

9   Detlev Julio K. Peukert, 'Anhelo de dependencia: Las ofertas de anexión de la República Dominicana a los Estados Unidos en el Siglo XIX,' *Jahrbuch für Geschichte von Staat, Wirtschaft und Gesellschaft Lateinamerikas*, vol. 23 (1986), p. 315. See also Mu-Kien Adriana Sang, *Buenaventura Báez: el caudillo del sur (1844–1878)* (Santo Domingo, 1991), pp. 113–46; and William Javier Nelson, *Almost a Territory: America's Attempt to Annex the Dominican Republic* (Newark, 1990).

'negrophobia'.[10] The American Commissioner in Santo Domingo in 1849 related that Haitian domination had made things black so anathema that a black Dominican could make the paradoxical proclamation that '*soy negro pero negro blanco*' or '*aunque tengo el cutis negro mi corazón es blanco*' ('I am black but white black,' or 'even though I have black skin my heart is white').[11] And in 1871 Dominicans were even able to persuade US senators against their own racial common sense that in the Dominican race mixture, as opposed to elsewhere, white blood predominated over black.[12] Yet I wish to argue that this identity developed for reasons quite different to those maintained in Dominican nationalist historiography.[13] A focus on the Haitian Occupation serves to naturalise anti-Haitianism, as if all nations have enemies, and former colonial powers are frequent favourites; or as Sander Gilman has argued, all selves (even national ones) require an other.[14] I will argue, however, that the period of Haitian domination was less constitutive than corroborative, and that to account fully for the image of Haiti one must return to the seventeenth century, when the meanings of the community that would eventually become Haiti were first defined in relation to an emerging popular proto-Dominican creole identity through inter-island trade.[15] In the Dominican case, creolisa-

10   Silvio Torres Saillant, 'Creoleness or Blackness? A Dominican Dilemma,' *Plantation Society in the Americas*, vol. V, no. 1 (Spring 1998), Special Issue: 'Who/What is Creole?' edited by James Arnold.

11   Sumner Welles, *Naboth's Vineyard*, cited in David Nicholls, *From Dessalines to Duvalier: Race, Colour and National Independence in Haiti* (New Brunswick, 1996), p. 80. David Howard notes that Dominicans today refer to '*negro negro*' and '*blanco blanco*' as defining parameters of the status economy; see David John Howard, 'Colouring the Nation: Race and Ethnicity in the Dominican Republic,' DPhil Thesis, Oxford University (1997), p. 136.

12   *Report of the Commission of Inquiry to Santo Domingo* (Washington, DC, 1871), p. 13.

13   Key texts include: Joaquín Balaguer, *La isla al revés: Haití y el destino dominicano*, 6th edition (Santo Domingo, 1990); Manuel Arturo Peña Battle, *Ensayos históricos* (Santo Domingo, 1989). For the contextualisation of Peña Battle and Balaguer's thought, see Michiel Baud, 'Manuel Arturo Peña Battle y Joaquín Balaguer y la identidad nacional dominicana,' in Raymundo González et al. (eds.), *Política, identidad y pensamiento social en la República Dominicana. Siglos XIX y XX* (Madrid, 1999), pp. 153–180; and Raymundo González, 'Peña Battle y su concepto histórico de la nación dominicana,' *Anuario de Estudios Americanos*, vol. XLVIII (1991), pp. 585–631.

14   Sander Gilman, 'Introduction: What are Stereotypes and Why Use Texts to Study Them?' in Gilman, *Difference and Pathology: Stereotypes of Sexuality, Race and Madness* (Ithaca, 1985), pp. 15–35.

15   Most of the work on Creole identity formation in Latin America has focused on elite factions, which frequently used popular symbols such as miraculous virgins or peasant iconography to legitimate their claim to authority vis-á-vis the Spanish '*gachupines*.' The Dominican case is different because by the eighteenth century the Spanish were so scarce that they were barely even a social category, and elites were so poor that they were hardly elite. For more on elite creole formation in Puerto Rico, see the insightful essay by Francisco Scarano, 'The *Jíbaro* Masquerade and the Subaltern Politics of Creole Identity Formation in Puerto Rico, 1745–1823,' in *American Historical Review*, vol. 101, no. 5 (December 1996), pp. 1398–1431. On popular black Creole identity as seen through popular cultural forms see the rich account by Richard D.E. Burton,

tion was both contentious and homogenising,[16] as it served both to unify Dominicans of all hues and castes and to it set things Haitian apart. While anti-Haitianism is frequently taken as flat racism, it was only beginning in the late nineteenth century with the rise of modern corporate plantations staffed by Haitian and West Indian labour that anti-Haitianism devolved into a feeling of racial superiority, as a new pattern of ethnic labour segmentation emerged which made Haitians appear absolutely degraded in Dominican eyes through their relation to an utterly servile labour form — cane cutting — associated with slavery.[17] Previous to this, anti-Haitianism was essentially a defensive fear of Haitian potency — military as well as religious and economic.

Anti-Haitianism is not the only story of race in the Dominican Republic. Analyses of Dominican racial ideology have tended to focus on anti-Haitianism, a style of racialised nationalism that structures Dominicans in segmentary opposition to Haitians.[18] In this Manichean construct Dominicans are white because Haitians are black, a contrast which has inspired a cluster of related metaphoric contrasts (purity vs. pollution, etc.).[19] However, even if Dominicans have effectively denationalised blackness by exporting it to the other side of the island, the story of race does not end

---

Afro-Creole: Power, Opposition and Play in the Caribbean (Ithaca, 1997). The classic text on the emergence of Creole identity in Mexico is, of course, Jacques Lafaye, *Quetzalcóatl and Guadalupe: The Formation of Mexican National Consciousness, 1531–1813* (Chicago, 1968). I am using the terms Dominican and Haitian here for lack of anything more accurate since this was a transitional moment in between colonial and Creole identity, when pirates, buccaneers and contrabandists — all in effect anti-nationalists — were very important within both the French and Spanish speaking populations of Hispaniola. I would say, however, that in the seventeenth century the Haitian community was predominantly constituted of buccaneers and corsairs, and the Dominican community was more settled, and thus by comparison the process of creolisation (thus the development of a protonational identity) was more advanced in the Spanish colony.

16   In contrast to Nigel Bolland, 'Creolization and Creole Societies,' in Alistair Hennessy (ed.), *Intellectuals in the Twentieth-Century Caribbean* (Basingstoke, 1992), pp. 50–79.

17   Michiel Baud, '"Constitutionally White": The Forging of a National Identity in the Dominican Republic,' in Gert Oostindie (ed.), *Ethnicity in the Caribbean* (London, 1996), p. 131. Aviva Chomsky also argues that Haitian immigration to the sugar industry in Cuba had a clearly derogatory impact on race relations there; see her essay, '"Barbados or Canada?" Race, Immigration, and Nation in Early-Twentieth-Century Cuba,' *Hispanic American Historical Review*, vol. 80, no. 3 (August, 2000), pp. 415–62.

18   It is the fact that anti-Haitianism is really nationalism that enables Dominicans who see themselves as patriotic to claim that they are anti-Haitian and not racist.

19   Particularly in the contemporary period for the Partido Reformista Social Cristiano; see Joaquín Balaguer, *La isla al revés*. For more on the 1937 Haitian massacre, see R. Derby and R. Turits, 'Historias de terror y los terrores de la historia: La masacre haitiana de 1937 en la República Dominicana,' *Estudios Sociales*, vol. 26, no. 92 (1993), pp. 65–76. For more on official anti-Haitianism, see M. Fennema and T. Lowenthal, *Construcción de raza y nación en la República Dominicana* (Santo Domingo, 1987); and Pedro L. San Miguel, *La isla imaginada: historia, identidad, y utopía en la Española* (Santo Domingo/San Juan, 1997).

there.[20] Indeed, even if Dominicans as a nation define themselves as 'constitutionally white',[21] I would argue that as an ethnos Dominicans do see
themselves as mixed-race *mestizo* or *criollo*, which stands in for black in this
context.[22] Creole identity is invoked when Dominicans refer to being *'blanco de la tierra'* (whites of the land) or *indio*, labels that may have evolved
from the colonial distinction between African-born slaves or *congos*, as
opposed to Creole slaves, or those born in the new world.[23]

Black and white are what the structuralists would term binary opposi-
tions that define the overarching framework of Dominican racial distinctions, but the unmarked yet subtly graded terrain in between is rich with
meaning, even if it is not perceived as a social category per se, and thus
remains for the most part invisible.[24] Yet true blackness and whiteness are

20   I am contrasting the Dominican Republic's exclusionary approach to blackness with
     Cuba's inclusionary approach; see Robin D. Moore, *Nationalizing Blackness:
     Afrocubanismo and Artistic Revolution in Havana, 1920–1940* (Pittsburgh, 1997). I am also
     distinguishing between anti-Haitianism as a form of racialised nationalism and atti-
     tudes towards colour within the Dominican community.

21   See Baud, 'Constitutionally White'.

22   Here I am diverging from Ronald Stutzman's compelling essay on *mestizaje* in Ecuador,
     where apparently 'ethnic identity [is exchanged] for membership in the nation-state', see
     Stutzman, *'El Mestizaje:* An All-Inclusive Ideology of Exclusion,' in Norman E. Whitten
     (ed.), *Cultural Transformations and Ethnicity in Modern Ecuador* (Urbana, 1981), pp. 45–94.
     Dominicans patently do not use the term *'mestizo'* or *'mulatto'* to describe themselves
     (Howard, 'Colouring the Nation', pp. 137, 71), however, deploying *'indio'* (i.e. *criollo*)
     instead. This is how poor Dominicans can identify the Dominican nation as white,
     while claiming simultaneously that they are *indio* or Creole mixed-race.

23   For evidence of the use of *'blanco de la tierra'* during the Haitian Occupation, see Jonathan
     Brown, *The History and Present Condition of Santo Domingo*, Source Books on Haiti no. 8
     (London, 1972 [1837]), vol. II, p. 286. Fennema and Lowenthal claim that the term *indio*
     was used by African slaves who fled enslavement from the French part of the island dur-
     ing the eighteenth century, although it could alternatively represent a feature common
     throughout the Americas whereupon maroons took refuge within frontier indian commu-
     nities, and then adopted indigenous identities since they were appealingly autochthnous,
     and hence legitimate, as opposed to African slavery. Moreau de St Mery notes during his
     visit to the Spanish side of the island, however, that by the eighteenth century a kind of
     indio masquerade had developed, whereupon many Creoles with indian features were mak-
     ing much of their purported indian descent (cf. Scarano, *'Jíbaro* Masquerade;' M.L.E.
     Moreau de St Mery, *Descripción de la parte española de Santo Domingo*, translated by C. Armando
     Rodríguez (Ciudad Trujillo, 1944), p. 95). And into the nineteenth century, Creole women
     filed their teeth to a point, considering it beautiful, which may have been a Taino practice
     (William Walton, *Present State of the Spanish Colonies, Including a Particular Report of Hispaniola*
     [London, 1810], p. 371). In contemporary usage, most informants I questioned who
     referred to themselves as having an 'indio' identity did not mean a genealogical connection
     to an indian past, but rather that their skin was brown. This is why the use of the term *indio*
     I would say implies a tacit recognition of a mulatto or Creole ethnicity.

24   Edmund Leach, 'Anthropological Aspects of Language. Animal Categories and
     Verbal Abuse,' in E.H. Lenneberg (ed.), *New Directions in the Study of Language*
     (Cambridge, MA, 1964); Marshall Sahlins, 'La Pensée Bourgeoisie: Western Society as
     Culture,' *Culture and Practical Reason* (Chicago, 1976), pp. 166–204, and Ferdinand de
     Saussure, *Course in General Linguistics* (New York, 1966).

seen as residing outside the nation, in Haiti and Europe/US Creole identity is perceived as brown — a composite of white and black 'lines' or personae that become salient in different contexts.[25] In *mestizo* cultures, the fact that there are multiple criteria for race-marking enables one to redefine one's racial identity in different contexts; thus, as self or person, in private or public. This is why mulatto Dominican dictator Rafael Trujillo, for example, was able to assert that he was a Spaniard, and a Haitian, on different occasions since both of these were legitimate lines of descent in his case. It also means that one may claim one racial marker as superordinate over others (such as lineage over phenotype) as when one a respondent stated, 'My parents are Spanish so even though I look like a *mulatta*, I am definitely *blanca*.'[26]

Just as civilisation was the mother of barbarism, the defining feature of Caribbean society, the sugar plantation, spawned its obverse, a frontier society of runaways, vagrants and half-castes who did not live within colonial society but rather in opposition to it in the refuge of the mountains, the depopulated coasts and the sea.[27] And it was here that a truly Creole society was founded in the sense of a novel social identity and culture that saw itself as autonomous from the metropole. As Antonio Benítez-Rojo has argued, it was the cattle economy and resultant contraband trade that emerged in the latter sixteenth century along the north coast of Hispaniola as the first wave of sugar *ingenios* and mines decayed that gave birth to a novel sense of community, one that was patently non-elite and even more expressly non-colonial.[28] This community was based on hide production, but it was also squarely a part of Gilroy's 'Black Atlantic' since it was deeply linked to the thriving maritime smuggling economy and the triangle trade.[29] In the eighteenth century, this illicit subculture became the basis of French settler identity in Hispaniola, emerging within the very interstices of Spanish mercantile restriction which imposed draconian measures to first quash, and when this was unsuccessful, tax these vibrant trade networks with Cuba, Jamaica, Puerto Rico, Curaçao, the Turcos and Caicos islands, France, Germany, the United States and most especially Haiti. These smugglers were

25 The notion of 'line' is from Erving Goffman, 'On Face-Work,' *Interaction Ritual: Essays on Face-to-Face Behavior* (New York, 1967), pp. 5–46; see also Goffman, *The Presentation of Self in Everyday Life* (New York, 1959).

26 Howard, 'Colouring the Nation,' p. 76.

27 Silvio R. Duncan Baretta and John Markoff, 'Civilization and Barbarism: Cattle Frontiers in Latin America,' *Comparative Studies in Society and History*, vol. 20, no. 4 (October 1978), pp. 587–620.

28 Antonio Benítez-Rojo, *The Repeating Island: The Caribbean and Postmodern Perspective*, translated by John Maraniss (Durham, NC, 1992), pp. 43–55.

29 Paul Gilroy, *The Black Atlantic: Modernity and Double Consciousness* (Cambridge, MA, 1993). For more on black seamen and their networks of communication during this period, see Julius Sherrard Scott III, 'The Common Wind: Currents of Afro-American Communication in the Era of the Haitian Revolution,' PhD thesis, Duke University (1986).

so successful that they soon cornered the market in specie, bullion, and luxury commerce, as merchants sought to avoid high taxes due to the fact that 'trading by stealth' could make for as much as a threefold increase in profits.[30] I wish to propose that a Dominican Creole idea of Haiti first arose through these networks of exchange, thus Haiti took shape in the Dominican imagination through the meanings implicit in eighteenth century intra-island trade. Bryan Edwards noted that there was 'a hereditary and inextinguishable animosity between the Spanish and French planters' on Hispaniola but this sense of difference was based primarily on colonial identity, or Spanish–French mutual stereotypes that were transported to the colonies.[31] The eighteenth century was key to defining a sense of what would later become Haitian and Dominican national alterity because this was when the two economies matured as very distinct but symbiotically interrelated. At a time when sugar was one of the greatest sources of global wealth, Haiti blossomed into the paramount sugar producer in the French colonial world, and the Dominican Republic became its foremost supplier of livestock products — meat, hides, cattle, mules and oxen. Just as Haiti came to be seen as embodying the cash nexus — which in the eighteenth century meant gold and silver, and sugar and slaves — Creole identity in the east was imaged through cattle, cacao and tobacco. Haitians drank coffee, while Dominicans drank cocoa.[32] This may be why today the dominant racial terms marking *lo criollo* in the Dominican Republic are all agricultural produce, foods that are consumed at home — chocolate, wheat, coffee and cinnamon.[33]

30   Marcus Rediker, *Between the Devil and the Deep Blue Sea: Merchant Seamen, Pirates, and the Anglo-American Maritime World, 1700–1750* (New York, 1987), p. 42.
31   Although an open question remains just how 'French' the buccaneers saw themselves as being in the period before the French actually acquired the western portion of the island in 1793, since they had rebelled previously when Tortuga Island was administered by the French West Indian Company. See Bryan Edwards, *An Historical Survey of the French Colony in the Island of Santo Domingo* (London, 1797), p. 188. See also Nicholas Canny and Anthony Pagden (eds.), *Colonial Identity in the Atlantic World, 1500–1800* (Princeton, 1987). For accusations that the buccaneers of Mole St Nicolas, Haiti, were monopolising specie to the detriment of everyone else, see Edward Long, *The History of Jamaica or General Survey of the Ancient and Modern State of that Island, with Reflections on its Situations, Settlements, Inhabitants, Climate, Products, Commerce, Laws and Government* (London, 1979 [1774]), esp. p. 535.
32   Moreau de St Mery, *Descripción de la parte española*, p. 97.
33   As noted by Howard, Introduction, 'Colouring the Nation'. The lingering importance of this opposition of identities is also noted by Melville Herskovits, who observed how 'deeply lodged' the 'pattern of a money economy' was in Haiti when he did his fieldwork in 1937; see his *Life in a Haitian Valley* (New York, 1971), p. 83. For more on Creole identity and food, see my essay, 'Gringo Chickens with Worms: Food and Nationalism in the Dominican Republic,' in Gilbert M. Joseph et al. (eds.), *Close Encounters of Empire: Writing the Cultural History of US–Latin American Relations* (Durham, 1998), pp. 451–93.

The most influential theorists of race in the Caribbean have considered the ways in which relations of production have shaped emergent notions of race. They have demonstrated how sugar boom periods corresponded with sharper patterns of social differentiation and increased racial distance.[34] These arguments help explain why anti-Haitianism became particularly noticeable from the 1870s onwards, as the Dominican Republic developed modern sugar *centrales* staffed primarily by Haitian and West Indian labour. Yet if anti-Haitianism became dominant during this period, it must have developed from some earlier trace associations. I consider here how relations of exchange and patterns of consumption can give rise to emergent ideas of racial or protonational difference, and thus how regimes of trade can shape ideas of racial otherness, as objects become signs of identity and difference marking discrete trading communities. The contraband economy focused upon here represented the Caribbean corner of the triangle trade, the nexus not only of competing colonial powers and their maritime mercenary representatives, but also the site of competing regimes of value of various kinds — as African paganism vied with Christianity, and feudalism sparred with mercantilism and emergent capitalism. As William Pietz has argued, the idea of the fetish originated in this conflictive moment in coastal West Africa as a form of value that remained stubbornly present amid the ebbs and flows of incessant bargaining. The fetish became a kind of anchor within a 'mercantile intercultural space created by the ongoing trade relations between cultures so radically different as to be mutually incomprehensible',[35] thus a dizzying multiplicity of different economies of valuation. It is not coincidental that parallel to the idea of the fetish arose another form of essentialism on the next stop along the same trade circuit, the beginnings of the ascription of fixed identity through race and nationality on Hispaniola. Indeed, as a form of fetishism, notions of essentialised race provided hierarchy, and thus stability, in a moment in which there was no common grammar of trade, and commensurability was so uncertain that trade itself was so frequently violent that it was given its own name — 'rescate' which shares an origin with the Portuguese term for kidnapping — during a period in which trade itself was described by many as a 'mild form of war'.[36]

---

34   Mintz and Hoetink are key proponents of this view; see, for example, Sidney Mintz, 'From Plantations to Peasantries in the Caribbean,' in Sidney Mintz and Sally Price (eds.) *Caribbean Contours* (Baltimore, MD, 1985); and Harry Hoetink, 'The Dominican Republic in the Nineteenth Century: Some Notes on Stratification, Immigration and Race,' in Magnus Mörner (ed.), *Race and Class in Latin America* (New York, 1970), pp. 96–121.

35   William Pietz, 'The Problem of the Fetish, I,' *Res* 9 (Spring 1985), pp. 5–17; Pietz, 'The Problem of the Fetish, II,' *Res* 13 (1987), pp. 23–45; and Pietz, 'The Problem of the Fetish, IIIa,' *Res* 16 (1988), pp. 105–123.

36   Rediker, *Between the Devil and the Deep Blue Sea*, p. 20.

What I wish to do here is trace the possible origin of certain ideas about Haiti that have become officialised in anti-Haitian policy, but which I argue originated during the formative period when Creole identity was first taking shape.[37] The idea of Haiti as a source of hidden potency and illicit value may well have arisen during the period when contraband was the central pillar of the economy and the only form of exchange with Haiti; just as the link between Haiti and monetary value may well have reinforced through the wildly successful sugar bonanza during the decades preceding the revolution, a phenomenon which Dominicans observed from the sidelines with amazement and no small measure of envy. While the Dominican Republic was still engaged in predominantly non-monetised exchange, and most of the peasantry lived from subsistence agriculture, the riches produced by the Haitian sugar boom were quite incomprehensible. Yet even before the sugar economy of Haiti overtook that of Jamaica, the buccaneers of northern Hispaniola were accused of hoarding specie, bullion, slaves, sugar and luxury goods in general, thus draining the value of the entire region and transforming what should be exchange value into inalienable possessions by taking these out of circulation and holding them in check.[38] Ideas about Haiti as monopolising illicit value were first established in the early eighteenth century, as accusations raged from as far away as Jamaica that smugglers trading with Haiti had provided her with most of the gold, silver and specie in circulation in the Caribbean. Haiti stood accused, thus, of secretly harbouring specie and driving up slave prices since she had become the only country able to purchase them. At a time when specie was scarce, and sugar or slaves were often used as a general money form, Haiti was seen as avariciously hoarding all the standards of value available within the eighteenth century grammar of West Indian trade — gold, silver, slaves and sugar — and thus underdeveloping her neighbours.[39]

The meanings transacted through trade, however, were not merely the result of the products themselves serving as symbols; the very terms of exchange itself were important. Eighteenth-century Haiti was a highly monetarised economy, with planters in possession of enough French francs to buy hundreds of slaves to work their sugar, coffee and cacao plantations. By sharp contrast, the Dominican Republic decayed into a

---

37 These ideas about Haiti are developed in my essay: 'Haitians, Magic and Money: Raza and Society in the Haitian-Dominican Borderlands, 1900 to 1937,' *Comparative Studies in Society and History*, vol. 36, no. 3 (July 1994), pp. 488–526.

38 This vision of Haiti as monopolising regional specie and value was not solely the province of Spanish colonists; the topic was of great concern in eighteenth century Jamaica. See Long, *The History of Jamaica*, p. 535. And Howard notes that even today Haitians are seen by Dominicans as having vampire-like qualities, such as blood-sucking and cannibalism (Howard, 'Colouring the Nation,' p. 63).

39 Even if these were calculated in pieces of eight, Spanish currency itself was rare.

colonial backwater after Spain's attention had shifted to the South American mainland, and specie was highly inflationary and hard to come by. In this largely barter economy, tobacco and other products were used as surrogate currency, and slaves were more frequently stolen from Haiti than purchased. These highly unequal terms of exchange served to establish rank on the island as Haiti achieved fame in part through her privileged relationship to France, which provided both economic backing and recognition.[40] Haitian opulence is clear in travel accounts such as Père Labat's who described the governor's palace at the north-western coastal town of Port-de-Paix as the 'most lovely he had seen in America', or in the fact that in the eighteenth century *'comme il faut'* meant distinguished in Dominican Spanish parlance.[41] I argue here that notions of protonational difference were first outlined through the paths of commodities exchanged across the island, and that ideas about Haitian potency derived from its perceived sumptuary monopolisation of certain highly prized items, especially sugar, slaves, specie and precious metals.[42] The effective monopoly of value of Haiti was severe enough to create a two-tier logic of exchange, within which Haiti traded with money, while other islands traded in barter, principally for agricultural produce, as well as cattle, tobacco and logwood.[43]

Contraband, Cattle and Creole Society

Before dealing with the problem of how Haiti came to be seen as the sole repository of blackness on the island, one must explain what enabled Dominican mulattos to see themselves as 'constitutionally white'.[44] The answer lies in the character of Dominican slavery, and the period of sixteenth and seventeenth century economic decline. After the first attempts at mining and sugar had petered out and Spanish colonial attention had shifted to the more profitable mainland, the Dominican economy devolved into a smallholder's mixed economy of subsistence agriculture, cattle and tobacco production. The first wave of sugar and mining had led to the importing of some 20,000 slaves by the mid-sixteenth century, fre-

40 As in Nancy Munn's formulation developed in *The Fame of Gawa: A Symbolic Study of Value Transformation in a Massim (Papua New Guinea) Society* (Durham, 1992), p. 116.
41 R.P. Labat, *Viajes a las isles de la América*, Colección Nuestros Paises (Havana, 1979 [1694]), p. 234.; Moreau de St Mery, *Descripción*, p. 85.
42 Arjun Appadurai, 'Introduction: Commodities and the Politics of Value,' in Appadurai (ed.), *The Social Life of Things: Commodities in Cultural Perspective* (New York, 1986), pp. 3–63.
43 Edward Long even proposed that British possessions be allowed to pay taxes to the metropole in produce (as they had been for a short time), since they could pay in sugar (Long, *The History of Jamaica*, pp. 536–7).
44 Baud, 'Constitutionally White'; Peter R. Galvin, *Patterns of Pillage: A Geography of Caribbean-Based Piracy in Spanish America, 1536–1718* (New York), American University Studies XXV, Geography, vol. 5 (1999), p. 109.

quently staffing plantations with as many as 200 slaves, an enormous number for the period. But as Spanish attentions turned elsewhere, and rich
planters moved on, the economy floundered due to mercantilist restrictions
leaving producers with no outlet for their products nor source for provisions. As a result a flourishing contraband economy developed along the
northern and southern coasts, in part in response to the rise of a thriving
smuggling economy spurred by Dutch, French and English pirates and mercenaries. In the 1590s the Dutch had some 20 ships trading solely with Santo
Domingo and Cuba. Indeed, the very term buccaneer derives from *boucaner*,
to smoke, referring to the wild oxen and boar hunters on Hispaniola and
subordinate northcoastal Tortuga Island. After the demise of sugar, many
former slaves became *cimarrones* (runaway slaves) and retreated into the
underpopulated mountains as itinerant peasants, while others found a highly lucrative outlet in this coastal pirate subculture. Labat noted that by 1693
most filibusters and corsairs in the Caribbean were mulatto.[45] By 1677
contraband had become *'una verdadera tradición'* principally in the seas
between Cuba and Hispaniola, and extending to Puerto Rico, Jamaica,
Cartagena and Veracruz, with its 'acropolis' at Tortuga.[46]

The rough and ready subculture of this hunting ecology flourished as
long as there were ample stocks of wild boar and cattle, and a highly
wasteful style of hunting developed, in which hundreds of boars were
felled in a day.[47] Hunters were classed into two groups; those who hunt-
ed bulls for hides (known as *boucaniers*, who were considered far more
skilled) and those who chased wild boar, for the sale of meat and fat to
the planters.[48] The latter were called merely hunters and were known for
their technique of forming the meat into long strips, the distinctive form
of smoking used and its delicious taste. The two groups appear to have
been quite distinct. Since the former was considered more skilled, it may
have been principally an occupation practised by Europeans who had run
away from positions as bond servants or ships' crew. The latter were frequently runaway slaves or half castes, locally known as *monteros*, who practised occasional swidden agriculture but were principally itinerant hunters
whose diet consisted of large quantities of meat (at times eaten raw

45   Labat, *Viajes a las islas de la América*, p. 238.
46   Quoted in Michiel Baud, 'Peasant Society Under Siege: Tobacco Cultivators in the
      Cibao (Dominican Republic), 1870–1930,' PhD dissertation, Utrecht (1991), p. 19.
47   While Oviedo said that in 1535 hunters could kill 500 animals in a morning, later
      accounts testify to as many as 100 per day (Moreau de St Mery, *Descripción*, p. 99;
      Galvin, *Patterns of Pillage*, p. 114).
48   Esquemeling, *The Buccaneers of America*, translated by Alexis Brown (London, 1969),
      p. 54; Labat, *Viajes a las islas de la América*, p. 234. Labat describes the smoking process
      and praises the quality of the meat.

apparently).[49] They would remain in the mountains for stints of a year or two and then descend to La Tortuga for necessities such as muskets and shot, where they were known for drinking to excess and womanising.

By the late seventeenth century Spanish mercantilist restrictions had spawned a thriving contraband economy in which the pillage of gold, silver and pearls was combined with a bustling contraband trade in hides. Frequently semi-officialised European corsairs and freebooters seeking to break the Spanish maritime stronghold combined with Spanish colonists in dire need of slaves and manufactured goods to develop a veritable sub-culture with its own rules and regulations that operated in the interstices of Spanish mercantilism. The larger ships would operate under cover of official trade, obtaining all necessary permissions for the bulk of the cargo and then trading the concealed contraband merchandise on the side. The smaller ships, which were typically English, Dutch, French or Danish, would trade far from the principal cities at subordinate ports or at the mouths of rivers. The ritual of contraband trade started with cannon fire to alert local colonists that a ship had arrived, and always occurred at night. Called '*tráfico á la pica*', this commerce occurred in cash, among heavily armed men in small groups. Only a small array of goods was displayed, most remaining on ship to facilitate rapid disembarcation if necessary, and large sales to distinguished individuals were honoured with cannonfire.[50]

Forged in opposition to Spanish rule, a truly Creole culture emerged through this prosperous contraband economy, one which provided ample space for former slaves to find upward mobility through a combination of smuggling and swidden agriculture and hunting, along with marooned shipmen and deserters, adventurers and runaway bondsmen who would try their fortune. As such a new symbiosis was forged between what Mintz has termed a 'protopeasant' economy based on shifting cultivation and wild boar and oxen hunting, scores of herds of which had multiplied in the wake of the withdrawal of the plantation economy, and the smugglers. A

49   William Walton describes the maroon hunting activities in some detail, especially those in the environs of Neyba; see his *Present State of the Spanish Colonies*, pp. 31–6. For more on the history and ecology of the *montero*, see Raymundo González, 'Ideología del progreso y campesinado en el siglo XIX,' *Ecos*, vol. 1, no. 2 (1993), pp. 25–43. The *jíbaro* is the Puerto Rican equivalent, for which there is a more developed literature than the Dominican version; see Scarano 'The *Jíbaro* Masquerade,' pp. 1398–1431, for a treatment that stresses the itinerancy and hunting features of the phenomenon. See Jorge Duany, 'Ethnicity in the Spanish Caribbean. Notes on the Consolidation of Creole Identity in Cuba and Puerto Rico, 1762–1868,' *Ethnic Groups*, vol. 6 (1985), pp. 99–123, esp. 112, for an account that describes the *jíbaro* as principally a small-scale agriculturalist. One should not fix unduly the boundary separating hunters and pirates, however, since a good many hunters became pirates, and presumably vice versa.

50   Labat, *Viajes a la isla de la América*, p. 144.

new subculture was forged in which, due to mercantilist restrictions that stymied commerce, those on the margins of colonial society — fugitives, runaway slaves and servants, and *mestizos* who had nothing to lose — fled to the coasts where finding their knowledge of local territory and skills with a cutlass highly useful, many freedmen joined ships. For example, Sir Francis Drake, who pillaged the shores of Santo Domingo in 1571, picked up during his travels a 'faithful negro', Diego, who helped him establish communication with runaway slave communities in Panama who kept watch on Spanish whereabouts while he was looting their gold.[51] After the stocks of wild game were depleted, diminishing the output of hides and smoked meat, Hispaniolan hunters scoured the coasts in small vessels seeking Spanish craft to plunder for gold and slaves. Indeed, these smugglers were so successful that the Spanish took to forcibly burning all settlements and their cattle along the northern coast in 1606 so as to force the population into the interior. But contraband continued to thrive and most likely even increased due to greater Caribbean Sea traffic.

With the rise of the Haitian sugar economy came a dramatic rise in trade to Hispaniola, and with it the stakes of freebooting. By the eighteenth century, corsairs from Hispaniola were not only notorious for their expertise as far afield as Mexico, but were capturing small fortunes. Not surprisingly, many were mulattos, especially among the small crews. In 1749 one Domingo Sánchez Moreno and his colleague took a British frigate of 22 cannon, 192 slaves, ivory, wax and dye, at an estimated worth of 32,000 pesos. Lorenzo Daniel was particularly fearsome due to his record capture of more than 70 English war and trade ships.[52] And the mulatto shoemaker Miguel Enríquez became one of the wealthiest men in Puerto Rico through piracy; he lent money to the Church and had his own fleet of corsairs in the service of the Spanish Crown; he even succeeded in expelling the English from Vieques Island on two occasions.[53] During the era of contraband, northern coastal towns such as Monte Cristi and Port-de-Paix became cosmopolitan metropoles, teeming with Portuguese money and exotic spices, and attracting many freedmen looking to find their fortune. One contemporary observer attributed the development of agriculture *in toto* during the mid-eighteenth century to the bounties of contraband, which made more specie available to purchase slaves, which in turn increased production.[54] While a wild speculation to be sure, one per-

---

51   Sir Richard Carnac Temple, *The World Encompassed and Analogous Contemporary Documents concerning Sir Francis Drake's Circumnavigation of the World* (London, 1926), p. xxi.
52   Antonio Sánchez Valverde, *La Idea del valor en la isla española* (Ciudad Trujillo, 1947 [1780s]), p. 142.
53   Juan Guisti Cordero, Department of History, University of Puerto Rico at Rio Piedras, personal communication.
54   Sánchez Valverde, *Idea del valor*, p. 146.

son maintained that contraband accounted for a full one-sixth of all commerce, although an even higher figure might be conceivable.[55] Trade in contraband eventually became so financially rewarding that it began to take its toll on farming. By the turn of the eighteenth century, a petition was filed to the Crown for black slaves 'on credit' to help stimulate agriculture.[56]

In the Spanish colony during the seventeenth and eighteenth centuries slavery devolved into a system that barely resembled the corporate model elsewhere. The feature that made the Dominican case distinctive was that the free black population constituted the majority by the eighteenth century.[57] Colonial poverty made slave imports prohibitive outside the largest of firms; most plantations could only afford to purchase a handful. A Dutch bondservant himself employed by the French West India Company, Exquemelin, noted how scarce African slaves were on Hispaniola even by the late seventeenth century. He also claimed that, due to their short-term contracts, white bondsmen were worked harder and punished more severely than slaves, particularly when under contract to the hunters.[58]

Ranching required a far looser regime of control than sugar, and thus consequently nurtured far more trust between masters and slaves. The fact that most slaves were employed singly or in pairs in cattle ranching encouraged paternalism and fostered identification with a patron who could offer various perks, privileges and upward mobility; it also helped forge vertical as well as horizontal ties of patron clientelism across the social divide.[59] On the cattle ranches, slave-master relations were quite intimate, particularly since the *hatos* typically only employed one or two slaves and the rancher and his men would spend weeks at a time on the road together.[60] In eighteenth-century Uruguay, for example, four or five slaves could control a herd of 250,000. Ranching was particularly appropriate to an economy in which capital was scarce and land was plentiful.[61] Indeed, labour

55   *Ibid*, p. 159.
56   Francisco Franco de Torquemada, 'Representación,' in Emilio Rodríguez Demorizi (ed.), *Relaciones históricas de Santo Domingo*, cited in Silvio Torres Saillant, 'Creoleness or Blackness?,' p. 30.
57   Moreau de St Mery claims that there were 'fewer *libertos* than whites, but many in relation to blacks,' although he could have been including many mulattos who passed as white in that category (Moreau de St Mery, *Descripción*, p. 92).
58   Esquemeling, *The Bucaneers of America* (1969), p. 64.
59   Michiel Baud notes that among the tobacco producers of the Cibao valley in the nineteenth century, cross-class interracial unions out of wedlock through the institution of the mistress were the norm (Michiel Baud, *Peasants and Tobacco in the Dominican Republic, 1870–1930* [Knoxville, TN, 1995]).
60   For more on slavery and *cimarronage* in the Dominican Republic, see Carlos Esteban Deive, *Los guerrilleros negros: esclavos fugitivos y cimarrones en Santo Domingo* (Santo Domingo, 1989); and Ruben Silié, *Economia, esclavitud y población: ensayos de interpretación histórica del Santo Domingo español en el siglo XVIII* (Santo Domingo, 1976).
61   Rodríguez Molas cited in Baretta and Markoff, 'Cattle Frontiers in Latin America', p. 599.

relations in not only cattle but also contraband tended toward intensely personal bonds. Considered inviolable, buccaneers were characteristically fiercely loyal to each other, sharing all booty together. Called *matelotage*, the bonds forged in the intimate ties of codependency among corsairs and pirates were highly ritualised and typically included homosexual ties.[62]

While it may not be fair to describe slavery in the Dominican Republic as more benign than elsewhere, one can say that relations with owners and employers tended to be intimate, if hierarchical. Most Dominican slaves were domestic, and many of those who relied on slave labour commonly rented it for the day, since they were too poor to purchase it outright. Slave labour was even rented by the day in fairly capitalised firms, such as cigar factories.[63] In the most technologically advanced enterprise of the period — sugar — the largest firm in the country was composed of 200 slaves — far inferior to Jamaica, for example. And even on the largest plantations, ties of ritual co-parentage actually linked whites and slaves, making for a less distanced style of authority relations than other slave regimes.[64]

Dominicans did own slaves, yet after the collapse of the early plantation economy, these were most often acquired illicitly. This fact must have fostered Dominicans' tendency to define slavery as something not really their own. Indeed, the bulk of slaves arriving in Santo Domingo during this period were not bought directly, but rather plundered as spoils at sea or stolen and resold. Given the shortage of slave labour, a thriving branch of the contraband economy was that of brigands who operated in the border regions of Haiti and the Dominican Republic who either captured runaways or stole slaves from large French plantations and then bartered them off for cash or cattle. They were also known for kidnapping whites and charging ransom in slaves. Some individuals based in Santiago boldly travelled to Haiti where they robbed slaves to sell in Spanish territory, presumably at locally affordable prices, undercutting slavers with high overheads to recoup. The problem became so severe under Toussaint Louverture that a formal complaint was lodged against the Spanish authorities. Many of these brigands were themselves black or brown, probably Spanish Creoles.[65] And most slaves purchased on Spanish terrain were not paid for in cash, but rather swapped for tobacco, cattle or other livestock

---

62   B.R. Burg, *Sodomy and the Pirate Tradition. English Sea Rovers in the Seventeenth-Century Caribbean* (New York, 1983), p. 128. For more on pirate culture during this period, see Rediker, *Between the Devil and the Deep Blue Sea*, and W. Jeffrey Bolster, *Black Jacks: African American Seamen in the Age of Sail* (Cambridge, MA, 1997).

63   Sánchez Valverde, *Ensayos* (Santo Domingo, 1988), pp. 249–50.

64   David Barry Gaspar, 'Slave Resistance in the Spanish Caribbean in the Mid-1790s,' in David Barry Gaspar and David Patrick Geggus (eds.), *A Turbulent Time: The French Revolution and the Greater Caribbean* (Bloomington, 1997), p. 142.

65   *Ibid.*, p. 143, note 197.

or otherwise acquired. This fact is particularly notable since both tobacco and cattle, as we shall see, are major symbols of Spanish Creole identity. If slavery in the Dominican Republic was associated with illicit wealth originating outside the nation, perceived as stolen booty, one can begin to see why. By the eighteenth century, slaves were rarely categorised generically as a unit, as 'esclavos', but rather it was always noted whether they were 'esclavos franceses' or Creoles, the former presumed to be fugitives escaping harsh crimes, runaways or illegitimately acquired. In the Dominican Republic, not only was slavery perceived as exogenous, as exotic and illegitimate, but blackness was not primarily associated with the slave condition since most Blacks in the Spanish colony were freedmen.

There was enough colonial legislation seeking to curb the advances of freedmen to indicate that they were not only doing well, but too well. Moreau de St. Mery, who visited Santo Domingo in 1783, reported that 'color prejudice, which in other countries has erected a barrier between whites and freedmen or their descendents almost does not exist.' But then, how could it, when 'the great majority of the Spanish colonists are mestizos'.[66] Laws were passed restricting blacks from wearing the finery of their social superiors such as gold jewellery, pearls, silk or draping shawls, which must have been quite commonplace to merit official intervention. There was also a law preventing freedmen from certain professions, such as secretaries, notaries, the judiciary, the military or the civil service. Yet clearly these juridical barriers were being frequently violated, since the assimilation and advance of mulattos was such that it drew protests from the metropolis when freedmen were encroaching on teaching and the priesthood by the early 1700s.[67] 'Racial drift' or the effective absorption of mixed-race into the social category of whiteness either by acquiring capital or adopting the demeanour of the upper class must have been commonplace given St Mery's observation that 'the political construction of the Spanish colony does not allow deference before the civil status of a white and a freedman'.[68] By 1794 there were nearly a third more freedmen than slaves, and the numbers of both greatly outstripped that of whites.[69]

The frontier nature of the economy provided more avenues for upward mobility than the more developed corners of the Spanish Empire. For example, given the lax disciplinary controls of the cattle economy, it was relatively easy for labourers to escape the ranches and either commence

---

66   Moreau de Saint Mery, *Descripción*, p. 93.
67   Hoetink, *The Dominican People, 1850–1900. Notes for a Historical Sociology*, translated by Stephen K. Ault (Baltimore, 1982) p. 183.
68   Moreau de Saint Mery, *Descripción*, p. 94. On 'racial drift', see Kuznesof and Schwartz, 'Race, Class and Gender: A Conversation,' *Colonial Latin American Review*, vol. 4, no. 1 (1995), pp. 153–201.
69   *The Dominican People*, p. 183.

their own herd, or start their own business selling cattle parts. This must have been quite commonplace, given ordinances specifically aimed at curtailing freed black cattle rustlers by resettling them on the outskirts of the capital city.[70] Indeed, the tension between agriculturalists and hunters, which was commonplace throughout Latin American frontiers, had a racial valence in this case, with whiter farmers, frustrated by wild boar herds, taking specific legislative aim at the coloured population. Complaints also arose in the world of commerce that 'the white population does not have useful employment because the mechanical trades and retail business are in the hands of free blacks and dark coloureds'.[71] Travellers were consistently shocked at the 'hauteur and overbearing pride' of the Creoles, who probably challenged their sense of appropriate demeanour for those who had only fairly recently escaped the shackles of slavery.[72]

However, the most important Afro-Creole domain was the backwoods, where many *cimarrón* communities had formed, one of which was even officially recognised by both French and Spanish authorities. Lundahl estimates that by the 1770s, Haitian maroons were the majority in Dominican border towns, and at mid-century 3,000 slaves from the French colony were resident in Spanish border areas (although to be fair the borderline itself was only really established in 1777 when the western area was ceded to France in the Treaty of Aranjuez).[73]

But to mention only the runaway slave communities presumes that black culture was merely an isolated enclave. Indeed, the fact that slavery was not practised in a discrete zone meant that blackness was patently not bounded, but rather (as Esteban Deive argues) touched Dominican culture as a whole.[74] Indeed, the free black and mulatto nomadic peasantry practising slash and burn cultivation and only occasional cash cropping as needed was neither marginal nor a minority. Rather, they formed the bulk of the rural population outside the Cibao valley, where the export crop tobacco was produced.[75] And even the proud Santiago de los Caballeros,

70   *Ibid.*, p. 146.
71   *Ibid.*, p. 183.
72   Walton, *Present State of the Spanish Colonies*, p. 380. Comments of this nature appear in nearly every travel account cited here. Bryan Edwards wages the same nature of complaint about West Indian Creoles, who he said suffered from 'ostentatious pride,' a 'ridiculous affectation of splendor' and an exaggerated 'consciousness of self importance' (*The History, Civil and Commerical, of the British Colonies in the West Indies*, vol. III [London, 1801]), p. 9.
73   Mats Lundahl, 'Haitian Migration to the Dominican Republic,' in his *The Haitian Economy: Man, Land and Markets* (New York, 1993), pp. 112–13.
74   Carlos Esteban Deive, *La eclavitud del negro en Santo Domingo (1492–1844)*, vols. I and II (Santo Domingo, 1980).
75   For a sense of the prevalence of the *montero*, see Sánchez Valverde, *Idea del valor*. Walton (*Present State of the Spanish Colonies*) describes the ubiquity of both *monteros* and maroons.

considered the seat of the agrarian aristocracy, was described in 1666 as a town of hunters and planters (in that order).[76] Called *monteria*, this style of rural existence was the bane of eighteenth and nineteenth century liberals, who saw its dispersion as anathema to a cultural grid that privileged urbanism as the seat of civilisation and culture. They lamented that the *monteros* 'never see the capital just like the first Indians' and worried incessantly about how to harness their labour for national development.[77] This free coloured community was also seen as patently dangerous because it could serve as a sponge for escaped slaves fleeing *ingenios* and haciendas. Yet it is clear that the *montero* mountain peasant was critical in defining a patently Creole lifestyle, one that resisted sedentary agriculture, developing small subsistence plots called *conucos* only as needed, and only partially entering market relations. Yet, contrary to protopeasants elsewhere in the Caribbean, these were first and foremost hunters, and only very partially agriculturalists.[78]

Contemporary observers vilified the *monteros* as the quintessential barbarians who refused to sell at market, wear proper clothes or live in towns. They were 'a funny sight', with their black rags, stained with blood and grease, a leather belt threaded with four daggers and a cartridge box and rough-hewn sandals.[79] They actually figure far more negatively than slaves because they resided completely outside the social order. The slave was subhuman but he at least was located within society — even if on the bottom rung. A 1793 rural report wrote,

> the free blacks are the worst ... they are hopeless; they usually live in the bush, as they desire total freedom and independence; they run around almost naked, and are the cause of all the problems that are committed and could be committed on the island. Estos negros son la mayor parte vagos, malentretenidos ... amancebados, ebrios y ladrones.[80]

To the *monteros'* credit, however, shifting agriculture was a sensible response to the low demographic density of eastern Hispaniola. As late as 1871 only one tenth of the land in La Vega province was in cultivation.[81]

76 Esquemeling, *The Buccaneers*, p. 24.
77 Sánchez Valverde, *Idea de valor*, p. 148. The state was too weak to effect a passbook system, which succeeded in sedentising the corresponding *jíbaro* population in Puerto Rico.
78 Thus this model resembles more the Puerto Rican style of peasantry than that of Haiti or the British West Indies, where provision grounds were the basis of market relations even within slavery, and thus the basis of the 'protopeasantry' for Mintz and Creole society for Trouillot; see Michel-Rolph Trouillot, 'Culture on the Edges: Creolization in the Plantation Context,' *Plantation Society in the Americas*, vol. V, no. 1 (Spring 1998), pp. 8–28.
79 Labat, *Viajes a las islas de la América*, p. 246.
80 Raymundo González, 'Hay tres clases de gentes en la campaña ...,' *El Caribe*, 23 November 1991, p. 18.
81 Hoetink, *The Dominican People*, p. 5.

Contrary to the fears of *hacendados* and *hateros,* however, free blacks in the Spanish colony appear to have rarely identified with slaves. Indeed, during the rural tumult caused by the Haitian Revolution in the 1790s, the *monteros* more often offered their services in the *marechausée* — groups formed to hunt slave runaways. In the view of a visitor to the island in 1828, there were:

> few slaves on this part of the island and these were living in so great a state of equality with the people that slavery was only known by name. They evinced no desire whatsoever to throw off their adherence to their masters and join their brethren of the west.[82]

Further evidence of the exemplary patriotism of free coloureds is that a group of upstanding mulattos helped fight the British to actually maintain Spanish colonial control in 1810.[83] Some notorious *moreno* criminals even focused their attacks primarily on slaves, killing and injuring them.[84] French minister Raybaud wrote that Dominican Blacks

> felt too proud of the social superiority that daily contact with their masters imparted them over the slaves in the French section to consent to imitate the latter whom they haughtily called '*los negros*'.[85]

If the Spanish colonists perceived the *monteros* as completely autarchic, that was not entirely the case. Spatially autonomous, these mountain peasants did maintain active if sporadic relations with the market. Indeed, the *monteros* commenced tobacco production for trading purposes in the latter sixteenth century, finding the British, French and Dutch avid purchasers.[86] Tobacco served their needs because it could be dried and easily transported, as well as saved; tobacco, alongside the pig, rapidly became the savings bank of the rural poor, a means of quick and ready cash. By 1678 some two million pounds of tobacco leaf were exported to France.[87] These two valuable exports — tobacco and livestock — created a symbiosis between

---

82   James Franklin, *The Present State of Hayti (Saint Domingo,) with Remarks on its Agriculture, Commerce, Laws, Religion, Finances, and Population, etc., etc.* (Westport, CT, 1970 [1828]), p. 184.

83   Fradique Lizardo, *Cultura africana en Santo Domingo* (Santo Domingo, 1979), p. 53, cited in Torres Saillant, 'Creoleness or Blackness?' p. 31.

84   I have in mind the case of the *'negro incognito'*; see Raymundo González, 'El "Comegente" atacaba personas y propiedades cerca de las poblaciones,' *El Caribe,* 28 September 1991. Although González argues that the attacks on blacks may have been an attack on the most precious property of Spanish colonial society, and thus not really on the blacks per se at all.

85   Raybaud cited in Hoetink, *The Dominican People,* p. 186.

86   Esquemeling states that tobacco production was begun expressly for the purposes of trade (*The Buccaneers of America,* p. 48).

87   Baud, 'Peasant Society under Siege,' p. 20.

the *monteros* and smugglers, as producers and traders, both of which were 'marked by vigorous, often violent antipathy against traditional authority'[88] — to Spanish colonial society and its mercantile restrictions.

As a result, tobacco and cattle came to symbolise an emergent Creole identity, one associated if implicitly with free blacks and mulattos and a racial democracy in which there were multiple opportunities for upward mobility, unlike plantation crops such as cacao or sugar which required slave labour and produced a rigid virtual caste system. This is clear in the writings of nineteenth century Dominican liberal Pedro Francisco Bonó, whose ideas regarding the virtues of tobacco cultivation influenced Cuban anthropologist Fernando Ortiz's musings about tobacco and sugar. In the words of Bonó, 'cacao is oligarchical and tobacco is democratic … all the workers work together, all of them earning, producing and consuming national produce and giving life to society'.[89] Bonó saw tobacco as one of the key formative influences in the development of this cosmopolitan society and new 'race', which was a mixture of the caucasian, the Indian and the African, which he contrasted to Haiti, which was seen as exclusively black.[90] Indeed, tobacco became a key trope for late eighteenth and nineteenth century liberal boosters who wanted to promote national development through challenging the pessimism of Eurocentric racial theorising. Just as tobacco was superior to sugar (which produced 'excessive profit and caused a risk to our nationalities'),[91] Dominican *criollos* were superior to the French colonists of neighbouring Haiti who were consumed by the tropics; Creoles, by contrast, live longer and get stronger the farther they are from their European origin.[92]

If intellectuals such as Bonó constructed tobacco and sugar as symbols of Creole identity and its antithesis, thus the Dominican Republic and its difference to Haiti, they did not entirely invent them. Given the pervasive

88   Rediker, *Between the Devil and the Deep Blue Sea*, p. 275.
89   Rodríguez Demorizi (ed.), *Papeles de Pedro F. Bonó*, p. 363.
90   *Ibid*, p. 399. Interestingly, while Bonó embraces tobacco and the racial democracy it helped forge, he vilifies its primary producers, the *monteros*, for their stubborn refusal to live in groups or towns. As he states, 'Nuestro pueblo, señor A., tiene prendas relevantísimas individuales, es bravo, audaz, es bondádoso, hospitalario, sencillo, trabajador, inteligente, emprendedor. Separadamente individuo por individuo, es de lo mejor que hay en el mundo, pero tomado colectivamente es casi inútil; no tiene la sociedad dominicana esa cohesión indispensable de toda agrupación humana que quiere ser definitivamente independiente, dueña absoluta de sus destinos. El fondo de nuestro carácter nacional lo constituye el particularismo, el individualismo. No se percibe en ninguno de sus actos la nota predominante que constituye el alma de las naciones estables' (p. 399).
91   *Ibid*, p. 610. For more on Bonó, see Raymundo González, 'El pensamiento de Bonó: Nación y clases trabajadoras,' in González et al. (eds.), *Política, identidad y pensamiento social*, pp. 41–64; and *Bonó, un intelectual*.
92   Sánchez Valverde, *Idea del valor*, p. 163.

poverty and lack of specie, Dominican traders more frequently swapped tobacco for slaves than bought them with cash. Indeed, tobacco, the key smallholder cash crop, and cattle, collected by free black hunters on the north coast or produced by southern ranchers, were the two most important surrogate currencies used for acquiring slaves.[93] It is not surprising, then, that cattle and tobacco became popular linked symbols of national value, race mixture and Creole identity. Evidence is the fact that Dominican peasants class their tobacco leaf into two varieties, *criollo* and *oler*. Being from local seeds (*oler* seeds were originally from Cuba) *criollo* is favoured for export due to its rich growth and large leaf. The language used to describe the Creole leaf not surprisingly invokes the *mestizo*: dark brown or dark cinnamon in colour and slightly chocolate in aroma. If both the kitchen garden or provision ground and its produce, food, are staple symbols of *lo criollo*, then it makes sense that the *montero* style of tobacco planting was to intersperse it with food crops such as manioc, corn and beans in the *conuco*, the small subsistence food plots of the itinerant *montero* or free black.[94] Significantly, tobacco was also planted inside the backyard pigpen.[95] Interestingly, there are other local tobacco varieties that are not exported and which all invoke cattle: *ranchero*, *lengua de vaca*, *rabo de mula* and *el hatero*.[96] The cross-pollination of tobacco and cattle names here is significant since it underscores their common identity as linked Creole symbols that form part of the same regime of value, which seemed to become even more Creole in the very act of exchange with outsiders. Tobacco and cattle were thus 'earmarked monies' which came to represent the emerging domestic Creole identity of the Spanish colonists, ones which were seen as distinct from the fabulous yet clandestine wealth of the illicit 'sweet trade' whose bounty of gold, silver, slaves, pearls, specie, sugar and other forms of treasure seemed to appear out of nowhere, and often vanished just as fast.[97] Although the *montero*-buccaneer relationship was symbiotic,

93   *Ibid.*, p. 157.
94   Baud, 'Peasant Production,' p. 24 and Baud, 'A Colonial Counter Economy: Tobacco Production on Española, 1500-1870,' *Nieuwe West-Indische Gids/New West Indian Guide*, vol. 65, nos. 1 and 2 (1991); pp. 27–49. Trouillot places the provision grounds at the centre of Creole identity production in 'Culture on the Edges'. Sánchez Valverde states: 'Conucos se llaman en Santo Domingo las labranzas de frutos del país, que en cierto número de varas de terreno hacen regularmente los negro libres, etc., o los esclavos jornaleros, a quienes lo conceden los proprietarios que no pueden cultivar la área de su pertenencia, por el precio de cinco pesos al año' (Sánchez Valverde, *Idea del valor*, p. 202).
95   Sánchez Valverde, *Idea del valor*, p. 157.
96   Baud, 'Peasant Society under Siege,' appendix: pp. 200–01. For more on Bonó and his contribution to the symbolics of Creole identity in the Dominican Republic, see my essay, 'Gringo Chickens with Worms'.
97   The notion of earmarked monies is from Viviana A. Zelizer, *The Social Meaning of Money: Pin Money, Paychecks, Poor Relief, and other Currencies* (New York, 1994), pp. 1–35.

they were distinguished by the fact that the latter had far more ready access to cash, the lack of which made for certain critical scarcities on land, particularly of manufactured goods. For example, the clothes of Spanish colonists were so ragged that mass was held before sunrise to avoid embarrassment and many women avoided mass altogether for lack of proper shawls.[98] While buccaneers sought exclusively treasure and high value luxury goods, *monteros* were quite particular about the goods they traded for, requesting only items useful to their hunting needs, such as cloth, shot and gunpowder; they were not interested in accumulation for its own sake.[99]

Indeed, cattle functioned as a virtual currency within the Spanish colony. Interestingly, the very term originated in the Mediaeval Latin *capitale*, which meant funds or holdings. Cattle and its byproducts from the Spanish colony were highly valued in the region, and were taken to be a standard of value, within the colony and without.[100] Indeed, even if payment was reckoned in terms of pieces of eight, seventeenth-century Spanish currency; leather was as good as silver when it came to reckoning ransom and was commonly used as specie.[101] Smoked meat was recognised to be the lifeblood of the economy.[102] The Church accepted tithe in calves. So central were cattle to the contraband economy that when the Spanish sought in vain to curtail the black market along the north coast of the island, they did so by ordering the slaughter of all cattle in 1684. Cattle were so singularly important that they served as a means of political currency and leverage by the state.[103] If slaves were the *ur*-commodity par excellence of the eighteenth century, cattle were their mirror, and the two were often coupled as related yet distinct in the imagination of the time. The commensurability of cattle and slaves, for example, was key to the exchange rate of the slave trade in the Caribbean; it was also taken for granted in contemporary parlance.[104]

The Haitian Occupation

The period when sugar and cattle were solidified as signs of alterity was the nineteenth century when Haiti entered the sugar bonanza and the

---

98　Moreau de St Mery, *Descripción*, p. 85.
99　Labat, *Viajes a las islas de la América*, p. 245. Galvin, *Patterns of Pillage*, mentions the fortunes of former buccaneers who retired to civil service on Tortuga Island (pp. 109–68).
100　See Labat's comments on how delicious and unique was the taste of the cured meat produced by Santo Domingo buccaneers, which he says 'is infinitely more delicious and delicate' than other smoked meats (*Viajes a las islas de América*, pp. 234–35).
101　Galvin, *Patterns of Pillage*, p. 132; and Edwards, *An Historical Survey*, p. 136.
102　Moreau de St Mery, *Descripción*, p. 105.
103　As when the Spanish governor froze all French cattle withdrawals to pressure them to sign the border Treaty of Aranjuez in 1773 (Moreau de St Mery, *Descripción*, p. 25).
104　Edwards, *British Colonies*, p. 151.

Dominican economy was cast as its primary source for oxen, mules, meat and hide. Sugar came to stand in for the cluster of associations surrounding the contraband economy. Deployed as a currency, West Indian planters even paid their taxes in sugar in the eighteenth century.[105] As surrogate specie, then, sugar invoked the economy of piracy that virtually monopolised most regional currency from the sixteenth to the eighteenth centuries. By the mid-eighteenth century, the spectacular growth of sugar production in Haiti had created a thriving market for skins and smoked meat products, and as a result the Dominican ranching economy expanded, especially in the frontier areas due to their proximity to Port-au-Prince, the Haitian capital. A guaranteed market also provided an incentive to improve herds, and cattle quality improved along with yields.[106] Ruben Silié describes the Dominican Republic as 'doubly dependent' during this period,[107] upon Spain as well as Haiti, which became the primary consumer of Dominican products, as well as its key link to global markets for products such as mahogany and dyewoods, which were shipped through Haiti to Europe. One observer estimated that the French purchased upwards of 25,000 head of cattle and 2,500 mules and horses, and that the Spanish spent some half a million dollars per year in Haiti purchasing manufactured goods, tools and slaves.[108] This trade was so profitable that the Crown tried hard to tax it, though in vain.[109] By the onset of the Haitian Revolution (1791–1804) there was a clear sense of symbiotically linked yet distinct modes of production on the island, with a flourishing and extensive ranching economy in the east, and a far more prosperous sugar economy in the west (even if the Haitian revolutionary period had been depressionary, since the frontier zones were evacuated and the east was drawn into the civil war). Although the Haitian Revolution itself, which brought successive waves of French, Haitian and British troops onto Dominican terrain, piqued nationalist sensibilities among Dominicans, most slaves actually allied with their owners.[110] In the aftermath of the Haitian Revolution fears of possible further foreign intervention drove Haitian leaders to invade and finally occupy the Dominican Republic (1822–44).

The Dominican response was complex and varied considerably by region and social group. In response to rumours encouraged by Haiti that free coloureds could be reenslaved by the French, there was popular support for the intervention in certain regions. Dominican slaves certainly

105 At a time when produce was inadmissible. See Long, *The History of Jamaica*, p. 537.
106 Franklin, *The Present State of Hayti*, p. 26.
107 Silié, *Economía, esclavitud y población*, pp. 35 and 24.
108 Franklin, *Present State of Hayti*, p. 35.
109 Sánchez Valverde, *Idea del valor*, p. 157.
110 Franklin, *Present State of Hayti*, p. 28. See Geggus 'Slave Resistance' for an account of slave revolts in Santo Domingo and Cuba during the revolution.

rejoiced at the unilateral abolition of slavery, which had been declared earlier by Louverture but not enforced. Dominicans in the border zones supported incorporation, since Haiti was their primary market. Moreover, many of the poor were captivated by promises of land grants to freedmen and the abolition of taxes. And some elites felt that union with Haiti would be progressive and could help spur economic development in the east. There was even intellectual support among certain liberals, who rallied in favour of an island confederation.[111]

The basic thrust of Haitian President Boyer's economic policy was the modernisation of land and labour in the Dominican Republic, in an effort to reinvigorate a sagging economy in Haiti. The privatisation of land tenure and the promotion of cash cropping for export became the key watchwords. The revolutionary war had rung the death knell for the plantation economy, as former slaves fled into the countryside to become subsistence farmers. At the same time, the government had agreed to pay an indemnity to France in exchange for recognition and needed to jump-start the ailing economy in order to commence these payments. The first step was the privatisation of land, which had dramatic repercussions in the east where most land was *ejido* or public land for ranching purposes, and most private property was held in common, as *terrenos comuneros*. Church properties were nationalised, and émigré and public lands were recouped, some of which were doled out to revolutionary war veterans instead of a pension. All land that could not prove private ownership was subject to nationalisation for the purposes of redistribution.[112] In an effort to conduct more effective taxation the government issued a new round of currency, a highly unpopular move since paper emissions were seen as inflationary, 'ruinous' and even 'fatal', and the new copper coinage was described as too 'diminutive' for Haiti's 'national greatness'.[113] The State sought to counter a widespread culture of economic subterfuge, such as the peasantry's proclivity to engage in 'subterranean investments in capital'.[114] Many merchants operated through exchanges of coffee credit rather than cash; and the peasantry frequently invested their earnings in

111   Bonóin Demorizi (ed.), *Papeles de Pedro F. Bonó*, p. 610.
112   For more on the land question during the Haitian period, see Frank Moya Pons' essay, 'The Land Question in Haiti and SantoDomingo: The Sociopolitical Context of the Transition from Slavery to Free Labor, 1801–1843,' in Manuel Moreno Fraginals et al. (eds.),*The Spanish Speaking Caribbean in the Nineteenth Century* (Baltimore, 1985), pp. 181–214; for more on *terrenos comuneros*, see Samuel Hazard, *Santo Domingo, Past and Present; with a Glance at Hayti* (New York, 1873), pp. 481–84, and Sánchez Valverde, *Idea del valor*, p. 149.
113   For a criticism of paper currency emissions, see Long, *History of Jamaica*, p. 533; for the rationale against copper coinage and Haitian national value, see Brown, *Santo Domingo*, p. 262.
114   *Ibid.*, p. 287.

'treasure', which they buried alongside their coinage. Great sums of cash did disappear in this way, even though this practice was prohibited by law. In 1837, for example, 20,000 gold doubloons — a considerable fortune — were discovered under a plantation near Cap François, and smaller troves were found hidden near Port-au-Prince and St Marc.[115]

The main obstacle to the effective execution of these measures was the confused system of land tenancy in the Dominican Republic. Called *terrenos comuneros*, much of the land in the east was held collectively, with each owner possessing shares (*pesos* or *acciones*) in usufruct, a system developing in the seventeenth century during a period when the man-land ratio was overwhelmingly in favour of the latter. The resultant lack of clear private property in land was seen by the Haitian regime as a major impediment to progress; as a result, legislation was introduced to force sales of all land for which tenancy could not be proved.[116] Simultaneous to clarifying private land tenure, the regime sought to require production for export. If former Haitian slaves withdrew from plantation labour due to its association with slavery, the Dominican problem was different: there simply was no widespread practice of commercial agriculture, market relations were not ubiquitous and there was a long history, as we have seen, of barter and contraband. To add muscle to this effort, Boyer then implemented the Rural Code, a vagrancy law requiring everyone to till the land, excepting only a few privileged categories of professionals, such as civil servants and professors. Boyer clearly had his own reasons for seeking to augment state revenues — the need to offset the repeasantisation of the Haitian economy and the resultant collapse of the sugar plantation economy. But these moves were most likely heralded by Dominican liberals who had long since tried to find a way to make peasants out of the *monteros* — to capture the labour of a group which had successfully resisted state capture. As José Ramón Abad lamented,

> The land should be the well-guaranteed property of the cultured man, the always fertile workshop of regular and orderly work, not the wrong-headed, unproductive and anonymous pastures of ranching, nor the silent theatre of a vagabond life.[117]

While the voices of liberal critics became louder over the course of the nineteenth century, a shrill minority at mid-century launched attacks on the itinerant black peasantry as an anti-national force, one which could only become 'true citizens' through the virtues of commercial agriculture and

115 *Ibid.*
116 This account derives from Frank Moya Pons, *La dominación haitiana: 1822–44* (Santiago, 1973).
117 José Ramón Abad, *La República Dominicana: reseña general geográfico-estadística* (Santo Domingo, 1888), p. 288.

participation in national markets.[118] Boyer's efforts were ultimately a failure, due to the monumentality of the task of overhauling and modernising the land system and the lack of state resources for surveying. And the *terrenos comuneros* were one issue that united elite and peasant Dominican opposition to Boyer alike, since anyone engaged in some sedentary agriculture used this archaic and deeply Creole system for apportioning usufruct, one in which rights to cultivate, harvest and cull wood, for example, on a single plot were discrete and could be assigned to different individuals.[119] If 1822 was a good year for the economy, by 1835 a general agricultural decline had set in throughout the island, exacerbated by the US economic crisis, which Boyer sought in vain to avert through inflationary money emissions — by devaluing the Haitian gourde 250 per cent. And the contraband economy based on cattle ground to a halt since unification eliminated trade with Haiti.[120]

The Haitian occupation created a head-on clash between two economic logics. As a result of the sugar plantation economy, Haiti had experienced a far more thorough integration into global commerce and commercial agriculture than the Dominican Republic — the strength of its national currency until the revolution being a prime example. A history of ranching, wild meat hunting and shifting agricultural production based on communal lands made for a radically different economic logic, one that clashed with the Haitian State's agenda when it sought to foster commercial agriculture. The occupation was to confirm the difference between these two regimes of value: if Haiti had a monopoly on what were considered the key seventeenth and eighteenth century commodities — bullion, specie, sugar and slaves — the independent state had money.[121] The impoverished east by contrast had only cattle, tobacco, mahogany and land — all of which had served as alternative protocurrencies in inter-island trade, but had more limited exchange value on the global stage. If the economic disruption brought by the Haitian Revolution had created a situation in which 'the widespread poverty was such that distinct classes almost

---

118 The 'true citizens' quote is from Hoetink, *The Dominican People*, p. 9. See also Raymundo González, 'Ideología del progreso y campesinado,' pp. 25–44. My thanks to Raymundo for sharing with me his extensive knowledge of nineteenth century Dominican primary sources.

119 Hazard, noted in Hoetink, *The Dominican People*, Hoetink argues that *terrenos comuneros* were a Creole invention in Mörner (ed.), *Race and Class*, p. 103, noting that Del Monte y Tejeda mentions fifty *hatos* or ranches that had been individually owned, but which subsequently devolved into *terrenos comuneros*. On the other hand, discrete and distinct overlapping forms of usufruct was a feature of mediaeval Spanish land tenure as well.

120 Franklin, *The Present State of Hayti*, p. 297.

121 The Dominican Republic got its first national currency in 1944, when the National Bank was formed by Rafael Trujillo; before that time a series of regional currencies and the US dollar circulated.

ceased to exist; the purchasing powers of the *hacendado* and the free mulatto were on a par'.[122] This process of social levelling was furthered by the
Haitian occupation due to the attack on the two key factors of production:
large landowners and slaves.

During the latter half of the nineteenth century, the racial topography
of the Dominican Republic witnessed dramatic change. But the major
change occurred in the 1870s, when US corporate firms began installing
enormous sugar *centrales* along the southern coast of the island. To staff
these enormous enterprises cheaply, they imported contract labour from
Haiti and the West Indies for seasonal work cutting cane during the milling
season. If the Dominican Republic successfully avoided the first wave of
plantation agriculture and the resultant pattern of sharp racial and class
stratification, they suffered the second acutely in ways that had dramatic
repercussions for the relationship between race and national identity. The
creation of a foreign labour niche almost exclusively staffed by Haitians
created a new association between blackness and a particularly opprobri-
ous form of labour — unskilled, underpaid, highly dangerous and back-
breaking — based on contracts resembling slavery. This new ethnic
enclave had been foisted upon the country by US firms and thus was perceived ultimately as yet another US insult to the national patrimony, as
Baud asserts, 'Anti-Yankee feelings thus confirmed and reinforced anti-
Haitian feelings'.[123] This new ethnic labour market segmentation had the
dual effect of both denationalising blackness, by making it synonymous
with Haiti (as well as the evil machinations of the USA), just as it enabled
Dominicans to claim whiteness as a result of the fact they could suddenly
see themselves as 'superior' to Haitians for avoiding any participation in
this new, disagreeable unskilled form of labour.[124]

This new triangle formed between the USA, Haiti and the Dominican
Republic was reinforced even further during the 1920s US military occupations of the two nations. In the US racial gaze, both countries were
equally black, since US racial taxonomies did not allow for mixed-race status. The new demeaning conflation between unskilled work and blackness
may have created a logic whereby Dominicans sought to reclaim social

---

122 Hoetink, *The Dominican People*, p. 168.
123 Baud, 'Constitutionally White,' pp. 131–2. Torres Saillant has another take on this,
     arguing that the ideology of Dominican whitening has arisen in relation to US impe-
     rial penetration, representing Dominican elites' need to be recognised and valued by
     the USA ('Creoleness or Blackness?', p. 40). Aviva Chomsky alleges that a similar mix
     of anti-imperialism and anti-Haitianism developed in Cuba as a result of contract
     labour; see her essay, 'Barbados or Canada?'.
124 See Noel Ignatiev, *How the Irish Became White* (New York, 1995), for a parallel argu-
     ment about Irish identity and labour market segmentation in nineteenth-century
     urban America.

honour by distancing themselves as far as possible from Haiti and Haitians, so as to move closer to whiteness. Only in this way could they avoid bearing the brunt of US sambo stereotypes at a moment when, under US direct rule, they were suddenly painfully aware of the US perception of them as black due to the imposition of Jim Crow segregation on their home terrain. Thus, by providing an avenue for accentuating their difference from Haiti, anti-Haitianism seemed to move Dominicans closer to whiteness on a scale of gradation. In sum, the contract labour scheme inaugurated an entirely new phase in the changing relationship between race and national identity in the Dominican Republic, as blackness was ethnicised through labour force segmentation, reinforcing Dominicans' proclivity to see blackness as a thing apart.[125]

Conclusion

'Of money, as a central sign of civilization.' [126]

Daniel Webb

While traditional Dominican historians have maintained that anti-Haitianism commenced with the Haitian occupation and continued unabated until the present, I would argue that this view accords far too much causal weight to the occupation itself. It provides a nationalist narrative that is sentimentally appealing, and one which assuages contemporary guilt for the 1937 Haitian massacre in which some 20,000 Haitian border migrants were slaughtered by Dominican troops (which then becomes the Dominican riposte to the 'domination'), but which is ultimately inaccurate. Boyer sought to impose a system of commodified property relations in a country in which this was deeply alien; one without a national currency, for which the lion's share of national trade was conducted surreptitiously through contraband; a nation without private property in land or even much sedentary agriculture to speak of. Even if this project ultimately failed, it reinforced the association between Haiti and processes of commodification as embodied in the key symbols of sugar, slaves and specie which originated in seventeenth-century inter-island trade, as we have seen. The paired contrasting terms of sugar and tobacco, and slavery

---

125 Hoetink places more stress on the stratification produced by sugar itself, than Haitian importation. See his essays: 'Race and Color in the Caribbean,' in Mintz and Price (eds.), *Caribbean Contours*, pp. 55–84; and 'The Dominican Republic in the Nineteenth Century: Some Notes on Stratification, Immigration and Race,' in Magnus Mörner (ed.), *Race and Class*, pp. 96–120.

126 Daniel Webb, esq., *A General History of the Americans, of their Customs, Manners, and Colours. An History of the Blafords, and White Negroes. History of Peru. An History of the Manners, Customs, etc., of the Chinese and Egyptians*, selected by M. Pauw. (Rochdale, 1806).

and ranching, were thus surrogates for the symbolic opposition of commodity versus gift exchange, key signs of difference which helped give
shape to emerging national distinctions on the island.

Nor were the symbols of sugar and slaves merely significant on the
island of Hispaniola; they were the very substance of West Indian colonial
commerce since slaves were used as a general form of value against which
quantities of other products were measured, and sugar itself was used as a
currency in the eighteenth century.[127] It was these two items that gave
Haitian products their market value and Haiti its national worth. In the
eighteenth century, slaves were unique since they were renewable property; they were commodities which themselves produced value. If Haiti had
slaves, the Dominican Republic had not even the cash to pay for them and
was forced to resort to stealing or kidnapping or bartering them for the
homely but trusted Creole products of mules, wild cattle and horses,
tobacco, wood and wax. Through its hypermodern industrial sugar *centrales,*
Haiti seemed to manufacture money in stark contrast to the natural economy of gathering that ruled in the east. Somehow this economy of swap-
ping came to appear as stealing to Dominicans, since the terms of
exchange seemed to make Haiti grow at Dominicans' expense. Haiti has
been marked ever since this formative period, making Dominicans feel
inadequate since, unlike Haiti, they could not afford to purchase (and the
Crown would not grant them) the *ur*-form of commodity — slaves —
which perhaps would have provided them the spectacular economic development Haiti witnessed (if hopefully not the revolution). In sum, this early
formative period marked Haiti as embodying a special kind of value —
one that seemed to beget money out of nothing, steadily but surreptitiously, leaving the Dominican Republic with just the evanescent phantasm
of its 'idea', in the words of Dominican mulatto priest Antonio Sánchez
Valverde. This early phase also posited the notion of Haitian value as illegitimate, as the very embodiment of primitive accumulation through the
plundering of gold, treasure and slaves since even though neither nation
had yet been formed at that time, Haiti has been blamed by subsequent
Dominican anti-Haitian writers as the key agent and instigator of that law-
less and thieving seventeenth-century economy of piracy.[128]

Anti-Haitianism was thus neither a product of the nineteenth-century
occupation, nor does it consist of flat racism. This idea of Haiti as the virtual
embodiment of commodity value — of gold, silver, specie and slaves — dates

---

127   Adam Smith, *An Inquiry into the Nature and Causes of the Wealth of Nations,* edited by
      Edwin Cannan (Chicago, 1976), p. 27. For more on the symbolics of sugar in the
      Dominican Republic, see my essay, 'Gringo Chickens with Worms'.
128   Arturo Manuel Peña Batlle, *La Isla de la Tortuga: plaza de armas, refugio y seminario de los
      enemigos de España en Indias* (Madrid, 1952).

from the early buccaneer economy; yet this derived initially from an attitude of reverence, not depreciation. Haiti also had the symbolic capital of the revolution — of having won their independence from Europe at gunpoint.[129] Anti-Haitianism was transformed into a racially-marked posture of superiority only after the idea of Haiti was ethnicised; when Haitian migrants become synonymous with large scale contract labour imports and the back-breaking and brutal task of cane cutting (which itself is reminiscent of slavery) in the late nineteenth-century. Before that date, it was far more an awe of Haitian potency — economic, political and religious — and a form of racialised national identity. Anti-Haitianism defined blackness as a Haitian monopoly, but it also recognised it as something Dominicans needed to have in order to develop (but continued to lack), given the eighteenth-century logic that great nations were made by plenty of slave labour — and bullion.

The expulsion of blackness from the Dominican nation had repercussions for the meaning of Creole identity. As we have seen, a history of colonial poverty and the openness of the ranching, *montería* and smuggling economies provided many opportunities for freedmen to advance socially and economically. The nineteenth-century multiple interventions and wars also helped enable the formation of an emergent black middle sector through the armed forces, for example, which used the military as a springboard to politics. Indeed, order and progress dictator Ulises Heureaux who ruled for most of the 1880s was but one example of a powerful conservative mulatto strongman; liberal Gregorio Luperón was yet another (not to mention dictator Rafael Trujillo, who ruled from 1930–61). Just as Joaquín Balaguer chided Francisco Peña Gomez in the penultimate Dominican elections as a 'secret Haitian' and thus not Dominican enough to rule, in the 1880s Luperón accused Heureaux as being a US stooge and squashing the 'mestizo race', the Dominican '*indio*', through black importation (not surprisingly, Heureaux himself had Haitian lineage). With the late nineteenth century sugar boom fuelling state formation and the resultant creation of effective party patronage machines, blacks became an important part of both liberal and conservative political factions. Of course, it was the very success of these Dominican mestizos, as well as the fact that all Dominicans have some 'black behind the ear' (as Dominicans say), that has made race so useful as an available negative political currency in electoral discourse.

The fact that creolisation occurred outside the plantation economy in the Dominican Republic shaped a uniquely open pattern of race and class

---

129 Jonathan Brown complained that 'The mass of the people are not only uninstructed, but so profoundly stupid as to give rise to doubts if they are furnished with any intellect whatever. They know nothing of their age or of the events of their life but by referring to some prominent epoch in the history of their country as the "*ancien regime*", the "*ouverture du nord*" or the "*temps de Toussaint*"'. (from *Santo Domingo*, vols. I and II.

stratification, one in which movement within the social order was surpris-ingly generalised, and blackness was not coincident with lowly class status. This was compounded by the fact that freedmen outnumbered slaves very early on, so blackness was not stigmatised in quite the same way as else-where by an association with slavery.[130] The fact of multiple criteria in race marking has meant that almost anyone can seek upward movement through the status order, either through class ascent, or through lineage claims.[131] Unlike white or black, what distinguishes the mulatto is his abil-ity to move into a higher social station than his ascribed status — that of the family he was born into.[132] A sign of this potential movement is that unlike the twin poles of the racial order — black and white — mestizaje is marked linguistically by shades of gradation — *trigueño, indio, indio claro, indio oscuro*, etc., even if hair, ear and lip characteristics are also markers. However, what determines one's ascribed identity in this system is more complicated than appears at first glance since Dominican relations of con-sanguinity are inherently unstable. They are typically defined by the moth-er, since the unmarried matrifocal family pattern is most common, but can be overridden by the father's family since it is a putatively patrilineal sys-tem.[133] Indeed, in popular terms the father's 'blood' is at times considered to have more weight in establishing the race of the child (unlike the British West Indies, where it is said that the mother's is decisive).[134] Moreover, the relationship between race as a status marker and familial identity is further complicated by the fact that Dominican families inevitably include multi-ple hues, and thus even sibling rivalries can become in a sense 'racialised'. In the colonial period, individuals of stature passed by acquiring *cédulas de gracias al sacar* by presenting public testimony of their respectable demeanour. Those without resources or friends in high places, today, as in the seventeenth century, change contexts and reinvent themselves, even if

130   While Silvio Torres Saillant makes this point, he places primacy on demography not mode of production. I would concur with Mintz and Hoetink that it is not just the numbers of freedmen in proportion to slaves, but rather the forms of class and race relation that are produced that are significant.

131   As Jonathan Brown stated in 1837, 'the inhabitants … make unceasing endeavors to appear whiter than they really are. No parvenu pretender ever laboured with more eagerness to gain admission into the highest ranks of fashion than these multi-col-ored republicans, to be included among those of the class next beyond them in approach to the whites' (*Santo Domingo*), p. 284.

132   Although the prestige value of one's region of origin is a factor as well.

133   See Raymond T. Smith, *The Matrifocal Family: Power, Pluralism, and Politics* (New York, 1996).

134   Although the practice of pregnant mothers drinking milk of magnesia to 'whiten' their unborn child may contradict this claim (Howard, 'Colouring'). This contrasts with Jamaica, where 'Mother-blood' is considered more significant; see Smith, *Matrifocal Family*, p. 47.

the rise of the sugar economy restricted these options considerably. Puerto Rican educator Hostos observed in the 1880s the distinctive style of identity this culture produced when he stated that the opportunities for abrupt mobility have created a species of 'secret respect for oneself' that dominates in all Dominicans, a feature which may not even have been noteworthy if they were white and not so very brown.[135]

135 Hoetink, *The Dominican People*, p. 170.

CHAPTER 2

The Influence of the Haitian Revolution on Blacks in Latin America and the Caribbean

David Geggus

Introduction

Despite its demographic and geographic limitations, the Haitian, or Saint Domingue, Revolution of 1789–1804 has several major claims to a prominent place in world history.[1] Played out in a population of some 600,000 people, it was confined to an area of less than 12,000 square miles, a speck of land compared to the swathes of North and South America freed from colonial rule in the preceding and succeeding decades. The French colony of Saint Domingue, however, was a powerhouse of the Atlantic economy and had been the leading exporter of tropical staple crops for most of the eighteenth century. The slave uprising that began in August 1791 and transformed the immensely wealthy colony was probably the largest and most dramatically successful one there has ever been. It produced the world's first examples of wholesale emancipation in a major slave-owning society (1793), and of full racial equality in an American colony (1792).[2] Of all American struggles for colonial independence it surely involved the greatest degree of mass mobilisation and brought the greatest degree of social and economic change. Twelve years of devastating warfare — much of it guerrilla warfare, a decade before the term was coined — cost the lives of some 70,000 European soldiers and seamen, and an assuredly larger number of local inhabitants. It left the most productive colony of the day in ruins, its ruling class entirely eliminated. Haiti became Latin America's first independent country, the first modern state in the tropics.

---

1   This introduction draws heavily on the two works cited below, note 8. French historians prefer the term Saint Domingue Revolution on the grounds that national independence was not an issue until the conflict's last 18 months. I find the term Haitian Revolution acceptable for the period after August 1791, when slaves first became involved and transformed what until then had been primarily a struggle between different white factions and the free coloured population.

2   The French *Code Noir* of 1685 did not recognise any distinctions between free persons based on phenotype, but it was not enforced in the Caribbean and was soon contradicted by local legislation. The French Legislative Assembly voted an end to white supremacy in the colonies on 28 March 1792 to encourage free men of colour in Saint Domingue to help suppress the slave uprising that began the preceding August.

On 1 January 1804 the former slave Jean-Jacques Dessalines declared Saint Domingue independent and gave it the aboriginal Amerindian name of 'Haiti' to emphasise the break with Europe and anchor the new state to the American past. Having defeated armies of the three main colonial powers, France, Spain and Britain, the former slaves and free persons of colour turned to making laws for themselves and building a state apparatus. A symbol of black freedom and anti-imperialism, Haiti's first constitution defiantly prohibited landownership by whites and was soon amended to offer citizenship to anyone of African or Indian descent who took up residence in the country.[3] All this occurred in a world dominated by Europeans, where slavery and the slave trade were at their apogee, and where ideas about racial hierarchy were gaining in legitimacy.

It is easy to list the reasons why the Haitian Revolution is important but it is much more difficult to define how it affected the wider world. Its repercussions were felt in a number of domains, from the economic to the intellectual; they were sometimes ambiguous or contradictory, and in the slave-owning Americas they were not always easy to disentangle from the effects of the French Revolution. José Luciano Franco and, more recently, the essays in Gaspar and Geggus, *A Turbulent Time* (1997) have gone some way in charting the interaction between the French and Haitian revolutions in the Greater Caribbean region. But to date there have been few attempts fully to explore its multifarious and complex influence, and only one, by Eleázar Córdova Bello, specifically devoted to Latin America.[4]

From the beginning of the great slave uprising in Saint Domingue's northern plain, the black insurgents seem to have felt they were acting on a world stage. 'The world has groaned at our fate', they told Saint Domingue's governor in the first month of the insurrection.[5] Two years later, the slave leader Georges Biassou looked back to those days as 'a period that will be forever memorable among the great deeds of the universe'. He informed the governor of Spanish Santo Domingo, 'All Europe and the entire world have their eyes turned toward us, watching what course of action we are going to take.'[6] And finally, at the revolution's end in 1804, Louis Boisrond-Tonnerre, author of the Declaration of Independence,

---

3   David Nicholls, *From Dessalines to Duvalier* (Cambridge, 1979); David Geggus, 'The Naming of Haiti,' *New West-Indian Guide*, vol. 71, no. 1/2 (1997), pp. 43–68.

4   Eleázar Córdova-Bello, *La independencia de Haití y su influencia en Hispanoamérica* (Caracas, 1967); José Luciano Franco, *La batalla por el dominio del Caribe y el Golfo de México*, vol. II (Havana, 1965); David Barry Gaspar and David Patrick Geggus (eds.), *A Turbulent Time: The French Revolution and the Greater Caribbean* (Bloomington, 1997).

5   Pamphile de Lacroix, *Mémoires pour servir à l'histoire de la Révolution de Saint Domingue*, vol. I (Paris, 1819), p. 102.

6   Biassou to García, 24 August 1793, in García to Acuña, 23 November 1793, Archivo General de Simancas, Guerra Moderna, 7157. Another copy exists in Audiencia de Santo Domingo 956, Archivo General de Indias, Seville.

finished his memoirs by addressing the 'slaves of all countries' with an incendiary message that encapsulated the Haitian experience: 'you will learn from this great man [Dessalines] that mankind by its nature carries freedom in its heart and the keys to freedom in its hands'.[7]

This confident self-awareness was not misplaced. In an age of tumultuous events, marked by world war and revolution, the deeds of Saint Domingue's slaves and descendants of slaves seized international attention. The repercussions of this tremendous upheaval ranged from the world commodity markets to the studies of poets and philosophers, from the council chambers of the Great Powers to slave quarters from Virginia to Brazil and most points in between. It generated waves of migration and opened new economic frontiers. It stimulated slave revolts and new expansions of slavery, while embittering the developing debates about race, emancipation and decolonisation.[8] This chapter surveys some of this diverse impact on people of African descent in Latin America and the Caribbean.

Early Responses of People of Colour

News of the Haitian Revolution spread wide and fast. Even if it was not quite the 'unthinkable event' Rolph Trouillot has called it, nothing remotely like it had happened before; and nobody could think about slavery in quite the same way again.[9] Within one month of the 1791 uprising, slaves in Jamaica were singing songs about it. The military commander in Spanish Town wrote home that, 'Many slaves here are very inquisitive and intelligent, and ... they have composed songs of the negroes having made a rebellion at Hispaniola with their usual chorus to it.'[10] In 1800, when the ex-slave Toussaint Louverture became the undisputed ruler of Saint Domingue, slaves sang on the streets of Kingston, 'Black, white, brown, all the same'.[11] Just weeks after Toussaint occupied Spanish Santo

---

7   Louis Félix Boisrond-Tonnerre, *Mémoires pour servir à l'histoire d'Haïti* [1804] (Port-au-Prince, 1991), p. 119.

8   David Geggus, 'International Repercussions of the Haitian Revolution', 1999 Elsa Goveia Memorial Lecture (Kingston, 2000); David Geggus (ed.), *The Impact of the Haitian Revolution in the Atlantic World* (Columbia, SC, 2001).

9   Michel-Rolph Trouillot, *Silencing the Past: Power and the Production of History* (Boston, 1995), pp. 70–107. Many people since the 1770s had predicted or warned of a major upheaval in the colony — rather more, I suspect, than ever predicted the coming of the French Revolution. If they did not imagine the emergence of a modern black State, the same might be said of the abolition of the French aristocracy and monarchy, which was the more remarkable in view of the popularity of egalitarian and republican ideas in the 1780s.

10   David Geggus, *Slavery, War and Revolution: The British Occupation of Saint Domingue, 1793–1798* (Oxford, 1982), p. 90.

11   Michael Craton, James Walvin and David Wright (eds.), *Slavery, Abolition and Emancipation: Black Slaves and the British Empire* (London, 1976), p. 138.

Domingo, early the following year, free blacks and slaves in the hills above Coro in western Venezuela rejoiced at the news and sang a refrain that punned on the leader's name, 'Look to the firebrand (*Tison*) ... They'd better watch out!'[12] And in the year of Haitian Independence, slaves in Trinidad were heard parodying the Catholic mass: 'The bread we eat is white man's flesh ... remember St Domingo.'[13]

Even in far-off Rio de Janeiro some free black and mulatto militiamen were found in 1805 to be wearing round their necks medallion portraits of the emperor Dessalines, who had been crowned only months before.[14] Nine years later Bahian merchants complained that slaves were talking openly about local revolts, Haiti and the elimination of all whites and mulattoes.[15] A more subtle example comes from long after the revolution, when in 1836 Cuban officials in Bayamo discovered that the local Carabalí *cabildo* (or Biafran association) had replaced the royal crown on its flag — symbolic of the Spanish monarchy — with a plumed cocked hat, representative of Haitian heads of State.[16] Some doubts remain as to how much news penetrated rural regions, and how news travelled from the Caribbean to Brazil seems to be a mystery. But the basic facts of the Haitian Revolution appear to have been rapidly disseminated along maritime trade routes by sailors, refugees and proselytising privateers of diverse origins.[17]

In many parts of the Americas whites began complaining in 1791 of a new 'insolence' on the part of their slaves, which they often attributed to awareness of the successful revolt. The military commander in Jamaica

12   '... que corre entre los libres y esclavos de la zerranía mui balida la noticia de la toma de la Ysla Española de Santo Domingo p[o]r el Negro Tusen, y qe manifiestan gran regocijo, y alegria con ella, husando del estribillo, de *anda fiate de Tison*, respondiendo el a q se lo dicen *eso es pa qe lo vean.*' See Academia Nacional de la Historia, Caracas, Sección Civiles, Signatura A13–5159–2, report of 24 February 1801. I am indebted to Jeremy Cohen of the University of Florida for this reference.

13   Michael Craton, *Testing the Chains: Resistance to Slavery in the British West Indies* (Ithaca, 1982), p. 236.

14   Luiz Mott, 'A revolução dos negros do Haiti e o Brasil,' *Mensario do Arquivo Nacional*, vol. 13 (Rio de Janeiro, 1982), pp. 5–6. These men are wrongly described as slaves in João José Reis, *Slave Rebellion in Brazil: The Muslim Uprising of 1835 in Bahia* (Baltimore, 1993), p. 48.

15   Mott, 'A revolução'.

16   José Luciano Franco, *Ensayos históricos* (Havana, 1974), p. 185.

17   Julius S. Scott III, 'The Common Wind: Currents of Afro-American Communication in the Era of the Haitian Revolution,' PhD dissertation, Duke University (1986). In 1800 whites in Martinique commented on 'a marked change [since the revolution] in the manners and conduct of the slaves and people of colour throughout the colony; they doubtless are awake to every circumstance that happens and to events that have taken place at the other three French West Indian islands.' Some specified they were less submissive and more aware. See Kieran Kleczewski, 'Martinique and the British Occupation, 1794–1802,' PhD dissertation, Georgetown University (1988), pp. 331–32, 340.

noticed this in November 1791, at the same time as the Island Assembly was complaining of 'a new temper and ideas' in the slave population.[18] The following year a visitor to Rio de Janeiro wrote that 'the secret spell that caused the Negro to tremble at the presence of the white man [had been] in a great degree dissolved' by the spectacle of 'black power'.[19] In 1795 a Cuban magnate wrote that, since the Saint Domingue uprising, 'The insolence [of Havana's blacks and mulattoes] no longer knows any bounds.' This opinion was echoed three years later by the island's governor, who commented on the excitement created by news of blacks' growing power over whites in the neighbouring colony.[20] Although the word recurs frequently, we are rarely told what form this 'insolence' took. Sometimes it meant, as in Havana, people of colour neglecting to remove their hats in the presence of whites or insulting soldiers sent to break up popular disturbances; elsewhere it could refer to slaves answering their owners back with predictions that things were going to change.[21] These were ways, I think, of signalling awareness of what was happening in Saint Domingue.

We can conclude that many blacks in different parts of the Americas reacted to the spectacle of self-liberation in Saint Domingue with subdued pride or open belligerence. If the French Revolution proclaimed the ideals of liberty and equality, the Haitian Revolution proved to African-Americans they could be won by force of arms; that things were perhaps not so immutable as they seemed. But if the revolution was an inspiration, did it also serve as an object lesson, or source of support, for insurgents in other places? To what extent did it play a causal role in the numerous slave rebellions and conspiracies of these decades?

Resistance to Slavery

The answer to this question partly depends on an empirical accumulation of evidence and partly on one's individual understanding of the perpetually elusive issue of why people suddenly choose to risk their lives at a particular moment. My reading of the evidence is that a 'Haitian influence' of varying sorts can be found in many rebellions of the period, but not to the degree that contemporaries and modern historians have sometimes

18   Geggus, *Slavery, War and Revolution*, pp. 90–91.
19   Kenneth Maxwell, *Conflicts and Conspiracies in Brazil and Portugal, 1750–1808* (Cambridge, 1973), p. 218.
20   Alain Yacou, 'Le projet des révoltes serviles de l'île de Cuba dans la première moitié du XIXe siècle,' *Revue du CERC* (Guadeloupe), no. 1 (1984), pp. 50–51; Archivo General de Indias, Seville (hereafter: AGI), Estado 1, exp. 80, Conde de Santa Clara to Príncipe de la Paz, 29 November 1798.
21   David Geggus, 'The French and Haitian Revolutions, and Resistance to Slavery in the Americas: An Overview,' *Revue Française d'Histoire d'Outre-Mer*, vol. 76, no. 282–3 (1989), p. 112; above, note 20.

claimed.[22] The frequency of slave revolts and conspiracies in the Americas certainly reached a peak in the 1790s and the largest uprisings all occurred in the 40 years following the Saint Domingue revolt of 1791. But there were many other influences at work in the rebellions of the period, both internal to the societies concerned and deriving from revolutionary France or from the antislavery movement. Eugene Genovese's argument that the Haitian Revolution marked a turning point in the character of slave resistance does not seem to be borne out by the evidence from Latin America or elsewhere.[23] In the Spanish Empire we find two striking upsurges in slave and free collared resistance in the years 1795 and 1811–12. In the aggregate, these reflected an increase in the sales tax and rumours of emancipation that derived from the *Gracias al Sacar* Law (in 1795) and from the discussions (in 1811–12) of the Cortes of Cadiz, as much as from news arriving from Haiti.[24] In Brazil the pattern of slave revolt reflected the rhythms of the slave trade and apparently owed nothing to Haitian example.[25]

We find, nevertheless, several types of linkage between the Haitian Revolution and slave resistance elsewhere. Transplanted so-called 'French' slaves and free colours show up in several rebellions in Spanish-, Dutch- and English-speaking territories from the 1790s to the 1820s. It is not always certain these 'French' blacks were from Saint Domingue and, despite the exaggerations of some scholars, they did not necessarily play key roles in these events. The several small Spanish West Indian revolts and conspiracies of the mid-1790s provide a case in point. Moreover, the contact once supposed between Haiti and maroons in eastern Cuba no longer looks very likely.[26] Francophone slaves, however, did lead a large rising on Curaçao in 1795, along with a local field slave who adopted the name of the Domingan revolutionary leader André Rigaud.

Slaves taken to Puerto Rico from Saint Domingue adopted a different tactic. In 1796, the island governor complained of

---

22   This section is primarily based on Geggus, 'French and Haitian Revolutions,' and David Geggus, 'Slavery, War, and Revolution in the Greater Caribbean, 1789–1815,' in Gaspar and Geggus, *Turbulent Time*, pp. 1–50.

23   Eugene Genovese, *From Rebellion to Revolution: Afro-American Slave Revolts in the Making of the Modern World* (Baton Rouge, 1979).

24   David Geggus, 'Slave Resistance in the Spanish Caribbean in the Mid-1790s,' in Gaspar and Geggus, *Turbulent Time*, pp. 136, 139; Geggus, 'Slavery, War, and Revolution,' pp. 8–10. The reference to Cuban revolts in 1792–93 in Jorge Dominguez, *The Breakdown of the Spanish Colonial Empire* (Cambridge, 1980), p. 160, derives from a confusion with later events.

25   On Brazil, see Stuart B. Schwartz, *Sugar Plantations in the Formation of Brazilian Society: Bahia, 1550–1835* (Cambridge, 1985), ch. 17.

26   Geggus, 'Slave Resistance in the Spanish Caribbean,' p. 142; Gabino La Rosa Corzo, *Los palenques del oriente de Cuba: resistencia y acoso* (Havana, 1991), pp. 115–18

la seducción de algunos esclavos franceses que se han introducido aquí; los que no contentos con importunar a los tribunales con los reclamos diarios de su imaginaria libertad, seducen a los esclavos españoles, para que practiquen lo mismo, y se sustraigan por quantos medios les sea posible del poder y dominio de sus legitimos amos. Por desgracia esta insolencia ... ha tomado demasiado cuerpo en esta Isla y [without tough measures] se aumentará cada día hasta su total ruina.[27]

In Cuba, too, at around the same time, some bold spirits among the slaves of French refugees similarly claimed they were free by virtue of the events in Saint Domingue, 'maliciously' confusing, in one official's words, the French Emancipation Decree of February 1794 with a local deportation order.[28]

Joaquín Chirino, sharecropper of Coro, Venezuela, exemplifies another type of linkage with the French colony. He was not from Saint Domingue but he had visited the colony with his owner, before he launched a bloody revolt in May 1795 supposedly demanding 'la ley de los Franceses', which meant slave emancipation. (One should note, however, this traditional interpretation has been recently challenged.)[29] The example of Saint Domingue was more explicitly invoked two years earlier by a creole slave conspirator in neighbouring Santo Domingo who declared that local slaves were *pendejos* for doing nothing while slaves in the French colony were killing whites. He further claimed (falsely) that Jean-François, the leader of the 1791 insurrection, was already preparing an uprising in the Spanish colony. That plot came to nothing, but when in 1796 Africans organised a slave rebellion in Boca Nigua, Santo Domingo, they sought to learn directly about the Saint Domingue rising from some of its former participants who had settled nearby.[30] Twenty years later slave conspirators who launched the 1816 rebellion in Barbados planned 'to set fire ... the way they did in St Domingo'.[31]

27 AGI Estado 10, exp. 12, f.18v, Ramón de Castro to Príncipe de la Paz, 15 June 1796.

28 Geggus, 'Slave Resistance in the Spanish Caribbean', p. 137.

29 For contrasting assessments, see Pedro Arcaya, *La insurrección de los negros de la serranía de Coro* (Caracas, 1949); Federico Brito Figueroa, *Las insurrecciones de los esclavos negros en la sociedad colonial venezolana* (Caracas, 1961); Pedro Gil Rivas, Luis Dovale Prado and Lidia L. Bello, *La insurrección de los negros de la serranía coriana: 10 de mayo de 1795* (Caracas, 1996). Although Brito Figueroa emphasises the French connection, Arcaya stresses false rumours of emancipation linked to Spanish reforms, and the latter work rejects the idea of any outside influence on the revolt. It makes an interesting case that local officials fabricated evidence to obscure the essentially local causes of the uprising.

30 However, I have seen no evidence that justifies Lester Langley's statement that the Haitian Revolution was invoked by leaders in the Malé Revolt (Bahia, 1835): *The Americas in the Age of Revolution, 1750–1850* (New Haven, 1996), p. 141. Supposition rather than fact, moreover, underlies the claim, found in Richard D.E. Burton, *Afro-Creole: Power, Opposition, and Play in the Caribbean* (Ithaca, 1997), p. 85, that Jamaica's Christmas Rebellion was Haitian-inspired.

31 Craton, *Testing*, p. 261.

The case with the most impressive Haitian connection is the 1812 conspiracy of the free black carpenter, José Antonio Aponte of Havana.[32] He
promised his followers Haitian soldiers would come to their aid, when they
plotted to take over the island of Cuba. Similar promises had been made the
previous year in Santo Domingo in the multiracial conspiracy of Manuel del
Monte, and would appear again in the Escalera conspiracy three decades
later.[33] Such predictions seem to have been a device employed by leaders for
winning recruits and stiffening resolve in the face of overwhelming odds.
One of Aponte's fellow urban conspirators appears to have visited plantation slave quarters pretending to be Jean-François, the main leader of the
1791 insurrection, who had long been an object of pride for blacks in
Havana.[34] Jean-François was in fact already dead but some of his former
officers were passing through Havana at this time and were approached by
the conspirators, though apparently without success.

Most interesting of all, Aponte, who was an artist, also used a sketch
book that contained paintings or drawings of Toussaint Louverture, Jean-
Jacques Dessalines and Henry Christophe, who had been crowned King of
Haiti the previous year. The crowning of a black king and creation of a black
aristocracy in the heart of the slave-owning Caribbean assuredly caught the
imagination of many black people across the Americas. Yet, even in this conspiracy where Haitian influence was most visible, other major causal factors
were in play, such as the considerable decline in Cuba's military garrison during the previous decade and the rumours of slave emancipation issuing that
year from the Cortes of Cadiz, which also sparked resistance in Puerto Rico
and Santo Domingo (as well as Martinique).

Although Aponte's promises of Haitian help were bogus, there were a
couple of instances of direct participation from Saint Domingue in resistance to slavery elsewhere. One involved the participation of mulatto and
black privateers from the French colony in a revolutionary plot in 1799 in
Maracaibo, where their intermediary was a local *pardo* tailor, Francisco

---

32   José Luciano Franco, *La conspiración de Aponte* (Havana, 1963); Matt Childs, "'A Black
     French General Arrived to Conquer the Island": Images of the Haitian Revolution in
     Cuba's 1812 Aponte Rebellion,' in Geggus, *Impact*, pp. 135–56.
33   AGI, Santo Domingo 1000, 3 August 1811, José Nuñez de Cáceres to Secretario de
     Estado, with enclosures; Robert Paquette, *Sugar is Made With Blood: The Conspiracy of
     La Escalera and the Conflict Between Empires over Slavery in Cuba* (Middletown, CT, 1988),
     p. 242. In late 1825, spokesman of the Cuban planter class Francisco de Arango
     expressed fear that a victorious Simón Bolívar might invade Cuba in alliance with
     President Boyer and 30,000 'hombres terribles': *Obras de D. Francisco de Arango y
     Parreño*, vol. II (Havana, 1952), p. 401.
34   In 1795, Cuba's governor wrote bitterly that his 'nombre resueña en los oídos del
     populacho como un héroe invencible, redentor de los esclavos …' See AGI Estado 5,
     exp. 176, 16 December 1795, Las Casas to Príncipe de la Paz.

Pirela.[35] The other instance concerns the slave revolt sparked the following year by the invasion of Curaçao by French Caribbean forces, in which participated, somewhat accidentally, the exiled future president of Haiti, Alexandre Pétion.[36]

During Pétion's presidency, Haitian soldiers also fought alongside Spanish American Creoles for the independence of (a slavery-free) Venezuela.[37] The politics of survival, however, generally prevented Haitian statesmen from seeking to spread slave rebellion overseas; they could not risk a retaliatory maritime blockade that would cut off their source of arms. Beginning with the Declaration of Independence itself, Haitian governments disavowed such intentions, even if Dessalines's early proclamations did express sympathy for those still enslaved in the remaining French colonies. The annexation of Spanish Santo Domingo, attempted by Dessalines in 1805 and achieved by President Boyer in 1822, which ended slavery in Hispaniola, strengthened fears of Haitian aggrandisement and subversion, but it was primarily motivated by the defensive concern of denying a convenient base to potential invaders.

Into the 1840s and beyond, endless rumours circulated regarding the activity of Haitian 'agents' and these have been taken seriously by some scholars.[38] Although Haitian governments attacked slavery vigorously in print, there is no evidence that they engaged in the sort of activism that characterised Victor Hugues's regime on Guadeloupe, which in the mid-1790s helped stir uprisings on Grenada and Saint Vincent. Toussaint Louverture and Henry Christophe, in fact, denounced republican attempts to invoke rebellion in Jamaica to the British.[39] Surprisingly perhaps, those who did most to export liberty from Saint Domingue were not the ex-slave rulers who dominated northern Haiti, but former free men of colour based in the south who had no inhibiting links with the British.

---

35   Brito Figueroa, *Las insurrecciones*, p. 79; Aline Helg, 'A Fragmented Majority: Free "of all Colors", Indians, and Slaves in Caribbean Colombia During the Haitian Revolution,' in Geggus, *Impact*, pp. 159–60.

36   Roberto Palacios, 'Ansia de libertad,' *Lanternu*, no. 1 (1983), pp. 20–7. These forces were mainly black troops from Guadeloupe.

37   Paul Verna, *Petión y Bolívar: cuarenta años de relaciones haitiano-venezolanas* (Caracas, 1969), pp. 201–98.

38   Guillermo Baralt, *Esclavos rebeldes: conspiraciones y sublevaciones de esclavos en Puerto Rico* (Rio Piedras, 1981); Christopher Schmidt-Nowara, *Empire and Antislavery: Spain, Cuba and Puerto Rico, 1833–1874* (Pittsburgh, 1999), pp. 40–1; Pierre Pluchon, *Toussaint Louverture: De l'esclavage au pouvoir* (Paris, 1979), p. 518; Jean Fouchard, 'Quand Haïti exportait la liberté,' *Revue de la société haïtienne d'histoire*, no. 143 (1984), pp. 43–6; Mott, 'A revolução'; Palacios, 'Ansia'; Yacou, 'Projet'; Paquette, *Sugar*, pp. 12, 246–8.

39   Pierre Pluchon and Gabriel Debien, 'Un plan d'invasion de la Jamaïque,' *Revue de la Société Haïtienne d'Histoire*, vol. 36, no. 119 (1978), pp. 3–72. An interesting confrontation between the French and Haitian Revolutions, Toussaint's actions reflected his need to maintain good relations with the British, which the French hoped to sunder.

It is entirely possible, even so, that Haitian individuals ventured where Haitian governments feared to tread. The shadowy presence of Haitian expatriates can be glimpsed in an attempted rising on Martinique in 1811 and in the Igbo conspiracy on Jamaica in 1815.[40] The most intriguing example is perhaps the case of Luis Gigaut and the Escalera conspiracy of 1843 in Cuba. Though some historians have doubted the existence of both Gigaut and the conspiracy, in Robert Paquette's masterly reconstruction he appears as a key player, although his identity as Haitian is not clearly demonstrated.[41]

Race

It is not easy to say if the Haitian Revolution helped to change ideas about racial difference or merely reinforced existing preconceptions. The revolution occurred at a critical juncture in European thought, when libertarian ideology and humanitarianism were gaining ground, but when the beginnings of biological science were weakening Christian teachings about the oneness of mankind and preparing the way for the so-called 'scientific racism' of the nineteenth century. The epic struggle for Saint Domingue fed both sides of this debate. Certainly the spectacle of a people freeing itself from bondage, waging a successful war and establishing an independent state inspired many existing opponents of slavery and racial discrimination. Other commentators, however, found it easy to rationalise the successes of the Haitians, and a selective reporting of the revolution's numerous atrocities provided vivid propaganda for diatribes about civilisation and barbarism. Moreover, the sharp divergence in mortality rates suffered by white and black soldiers in the tropics, which was highlighted by the conflict, may also have encouraged people to think in terms of immutable racial differences.[42] In Hispanic America, where this epidemiological gap was narrower and where secularism made slower progress, modern racism was perhaps less widespread than among Anglo-Saxons. Some Cubans claimed so, but others among its most liberal thinkers dismissed Haiti for having a 'stupid ... impotent government of orangutans'.[43]

The half-century after the Haitian Revolution witnessed divergent trends in race relations in Latin America and the Caribbean. In the new Spanish American republics the legal caste system of the colonial era gave

40 David Geggus, 'Esclaves et gens de couleur libres de la Martinique pendant l'époque révolutionnaire et napoléonienne: trois moments de résistance,' *Revue Historique*, vol. 295, no. 2 (1996), pp. 105–32; Richard Hart, *Slaves Who Abolished Slavery* (Kingston, 1985), pp. 225–7.
41 Paquette, *Sugar*, pp. 246–8, 255.
42 Geggus, *Slavery, War and Revolution*, p. 287.
43 Paquette, *Sugar*, pp. 115, 180.

way before official ideologies of racial democracy. Institutionalised racial discrimination was ended in the British, Dutch, Danish and French Caribbean around 1830 following (in the British and French cases) lengthy local campaigns and piecemeal reform. In the Spanish West Indian colonies, on the other hand, the legal situation for free blacks tended to worsen with the introduction of harsher regulation, less frequent manumission, declining use of black militia, forced labour in Puerto Rico and ferocious repression in Cuba after the Escalera conspiracy of 1843.[44]

Both positive and negative influence on these contrary developments have been attributed to Haiti and its revolution. Its impact is thus ambiguous and uncertain. The worsening climate for free blacks in the Spanish West Indies, especially the growing hostility to the black militia that emerged in the 1790s, doubtless owed something to Haitian-inspired fears, but it could also be explained simply by the growth of the slave economy in these decades, especially as comparable developments had occurred in French and British colonies a century earlier. Even in the Dominican Republic, where the Haitian Revolution had its most direct impact, the revolution's influence remains unclear. Some twentieth-century Dominican historians have accorded to massacres apparently perpetrated by Haitian invaders in 1802 and 1805 a major role in generating the much-publicised antipathy between the two nations of Hispaniola.[45] However, as some white Dominican revolutionaries looked to Haitian aid in 1811, and others in 1821 chose to name their briefly independent State 'Haití Español' — something unimaginable for later generations — it may be that this enmity did not develop before the Haitian annexation of 1822–43, if not later.[46]

On the mainland, the Spanish creole revolutionaries' sudden acceptance of racial equality after 1810 — in striking contrast to their hostility to the *Gracias al Sacar* Law of 1795 — surely was informed by their reaction to events in Haiti, even if the military and demographic circumstances they faced provided sufficient cause for the change, and disputes over the franchise for the Cortes of Cadiz provided the occasion.[47] As far away as Michoacán the local bishop cited the case of Saint Domingue and his desire to avoid a local race war, when he advocated in 1810 abolition of racially-discriminatory taxation.[48] On the other hand, the Haitian example

44   *Ibid.*, pp. 119–27; Schmidt-Nowara, *Empire and Antislavery*, p. 41.
45   Emilio Rodríguez Demorizi, *Invasiones haitianas de 1801, 1805 y 1822* (Ciudad Trujillo, 1955).
46   Above, note 33; Geggus, 'Naming', p. 56.
47   Jaime E. Rodríguez O., *The Independence of Spanish America* (Cambridge, 1998), pp. 115–16; Manuel Chust, *La cuestión nacional americana en las Cortes de Cádiz* (Valencia, 1999), pp. 54–5, 71–4, 150–7, 164–7; John Lynch, *The Spanish American Revolutions, 1808–1826* (London, 1973), pp. 21–2, 196, 210–12, 263, 332–3.
48   David Brading, *The First America: The Spanish Monarchy, Spanish Patriots, and Liberal State, 1492–1867* (New York, 1991), pp. 570–71.

of racial conflict and political instability, which the Coro revolt of 1795 had brought even closer to home, perhaps more obviously inflected Simón Bolívar's private fears of *pardocracia* that led to his execution of his non-white allies and potential rivals, Píar and Padilla. In Bolívar's correspondence Haiti frequently appeared as an example to be avoided and, at least once, as a direct threat.[49] Such fears were no doubt strengthened by the popular republicanism that developed among non-whites in Gran Colombia and, as Marixa Lasso's work reveals, expressed itself in several local conflicts with the post-revolutionary elite in rhetorical appeals to the Haitian Revolution.[50]

In the British Caribbean, too, Mimi Sheller argues, the presence of an independent black State and memories of the Haitian Revolution encouraged the development of both black political activism and a 'pervasive fear' among whites that caused 'intense resistance' to it. Like Mary Turner, Sheller further notes the contribution of Haitian exiles in Jamaica to the political organising of local free blacks. Lecesne and Escoffery, two men of Haitian descent, were deported from Jamaica in 1824, accused of fostering slave rebellion and of links with the Haitian government.[51] The same year (when Cyrille Bissette and his colleagues were also deported from Martinique under similar circumstances) the mulatto politician Antonio Rebouças was accused in Sergipe, Brazil, of praising the king of Haiti and stirring up hostility to whites by saying that 'any mulatto or black could become a general'.[52] Down to the end of the century, black leaders like George William Gordon in Jamaica and Antonio Maceo in Cuba would be accused by their white enemies of seeking to emulate and being secretly in league with the black republic.[53]

The 'meaning of Haiti' of course was radically different for whites and blacks. At the same time as Gaspar de Betancourt was holding forth about

49 Harold A. Bierck (ed.), *Selected Writings of Bolívar* (New York, 1951), pp. 140, 229, 267–8, 307–8, 499, 624. Usually a byword for anarchy in his letters, Haiti was nonetheless once praised by Bolívar for its political stability, when he was advocating the lifetime-presidency system (p. 599).

50 Marixa Lasso, 'Haiti as an Image of Popular Republicanism in Caribbean Colombia: Cartagena Province (1811–1828),' in Geggus, *Impact*, pp. 176–90.

51 Mimi B. Sheller, 'Democracy After Slavery: Black Publics and Peasant Rebellion in Postemancipation Haiti and Jamaica,' PhD dissertation, New School for Social Research (1996), pp. 22–65; Mary Turner, *Slaves and Missionaries: The Disintegration of Jamaican Slave Society, 1787–1834* (Barbados, 1998 [1982]), p. 27.

52 On Rebouças, see Mott, 'A revolucão,' pp. 7–8. On Bissette, see Lawrence C. Jennings, *French Anti-Slavery: The Movement for the Abolition of Slavery in France, 1802–1848* (New York, 2000).

53 Sheller, 'Democracy,' pp. 339–43; Ada Ferrer, *Insurgent Cuba: Race, Nation, and Revolution, 1868–1898* (Chapel Hill, 1999), pp. 59–60, 94; Aline Helg, *Our Rightful Share: The Afro-Cuban Struggle for Equality, 1886–1912* (Chapel Hill, 1995), pp. 48–54.

Haitian orangutans he also noted that Haiti was an object of pride for black Cubans. Along with news of government reforms and abolitionist activity, he thought it responsible for their 'swagger'.[54] Some black Jamaicans were said to be talking of Haiti as a sort of paradise, shortly after Thomas Carlyle had labelled it a 'tropical dog-kennel and pestiferous jungle'.[55] Even among Cuban insurgents of the 1890s, blacks and whites differed in their tendencies to make positive or negative references to Haiti.[56] Yet opinion among blacks was not uniformly positive. Sheller mentions that ordinary Jamaicans and the Jamaican black press also discussed news of agricultural backwardness, political repression and social conflict in Haiti.[57] Moreover, although the image of King Christophe resonated strongly in Cuba, Brazil and elsewhere, Haiti's two periods of monarchy (1811–20, 1848–59) could hardly inspire enthusiasm among republicans. Jamaican radical Robert Wedderburn warned in 1817 in his London-published newspaper that black kings could be as tyrannous as white. And while he predicted for his native isle a Haitian-style rebellion, he at least made a show of counselling Jamaican slaves to adopt peaceful collective resistance and not follow their neighbours' violent example.[58]

The examples of Chirino, Pirela, Aponte and other free blacks who organised slave rebellions do provide evidence of free persons apparently inspired by Haiti opting for violent resistance. However, no such Haitian connection emerges in those cases where free colours conspired with whites rather than slaves, such as the Gual and España plot in La Guaira in 1797, the Bahia Tailors' Rebellion of 1798, or Cuba's Masonic plots of 1810 and the 1820s, whose principal points of reference were the French and mainland American revolutions.[59] As for the conspiracy of mulatto farmer Nicolás Morales that was uncovered near Bayamo, Cuba, in August 1795, I would agree that Morales doubtless was 'heartened' by the achievements of his counterparts in Saint Domingue, as Robert Paquette and other scholars argue. Nonetheless, the surviving sources provide no certain evidence of this, whereas they do demonstrate the critical impact of local issues (land, tax and racial discrimination). It seems a safe counterfactual proposition that the conspiracy could well have

---

54   Paquette, *Sugar*, p. 179.
55   Sheller, 'Democracy', pp. 59–60; Thomas Carlyle, *The Nigger Question*, edited by Eugene R. August (New York, 1971 [1849]), p. 29.
56   Ferrer, *Insurgent Cuba*, p. 134.
57   Sheller, 'Democracy,' pp. 49–58.
58   Iain McCalman (ed.), *The Horrors of Slavery and Other Writings by Robert Wedderburn* (Edinburgh, 1991), pp. 81, 86–7.
59   Pedro Grases, *La conspiración de Gual y España y el ideario de la Independencia* (Caracas, 1997); Maxwell, *Conflicts*, pp. 217–23; José Luciano Franco, *Las conspiraciones de 1810 y 1812* (Havana, 1977) and *Ensayos históricos*, pp. 23–9.

occurred without the Haitian Revolution but not without the *Gracias al Sacar* Law and its local suppression.[60]

It is rather less sure that, without the Haitian Revolution, there would have occurred the major multi-class risings of the mid-1790s on Grenada and St Vincent, Fédon's Rebellion and the Black Carib Rebellion, which were the most destructive and difficult to suppress of the decade outside Saint Domingue. Yet there, too, clearly predominating among causal factors were local issues (land disputes, increasing discrimination against Catholics) and, more especially, the help sent the insurgents by French commissioners in Guadeloupe and St Lucia, who helped to organise the risings. The causal link to Saint Domingue's revolution, beyond the inspiration and emboldening of non-whites that we can presume but not prove, was of a rather indirect nature. The assistance the insurgents received from Guadeloupe and St Lucia resulted from the French Republic's decision to use black liberation as a weapon of war. This derived from the French Republic's adoption of racial equality and slave emancipation, which were largely responses to events in Saint Domingue. The contribution of the Haitian Revolution was thus critical, but mediated through the French Revolution and French activism in the Windward Islands. No historian has so far shown that either party in those conflicts so much as mentioned events in Saint Domingue.[61]

There is an epistemological or methodological problem here. As it is scarcely credible that Nicolás Morales or Julien Fédon did not know of the Saint Domingue Revolution, some may feel it beyond question that the unprecedented success of black rebels in the French colony must have played a major role in motivating those leaders' resistance. The same might be said of Sam Sharpe, leader of Jamaica's Christmas Rebellion, or of the protagonists in any post-1791 black-white conflict.[62] Others may feel that historians should not put into the historical record what is not there, and that it was not simply the arbitrariness of colonial document-making that has linked Aponte and Chirino but not Fédon and Morales to Haiti. I incline hesitantly towards the second view. Similarly plausible, but lacking documental support, is the idea the revolution had a conservative impact not just on whites but on many free people of colour, too. Since the revolution divided free blacks in Saint Domingue itself and caused the migration of many,

60 Geggus, 'Slavery, War, and Revolution,' p. 16; Franco, *Ensayos históricos*, pp. 93–100. Paquette, *Sugar*, pp. 75, 124–25, 304, misdates the conspiracy. Alain Yacou, 'Révolution française dans l'île de Cuba et contre-révolution,' in Alain Yacou and Michel Martin (eds.), *De la Révolution française aux révolutions créoles et nègres* (Paris, 1989), pp. 31–3, misdates the *Gracias al Sacar* Law.

61 See Raymund Devas, *The Island of Grenada (1650–1950)* (St George's, 1964), pp. 103–155; Edward Cox, *Free Coloreds in the Slave Societies of St Kitts and Grenada, 1763–1833* (Knoxville, 1984), pp. 80–88; Curtis M. Jacobs, 'Fédon's Rebellion,' PhD dissertation, University of the West Indies, Barbados (2000).

62 See above, note 30.

the idea is worth pondering. Moreover, as Aponte, Morales and Pirela were each betrayed by *pardo* militiamen, and collared militia generally were involved in suppressing the rebellions of the period, there is ample reason to think not all in the non-white population responded enthusiastically to the Haitian spectacle of slave emancipation and black power.

All in all, it seems difficult to argue that the creation of Haiti had a decisive impact, either on the activities of Latin American free blacks or on the political or social climate in which they lived. Just as it proved to be a widespread influence on slave resistance but not the most important, so too was it a contributory factor reinforcing other influences affecting free populations of colour but not one of unique significance. Its impact, moreover, was ambiguous; it stimulated contrary tendencies. However, if this meant the revolution's impact was not clear-cut, it also gave it greater intensity.

Migration

Throughout the Haitian Revolution, waves of refugees and deportees left Saint Domingue and neighbouring Santo Domingo seeking temporary shelter or new homes elsewhere in the Caribbean or in North America. Intermittently, governments sought to restrict immigration from Saint Domingue, or from all French colonies, and to expel refugees, particularly if they were of African descent.[63] Nevertheless, such restrictions often were bypassed, especially when immigration promised economic rewards. Carlos Deive estimates that 4,000 Dominicans settled in Cuba and perhaps 6,000 more in Venezuela, Colombia and Puerto Rico. The number of French who came to Cuba from Saint Domingue has been put as high as 30,000.[64] By no means all were of European descent. Blacks, equally divided between slave and free, formed 70 per cent of the 10,000 who migrated from the French colony to Cuba and, in 1809–10, were deported to Louisiana because of the Napoleonic invasion of Spain.[65] The proportion of non-whites among the Spanish who moved from Santo Domingo to Cuba was probably similar.[66] Men of colour were also prominent among

63   A Spanish decree of 21 May 1790 banned immigration of blacks from French colonies, or of any other non-white viewed as dangerous. Apparently motivated by fear of the French rather than the Saint Domingue Revolution, it undercut Spain's century-old sanctuary policy of welcome for foreign fugitive slaves. The next year a treaty with the Dutch sought to close the Orinoco to fugitives. See AGI, Estado 5, Las Casas to Príncipe de la Paz, 3 January 1796; Alvin Thompson, *Some Problems of Slave Desertion in Guyana, c. 1750–1814* (Barbados, 1976), p. 27.
64   Carlos Esteban Deive, *Las emigraciones dominicanas a Cuba (1795–1808)* (Santo Domingo, 1989), p. 132; Domínguez, *Insurrection*, p. 161.
65   Paul Lachance, 'Repercussions of the Haitian Revolution in Louisiana,' in Geggus, *Impact*, p. 214.
66   In a sample of 683 Spanish refugees on five ships only 26 per cent were white and two per cent were 'indios blancos'. AGI, Estado 5, expedientes 95, 99, 138, 187 and 189.

the POWs who were packed into the region's jails and prison ships. Within months of the outbreak of war in 1793, more than 900 were sent to La Guaira, where their 'subversive shouts from inside the prison' greatly annoyed the captain-general. Thousands more were shipped in the following decade to Vera Cruz, Havana, Puerto Rico and Jamaica, where they were accused of spreading 'French principles'.[67] Slaves from Saint Domingue who had borne arms, or were just war booty, or who migrated with refugees, were sold in Cuba and the south Caribbean.[68] Other groups of blacks, impossible to sell, were relocated from Saint Domingue and other revolutionary hotspots to Central America, or simply abandoned on its coast or that of New Granada.[69]

This very diverse group of people affected local populations in different ways, but all made more palpable the drama of what was happening in Saint Domingue. 'Nothing has such a vivid effect on most men as the perceptions they receive via the sense of sight', remarked the Governor of Havana.[70] He was writing about the most feared group of migrants, the *tropas auxiliares* Spain had recruited among the original slave insurgents during its failed attempt to conquer the French colony. In 1796, after the loss of Santo Domingo, the Spanish government agreed to relocate an elite group of 800 (including women and children). Governor Las Casas was alarmed lest they end up in Cuba:

'la aparición de estos personages, esclavos miserables ayer, héroes hoy de una revolución, triunfantes, opulentos, y condecorados; tales objetos no son para presentarlos a la vista de un pueblo compuesto en el mayor parte de hombres de color que viven en la opresión de un número más corto de blancos'. With envious disapproval, he imagined the black officers *'deslumbrando con un fausto asombroso de magnífico coche de seis caballos, gran tren de casa, mesa, etc. muy superior al que ha visto jamás este público en el gefe y cabeza principal de la Isla.*[71]

Though the governor succeeded in keeping the group out of Cuba, where the slave economy was booming, more than 300 of the former insurgents

67   Angel Sanz Tapia, *Los militares emigrados y los prisioneros franceses en Venezuela durante la guerra contra la revolución* (Caracas, 1977), p. 77–80, 103 (citation), 147, 263–64; 'The Enigma of Jamaica in the 1790s: New Light on the Causes of Slave Rebellions,' *William and Mary Quarterly*, vol. 44, no. 2 (April 1987), pp. 275, 280–1.

68   David Geggus, 'The Great Powers and the Haitian Revolution,' in Berndt Schröter and Karin Schüller (eds.), *Tordesillas y sus consecuencias: La política de las grandes potencias europeas respecto a América Latina (1494–1898)* (Madrid, 1995), p. 121, no. 43; AGI, Estado 5, Las Casas to Príncipe de la Paz, 3 January 1796.

69   Geggus, 'Slavery, War, and Revolution,' pp. 26–7, and 'The "Swiss" and the Problems of Slave/Free Colored Cooperation,' in Geggus (ed.), *Haitian Revolutionary Studies* (Bloomington, 2001); Helg, 'A Fragmented Majority'.

70   AGI, Estado 5, Las Casas to Príncipe de la Paz, 16 December 95.

71   *Ibid.*

were resettled in Guatemala, more than 100 in Campeche and smaller groups in Panama and Florida. In Guatemala and Florida they provided valuable military services but everywhere that they settled they created considerable unease among whites, despite their ostentatious royalism, and great curiosity among blacks. Their pride was often singled out for criticism. The pension paid 'general' Georges Biassou in St Augustine was almost as much as the local governor's salary.[72] Jean Kina, a more conservative ex-slave caudillo employed by the British in Saint Domingue, also created a stir, when in 1800 he disembarked in Martinique wearing a colonel's uniform accompanied by a white secretary. Only months after marrying into the local free collared community, he staged a revolt on its behalf and was deported to Europe.[73]

The economic impact of the Saint Domingue diaspora was felt chiefly in Cuba and Jamaica through its contribution of skilled personnel to the sugar industry and, more particularly, its expansion of coffee production on the two islands. Coffee cultivation had been almost a French monopoly until the revolution but, stimulated by high prices and new migrants, Jamaica and Cuba would largely fill the shortfall in world production until Brazil overtook them in the 1820s. Among the owners of the new plantations that sprang up, French blacks can be found in Cuba's Oriente, where many fled after defeat by Toussaint Louverture in the War of the South (1799–1800). A few also acquired properties in western Cuba and Jamaica, including the wealthy Jean-Baptiste Lapointe. Free blacks were more commonly artisans; one worked as refiner on the famous *Ninfa* sugar estate; their womenfolk did laundry and sewing.[74] The greatest infusion of labour came from the slaves the refugees brought with them. The newcomers' harsh exploitation of slave workers attracted comment from the Spanish and perhaps also left its mark on the evolution of Cuban mores.[75]

Plantations where Domingan slaves predominated became islands of French Creole culture. In the mountains of Jamaica, French creole continued to be spoken for several decades. A few traces can still be found in

72   Jane Landers, 'Rebellion and Royalism in Spanish Florida: The French Revolution on Spain's Northern Colonial Frontier,' in Gaspar and Geggus, *Turbulent Time*, pp. 156–77; David Geggus, 'The Slave Leaders in Exile: Spain's Resettlement of its Black Auxiliary Troops', in Geggus (ed.), *Haitian Revolutionary Studies* (Bloomington, 2001).
73   Geggus, 'Esclaves et gens de couleur libres,' pp. 118–27.
74   Alain Yacou, 'Esclaves et libres français à Cuba au lendemain de la Révolution de Saint Domingue,' *Jahrbuch für Geschichte von Staat, Wirtschaft und Gesellschaft Lateinamerikas*, vol. 28 (1991), pp. 163–97; Alain Yacou, 'La présence française dans la partie occidentale de l'île Cuba au lendemain de la Révolution de Saint-Domingue,' *Revue Française d'Histoire d'Outre-Mer*, vol. 84 (1987), pp. 149–88; Jacques de Cauna, 'La diaspora des colons de Saint-Domingue et le monde créole: le cas de la Jamaïque,' *Revue Française d'Histoire d'Outre-Mer*, vol. 81 (1994), p. 351.
75   Yacou, 'Esclaves et libres français,' 184; Gabriel Debien, 'Les colons de Saint-Domingue réfugié à Cuba, 1793–1815,' *Revista de Indias*, vol. 13, no. 1 (1954), pp. 559–605, vol. 13, no. 2 (1954), pp. 11–36.

regional folklore and items of vocabulary, like 'leggins' meaning vegetables (from *légumes*).[76] The French Creole legacy in eastern Cuba extends to names, religion, music and dance, notably the carnival *tumba francesa*. However, a later influx of French migrants to the region in the 1830s and the migration of Haitians in the early twentieth century makes it difficult to precisely assess the Haitian Revolution's influence on regional culture.[77] Saint Domingue's influence on Trinidad, where Francophone culture remained dominant through much of the nineteenth century was clearly small. Although some refugees and their slaves, and some demobilised black troops, moved from one colony to the other, most migrants to Trinidad during, as before, the revolution came from the French Windward Isles. Even in Puerto Rico, much closer than Trinidad to Saint Domingue, fewer than 40 per cent of French migrants who arrived around 1800 came from Saint Domingue.[78]

The main American migration movement during the Haitian Revolution continued to be the Atlantic slave trade. The revolution considerably changed distribution patterns in the trade by removing the trade's major market (the destination of a third or more of incoming Africans in 1785–90), and by encouraging plantation development on new lands. Slave imports into Jamaica more than doubled between the 1780s and '90s, 're-Africanising' its slave population.[79] A similar process occurred in northeast Brazil. New frontiers opened to slavery in central Brazil and the Guianas, and blacks became a majority of the population of Cuba, as Spanish West Indian sugar exports tripled in the quarter-century ending in 1815. The Haitian Revolution, along with increasing world demand for tropical staples and commercial liberalisation, thus altered the pattern of the slave trade but it had relatively little impact on the aggregate demand for slaves in Latin America and the Caribbean. Despite the near-closure of the huge Saint Domingue market, the inflow of enslaved Africans into the Caribbean declined in the 1790s by less than 20 per cent from its (probable) peak in the 1780s, while arrivals in Brazil increased.[80] Contemplating

76 De Cauna, 'La diaspora des colons', p. 355.
77 Jean Lamore (ed.), *Les français dans l'Oriente cubain* (Bordeaux, 1993); Carlos Padrón, *Franceses en el suroriente de Cuba* (Havana, 1997); Judith Bettelheim, *Cuban Festivals* (New York, 1993); Fernando Ortiz, *Los negros esclavos* (Havana, 1975), pp. 216–18.
78 María Luque de Sánchez, 'Colons français réfugiés à Porto Rico,' in Martin and Yacou (eds.), *De la Révolution française*, pp. 41–8.
79 Barry Higman, *Slave Population and Economy in Jamaica, 1807–1834* (Cambridge, 1976), pp. 75–6; David Geggus, 'Jamaica and the Saint Domingue Slave Revolt,' *The Americas*, vol. 38, no. 2, p. 222.
80 David Eltis, *Economic Growth and the Ending of the Transatlantic Slave Trade* (New York, 1987), pp. 37–8, 243–5, 249. The more recent figures in David Richardson, 'Slave Exports from West and West-Central Africa, 1700–1809: New Estimates of Volume and Distribution,' *Journal of African History*, vol. 30, no. 1 (1989), pp. 1–22, suggest a less abrupt shift between the '80s and '90s and that Caribbean imports may have peaked in the 1760s.

the lure of the world market, colonists in Puerto Rico and Cuba certainly debated the wisdom of turning their islands into fully-fledged plantation colonies, in view of what had happened to their powerful neighbour. In both cases, however, they concluded in the famous words of Francisco Arango y Parreño that 'la hora de nuestra felicidad ha llegado'.[81] Only Spanish Louisiana tried suspending the influx of Africans, and then only briefly.[82] Only in the next decade, with the ending of the British, US, Dutch and Danish slave trades, did the volume of the Atlantic Slave Trade appreciably decline. However, it is by no means certain that the Haitian Revolution was an influential factor in this development.

Abolition, Emancipation and Decolonisation

Did the violent self-liberation of Haiti hinder, or advance, the struggle to end slavery and the slave trade elsewhere? As in the debate about race, the revolution provided propaganda to both sides in the antislavery debate and had paradoxical results. During the 1790s the uprising in Saint Domingue caused the success of abolitionism in France, yet it was a significant factor in its failure in Britain, in the Cortes of Cadiz and in Cuba. In Cuba it assisted the thousands or so Cobreros to gain ratification of their freedom in 1800, but in the Cortes of Cadiz and in nineteenth-century Cuba the dangers supposedly demonstrated by the Haitian example tended to be used as an argument for abolishing the slave trade and for not abolishing slavery. That argument appears to have helped Spanish ministers agree in 1817 to end the slave trade.[83] However, strong financial inducement from the British government was perhaps a more influential factor, and the decision anyway had no practical effect. Moreover, the argument from fear was clearly not an essential part of the abolitionist case even for those like José Antonio Saco, motivated by racism not humanitarianism, who switched, when it was convenient, from predicting race war to arguing that enslaved Africans were not dangerous but inefficient.[84] Fear does seem to have motivated Venezuela's governor in 1804 to quietly prevent slave imports

81   Arango y Parreño, *Obras,* vol. 1, p. 134; Michael Zeuske and Clarence Munford, 'Die "Grosse Furcht" in der Karibik: Saint Domingue und Kuba (1789–1795),' *Zeitschrift für Geschichtswissenschaft,* vol. 39, no. 1 (1991), pp. 51–9; Manuel Moreno Fraginals, *El ingenio: complejo económico social cubano del azúcar,* vol. 2 (Havana, 1978), p, 108; Schmidt-Nowara, *Empire and Antislavery,* pp. 40–1.

82   Paul Lachance, 'The Politics of Fear: French Louisianians and the Slave Trade,' *Plantation Society in the Americas,* vol. 1 (1979), pp. 162–97.

83   José Luciano Franco, *Las minas de Santiago del Prado y la rebelión de los Cobreros, 1530–1800* (Havana, 1975), pp. 131, 142; Hubert H.S. Aimes, *The History of Slavery in Cuba, 1511–1868* (New York, 1967), pp. 64, 73.

84   *José Antonio Saco: el autor y su obra* (Havana, 1973), pp. 6, 35–6; Schmidt-Nowara, *Empire and Antislavery,* pp. 8–9, 24, 31.

but the regional trade had already ceased several years before, to the dismay of the planter class.[85] Whether the revolutionary congress in Caracas was similarly motivated when it definitively banned the slave trade in 1811 is unclear, but the ban was likewise an event after the fact, and as with similar abolitions in the Southern Cone, it probably owed more to liberal ideology and the desire for British support.[86]

Considerable controversy continues to surround Haiti's influence on the abolition in 1807 of the British slave trade, the Americas' main source of bonded labour, and on the ending of British Caribbean slavery in the 1830s. Robin Blackburn stresses the cumulative character of the antislavery struggle and the Haitian Revolution's chronological primacy as the first major breakthrough in that struggle. Besides enhancing metropolitan opinion of blacks, and inspiring abolitionists, the revolution's legacy, reinforced by continuing slave resistance elsewhere, contributed to a cumulative weariness among politicians and discrediting of slave-owners that was an important factor in slavery's eventual abolition. Seymour Drescher, on the other hand, contends that Haiti featured little in the legislative debates that outlawed the trade and then slavery. He adds that there is little reason to think that colonists who continued where possible to buy enslaved Africans in record numbers were somehow scared into acceptance of abolition and emancipation by fear of 'another Haiti'.[87] Probably the strongest argument for linking the Haitian Revolution to the eventual success of antislavery in Britain is that it acted as an enabling factor, in the sense that it destroyed France's status as a major colonial power and that parliament might never have ended the slave trade, still less slavery, if France had remained a significant rival as a producer of tropical products.[88]

The most direct Haitian contribution to ending slavery elsewhere concerns the aid that President Pétion gave to Simón Bolívar, when he took refuge in Haiti in 1815–16. The payment Pétion stipulated for the arms, supplies and soldiers he provided to the two expeditions of that year was the future abolition of slavery in the liberated colonies. Creole revolutionaries in other parts of Latin America (Chile, Buenos Aires, Antioquia) had

---

85 Domínguez, *Insurrection*, pp. 99–100.
86 Hebe Clementi, *La abolición de la esclavitud en América latina* (Buenos Aires, 1974), p. 30; David Bushnell, *Reform and Reaction in the Platine Provinces, 1810–1852* (Gainesville, 1983), p. 10.
87 Robin Blackburn 'The Force of Example', and Seymour Drescher, 'The Limits of Example,' in Geggus, *Impact*, pp. 10–20; David Geggus, 'Haiti and the Abolitionists: Opinion, Propaganda and International Politics, 1804–1838,' in David Richardson (ed.), *Abolition and its Aftermath: The Historical Context 1790–1916* (London, 1985).
88 Michael Duffy, *Soldiers, Sugar and Seapower: The British Expeditions to the West Indies and the War against Revolutionary France* (Oxford, 1987), pp. 391–3; Franklin Knight, *The Caribbean: Genesis of a Fragmented Nationalism* (New York, 1990), p. 212; Robin Blackburn, *The Overthrow of Colonial Slavery* (London, 1988), p. 145.

already passed emancipation laws, but they were unsuccessful or had very limited impact. Bolívar's belated adoption of abolitionism, though similarly piecemeal, was a more significant turning point. But how much did it owe to Haiti? One can argue Bolívar's acceptance of an antislavery stance was essentially mandated by the military/political situation he confronted within Venezuela, that it was the logical development of the military manumission with which both insurgents and royalists had experimented from the beginning of the Independence Wars. An alternative view is that no other Venezuelan leader showed Bolívar's commitment to slave emancipation, and that, whatever the political dynamics within Venezuela, he might never have returned there without Haitian help.[89]

This question of Pétion's assistance to Bolívar is also central to assessing Haiti's contribution to the decolonising process. As Bolívar already had ships at his disposal, and the Haitian government was hardly his sole source of arms and soldiers, the episode was perhaps not indispensable to the liberation of Spanish America. On the other hand, it is difficult to see how else these two expeditions could have been launched from within the Caribbean at a time when the European colonies were hostile to the insurgents' presence.[90] Furthermore, this was not Haiti's only role in the Spanish American independence struggle. Pétion had already given modest assistance to Francisco Miranda's abortive invasion of Venezuela in 1806, and he and his successor, Boyer, helped equip other insurgent expeditions in the period 1816–19, including that of Francisco Mina to Mexico. Numerous Haitians also took part as private individuals in the revolution in New Granada and Venezuela. They participated as seamen, shipowners and soldiers; and Venezuela's first printer (whose first book was *The Rights of Man*) was also a Haitian citizen.[91]

On the other side of the balance sheet, it may be said that the Haitian Revolution indirectly contributed to keeping Cuba a colony through the nineteenth century in that memories of the revolution reinforced the fears of slave rebellion and race war which deterred and divided Creole resistance. The revolution's example was also used as an excuse in Spain not to extend political liberties to the island.[92] Finally, although President Geffrard helped the Dominican Republic win its Independence War of 1863–65, it was ironically the Haitian annexation of 40 years earlier that

89   John Lombardi, *The Decline and Abolition of Negro Slavery in Venezuela, 1820–1854* (Westport, 1961), pp. 13, 41; Blackburn, *Overthrow*, pp. 340–50; Verna, *Petión y Bolívar*, pp. 228–35, 257–9.

90   Rodríguez O., *Independence of Spanish America*, pp. 185–7; Verna, *Petión y Bolívar*, pp. 175–77, 257–9.

91   Verna, *Petión y Bolívar*, pp. 92–100, 299–321; Grases, *Conspiración de Gual y España*, pp. 67, 75.

92   Ferrer, *Insurgent Cuba*, pp. 8, 94, 112; Schmidt-Nowara, *Empire and Antislavery*, p. 25.

had extinguished the Dominicans' first brief experience of independence, as well as their far longer experience of slavery.

Conclusion

The Haitian Revolution had a complex and multifarious impact on blacks in Latin America and the Caribbean. Its influence was often ambiguous, its repercussions contradictory. From Rio to Spanish New Orleans, it rapidly became an object of pride for many, though surely not all, people of colour. The revolutionaries and the state they created served quite frequently as a stimulus to slave resistance, though rarely as an actual source of support. The revolution's impact on race relations was both positive and negative, and thus remains elusive. Although it destroyed the main slave mart in the Americas, the revolution did little to reduce the volume of the Atlantic slave trade; while liberating hundreds of thousands from bondage, it simultaneously encouraged the spread, and intensification, of slavery elsewhere. At the same time, it both encouraged and impeded in different ways the development of antislavery activism, and of the impetus toward independence of other colonial subjects. The influence of the Haitian Revolution was perhaps of no singular significance in any of the domains it impacted: slave resistance and antislavery, racism and antiracism, the expansion of slavery and of Francophone culture, decolonisation. But it left a rich legacy that is still far from fully understood.

CHAPTER 3

Entre pueblo y plebe: patriotas, pardos, africanos en Argentina (1790–1852)

Carmen Bernand

El tema de la gestación de las identidades nacionales en los primeros años de las luchas independentistas ha sido tratado por numerosos autores, pero recién empezamos a tener enfoques específicos sobre la manera en que las castas y los negros fueron integrados o excluidos de las nuevas definiciones nacionales. Jeremy Adelman, en un libro reciente, expone el problema al cual se enfrentaron los patriotas de 1810: crear un pueblo a partir de una masa desorganizada y heterogénea. Este autor muestra la flexibilidad de la representación popular a partir de los límites confusos de lo que se entendía por ciudadanía, término que en 1815 desplazó al de 'vecinos', en su sentido colonial de familias 'afincadas, arraigadas y enraizadas'. Teóricamente todos los hombres libres podían votar, pero la ciudadanía podía no ser reconocida para aquellos que vivían de su salario y no poseían bienes raíces.[1]

El análisis de la transición política que sigue la caída del virreinato, y los debates sobre la soberanía popular son cuestiones fundamentales que no pretendemos ahondar aquí. Nuestro propósito es más modesto y se limitará a rastrear la emergencia del 'pueblo' como categoría ideológica y política, a partir de ejemplos concretos sobre la población de color que nos ofrece la documentación colonial y republicana del Archivo General de la Nación de Buenos Aires (AGN-A). Insistiremos en los mecanismos de identificación y en el carácter segmentario de las identidades, sin intentar proyectar una determinada concepción de la identidad nacional forjada en el curso del siglo XIX sobre realidades más complejas.[2] De más está decir que los temas que presentaremos necesitan mayor ampliación. Por ejemplo, hemos iniciado una investigación sobre la propiedad de los negros y pardos a través de las testamentarías porteñas que aún no hemos concluido. Otros puntos como el funcionamiento de las cofradías y sus relaciones con las sociedades africanas fundadas en los años 1920 deberán ser profundizados en los años venideros.

---

1   Jeremy Adelman, *Republic of Capital. Buenos Aires and the Legal Transformation of the Atlantic World*. (Stanford, 1999).

2   Como lo recomienda José Carlos Chiaramonte, 'Modificaciones del Pacto Imperial,' en Antonio Annino, Luis Castro Leiva y François-Xavier Guerra, *De los imperios a las naciones: Iberoamérica* (Zaragoza, 1994), pp. 126–7.

Hablar de integración o de exclusión de la gente de color en la construcción de las identidades nacionales implica aclarar los términos utilizados. En primer lugar, la expresión que empleamos aquí por razones de comodidad, 'gente de color', no aparece con frecuencia en los documentos, pero tampoco es anacrónica ya que la encontramos por lo menos desde la segunda mitad del siglo XVIII con referencia a las castas. Estas gentes, de origen vil, pues derivan de mezclas con indios y sobre todo, negros, son 'pardos' de piel, es decir, de color indefinible, grisáceo y sucio. La ambigüedad de gentes que escapan a toda tentativa de clasificación somática (o cromática) los hace potencialmente peligrosos.[3] Esta categoría global de 'castas de color' reúne a todos los frutos del mestizaje, de la cual las referencias antiguas al origen han desaparecido, reemplazadas por un indicador racial impreciso que tendería a revelar una identidad colectiva.

Naturalmente, los miembros de las castas no se definían como tales sino que empleaban términos que indicaban una mayor o menor distancia respecto al calificativo de 'negro', considerado como marca de infamia. Pero tampoco las autoridades eran demasiado estrictas en la atribución de categorías raciales, como lo demuestran los registros matrimoniales de Buenos Aires, que reúnen en un mismo volumen a españoles y castas, sin introducir la separación habitual en la colonia. Por lo tanto, es imposible establecer un recuento exacto de los 'pardos' y otros mestizos.[4] En otro tipo de documentos (causas, litigios), los españoles emplean el término de 'negro' para describir a una persona que se autodefine como 'morena'. El nombre de 'africano' gozó de una cierta popularidad en los años consecutivos a la independencia, paralelamente al de 'americano'. A estas distinciones se suman otras, fundamentales, que tienden a fragmentar la colectividad negra en criollos y bozales y, sobre todo, entre esclavos y negros libres. Por último no hay que olvidar el menosprecio que la 'gente decente' sentía por las 'artes mecánicas', es decir, los trabajos manuales de distinta índole, ejecutados en gran parte por negros y mulatos.

Pueblo, nación, patria

El término de 'pueblo' es impreciso ya que contiene varias acepciones. En los años que preceden las luchas independentistas, el pueblo tiende a iden-

---

3   'Muchedumbre que llaman del color' (Plano geográfico e hidrográfico del distrito de la Real Audiencia de Quito [1766], en *Relaciones Geográficas de la Audiencia de Quito*, tomo II (CSIC, Madrid, 1992) pp. 456–57. Esta ambigüedad que se supone intrínseca a los híbridos ha sido tratada por Paul Gilroy en su análisis de la 'double consciousness' de los afroamericanos, *The Black Atlantic. Modernity and Double Consciousness* (Harvard, MA, 1993).

4   Marisa Díaz, 'Las migraciones internas a la ciudad de Buenos Aires, 1744–1810,' *Boletín del Instituto de Historia Argentina y Americana 'Dr. Emilio Ravignani'*, tercera serie, nos. 16 y 17 (1997–98), p. 18.

tificarse con la institución que lo representa, el ayuntamiento o cabildo. De ahí que sea en cierto modo sinónimo de 'vecindario', categoría que excluye a los esclavos y a los que vivían de su jornal, es decir, gente dependiente de un amo o de un maestro. Sin embargo, ya en los años 1780 aparecen citados como vecinos los sargentos mayores negros y algunas personas libres de color que han adquirido bienes. Este último fenómeno se incrementa en la primera década del siglo XIX. Los documentos notariales nos muestran generalmente mujeres casadas legítimamente, que pueden haber sido esclavas en algún momento de su vida y que poseen un terreno y una casa, y que pueden por consiguiente testar.

Pero 'pueblo' es también, en los primeros años del siglo XIX, un referente colectivo dotado de un alcance ideológico muy grande, y tiende a abarcar a todos aquellos que han sido marginados por las autoridades españolas, principalmente los criollos y los mestizos. El caso de la pertenencia de la gente de color y de los indios al 'pueblo soberano', se planteó durante la primera década del siglo XIX, a raíz de dos acontecimientos excepcionales: las invasiones inglesas y los combates independentistas. Estas luchas en las que intervinieron gentes de las clases bajas y 'viles', trastocaron los límites políticos y simbólicos del pueblo, como entidad colectiva, lo cual facilitó la integración, fugaz o duradera según los casos, de todos aquellos que no estaban necesariamente incluidos en el 'vecindario'. Pero por otra parte, 'pueblo' tenía su faceta negativa: el vulgo, el populacho, la plebe. El estatus civil de la gente de color osciló entre esos dos polos, el de la fidelidad a la patria y el del salvajismo de su conducta, según las circunstancias.

También es necesario resituar en su contexto los conceptos inclusivos y globalizantes de nación y de patria. La 'nación', en la época que nos interesa, tiene por lo menos tres acepciones, cultural, institucional y territorial, como lo muestra Mónica Quijada.[5] Por dimensión cultural de la nación se entiende el reconocimiento de una comunidad de origen en el sentido amplio (nación de los franceses, pero también nación de Guinea, etc.), caracterizada por su lengua y sus costumbres. La acepción institucional es, según esta autora, menos importante y aparece tardíamente en Hispanoamérica en el sentido de 'Reino' o 'Estado' sujeto a un príncipe. Por último, la definición territorial que supone un vínculo con la tierra natal se confunde con 'patria'. El caso de los negros y mulatos, esclavos o libres, encaja parcialmente en este esquema.

Recordemos por último que estas nociones incluyentes como nación y patria (y en cierto modo 'pueblo') implican algo más que una definición jurídica. El vínculo entre un individuo y la tierra donde nació implicaba

<hr>

5   Mónica Quijada, '¿Qué nación? Dinámicas y dicotomías de la nación en el imaginario Hispanoamericano del siglo XIX,' en M. Quijada y F-X; Guerra (compil.), *Cuadernos de Historia Americana*, no. 2, Asociación de Latinoamericanistas Europeos (1994), pp. 15–51.

desde el siglo XVI un conjunto de valores y de sentimientos que no pueden dejarse de lado en este tipo de discusiones. Se pensaba que 'a cada uno su patria, porque naciendo en ella sale aparejado a los ayres della, y assí lo cría como madre'.[6] A partir de numerosos ejemplos, José Antonio Maravall desarrolla el tema del amor como sentimiento patriótico. Toda patria se sirve con amor y se defiende contra los extranjeros. Por otra parte, se creía que la tierra y el clima tenían una influencia cierta en la formación de los temperamentos humanos y en las afecciones patológicas. El Nuevo Mundo, por ejemplo, es más fértil que España; allí se multiplican en libertad hombres y ganados, y la fuerza genésica de la tierra se transmite a los que nacen en ella. No podemos aquí desarrollar estas concepciones relativas al cuerpo humano y a sus diversas patologías en función de estas características precisas, y citaremos solamente la opinión de López de Velasco sobre las relaciones entre tierra, temperamentos y apariencias:

> Los españoles que pasan a aquellas partes y están en ellas mucho tiempo con la mutación del cielo y del temperamento de las regiones, aún no dejan de recibir alguna diferencia en la color y calidad de sus personas; pero los que nacen dellos, que se llaman criollos y en todo son tenidos y habidos por españoles, conocidamente salen ya diferenciados en la color y tamaño, porque todos son grandes y la color algo baja declinando a la disposición de la tierra; de donde se toma argumento que en muchos años aunque los españoles no se hubiesen mezclado con los naturales, volverían a ser como son ellos; y no solamente en las calidades corporales se mudan, pero en las del ánimo suelen seguir las del cuerpo y mudando él se alteran también.[7]

Esta relación entre la tierra natal, la fisionomía, el temperamento y, en definitiva, la identidad, también incluye en cierto modo a los criollos de color, que siempre tendieron a considerarse distintos de los 'bozales de Guinea'. Sin embargo la mancha de la esclavitud, transmitida por vía hereditaria a los negros libres, impidió una identificación total entre los diferentes grupos americanos.

La patria tenía pues varias acepciones. Una, amplia, que incluía a todos los naturales de América, ya la que Castelli se refirió en su proclama de Tiahuanaco, y otra, más restringida y más local, la ciudad de Buenos Aires, con la cual la gente de color podía identificarse más fácilmente, sin perder la referencia a la patria originaria y 'mítica' de Guinea. Esta 'patria chica' implicaba una clara separación entre los de dentro y los de fuera, los vecinos y residentes, pero también los simples moradores por un lado y los

---

6   José Antonio Maravall, *Estado moderno y mentalidad social*, vol. I (Madrid, 1971), p. 476.
7   López de Velasco, *Geografía y descripción universal de las Indias* (Madrid, 1971), pp. 19–20. Carmen Bernand, 'De l'ambigüité: à propos des hybrides dans le Nouveau Monde,' *Le Temps des Savoirs*, no. 1 (Paris, 2000), pp. 171–90.

extranjeros, los forasteros y transeúntes, por otro lado. La definición local de patria permitía la recomposición de las identidades por oposición a los recién llegados de España o de otros países europeos con el fin de competir con los porteños en el mercado laboral, de crear gremios, o, en última instancia, de complotar contra el gobierno. Todas estas situaciones se dieron y facilitaron la integración de la gente de color en un conjunto protonacional.

Nación como comunidad: las cofradías y sus rivalidades internas

La inclusión de los negros esclavos y libres en hermandades religiosas es un fenómeno característico de Hispanoamérica. En Buenos Aires, como en toda Hispanoamérica, existieron cofradías negras, siendo las más representativas de los últimos años de la época virreinal las de las naciones Congas y Angolas. Aquí la palabra 'nación' está empleada en el sentido 'cultural' para designar a gente de un mismo origen. Las funciones que desempeñaban estas asociaciones eran: la celebración pública del culto en determinados días de fiesta, la obligación para los cofrades de socorrerse mutuamente, y la posibilidad de poder celebrar danzas 'a su usanza'. En el Río de la Plata estas festividades llevan los nombres de 'tambores', 'tangos' y 'candombes'. Durante la época barroca, las 'naciones' solían participar en espectáculos públicos, descritos por los viajeros como Louis de Bougainville. Pero con la instauración del virreinato esos espectáculos fueron considerados como 'obscenos' y reiteradamente se trató de impedirlos.

Las cofradías tendían a la segregación de sus miembros en base al estatus pero también al color. En una misma iglesia, Santo Domingo, el culto de Nuestra Señora del Rosario estaba bajo la advocación de dos cofradías distintas, una de vecinos españoles y criollos, y otra, de negros esclavos y libres. Esta separación se había producido por el rechazo, por parte de los blancos (y quizás también de los negros) de entremezclarse. La cofradía del Socorro, abierta en principio a todo el mundo, sin distinción de calidades, se convirtió en una congregación de negros. Las otras cofradías de morenos que existían en Buenos Aires fueron las de San Francisco, divididas en dos hermandades, consagrada una a San Benito de Palermo, y la otra, formada por pardos, a Santa Rosa de Viterbo. En la iglesia de La Piedad, la cofradía de San Baltasar estaba constituida en su mayoría por negros de la nación Conga.[8] Las fiestas religiosas les brindaban la ocasión de realizar juntas en lugares cerrados, como los tambos, o en los huecos, es decir, solares descampados de la ciudad. Hasta los últimos decenios del siglo XVIII, los cofrades solían elegir un 'rey' con sus emblemas, la corona y el quitasol, costumbre que en los últimos años de ese siglo fue reprimida por las autoridades españolas, que temían que se crearan focos subversivos. Pero a pesar de los

8   Ricardo González, Daniel Sánchez y Cristina Fükelman, *Arte, culto e ideas. Buenos Aires, siglo XVIII* (Buenos Aires, 1998), p. 97.

bandos que prohibían la elección de 'reyes', éstos continuaron a ejercer una autoridad sobre sus gentes, cuyo alcance es difícil de determinar.[9]

El criterio para admitir a los negros esclavos así como a los morenos, pardos e indios, era el ser de 'buena vida y costumbres'. Es decir, se buscaban gentes integradas a la vida colonial. Hacia 1783 los morenos libres se separaron de los cofrades de la nación Conga de La Piedad y fundaron, en la misma iglesia, la cofradía de las Ánimas. El pretexto de la ruptura fue el deseo, por parte de los morenos, de no mezclarse con gentes que provocaban 'desacatos públicos' con sus danzas y músicas obscenas. Los morenos contaban con el apoyo del cura de la Piedad; los Congos bulliciosos, en cambio, eran tolerados por el sacristán de la Iglesia.[10] El principal argumento de los cofrades de las Ánimas para legitimizar sus demandas era el rechazo de la africanización. Los Congos, pero también otros grupos como los negros del Rosario, eran conocidos por sus ritmos y sus comparsas.

Los suplicantes de la nación Conga 'con el pesado yugo de la esclavitud que sufren perpetuamente' pedían hacer una capilla a San Baltasar y Ánimas 'para que en ella concurran los días de fiesta los hermanos esclavos e indios'. En vistas de solicitar la autorización, los morenos recordaban que 'desde tiempo casi inmemorial han acostumbrado con precedente permiso de varios gobernadores hacer sus funciones a imitación cada uno de sus respectivas naciones'. Reconocían que hubo desórdenes que se lograron contener, y los achacaban a otros cofrades, pero afirmaban que siempre rindieron servicios a la Real Corona, 'ya asistiendo a las guerras que se han ofrecido con los Portugueses y contra los enemigos bárbaros que invaden esta jurisdicción, ya haciendo las fatigas que se ofrecen en honor de la Corona.[11]

Estos comentarios revelan rivalidades entre distintas cofradías que se distinguen no sólo por las calidades de sus miembros sino por ciertas prácticas sobre las cuales tenemos pocas indicaciones detalladas. La documentación sobre cofradías menciona, por un lado, a ciertas 'naciones', es decir grupos con ciertas características de comportamiento, y por otro, a gentes no definidas según un criterio 'étnico', como eran los pardos o los morenos libres, gentes en proceso de 'blanqueamiento'. Las 'naciones' tienen sus pasos, sus músicas y sus propios ritmos, y la literatura que trata

9   Hemos estudiado al respecto el interesante documento 'Información hecha para esclarecer lo que expone Farias en su memorial contra Pablo Agüero, ambos a dos negros, hecha en Buenos Aires a 23 de enero de 1787', Archivo General de la Nación, Argentina (AGN–A), IX–36–4–3, Tribunales, Leg. 74, Exp. 10, 17 fols. Está en vías de publicación en Sevilla.

10 Miguel Ángel Rosal, 'Algunas consideraciones sobre creencias religiosas de los africanos porteños (1750–1820),' *Investigaciones y ensayos, Academia Nacional de Historia,* julio-diciembre, no. 31(Buenos Aires, 1981), pp. 372–79.

11 AGN–A, IX–31–4–6, 'Expediente en que los morenos cofrades de san Baltasar solicitan hacer una capilla para celebrar en ella sus funciones,' Justicia, Exp. 436, Legajo 17 (1785).

de estas cuestiones describe los candombes del Río de la Plata como bailes profanos de los negros, destinados a distraer al público. Sin embargo es lícito interrogarse sobre la exactitud de estas interpretaciones que parecieran atribuir únicamente a los negros de Buenos Aires rasgos festivos no religiosos, como si no estuviesen contaminados por rituales africanos, que en otras partes se desarrollaron durante la misma época. La arqueología urbana que se está desarrollando actualmente en Buenos Aires brinda testimonios materiales de ritos mágicos, tal como aparecen en el Brasil.[12]

A pesar de carecer de documentos precisos sobre estos puntos, sabemos la importancia que desempeñaron los 'reyes' negros en la perpetuación de los bailes, de las casas de tango y de los tambores. El término de 'candombe' utilizado en el Río de la Plata para designar estas 'juntas', es similar al de 'candomblé' corriente en el Brasil. Es probable que el término de 'nación', en Buenos Aires como en Porto Alegre, no corresponda a una categoría étnica precisa sino a una comunidad que comparte ciertas tradiciones que en todo el Brasil están asociadas a terreiros. Los documentos mencionan efectivamente, para Buenos Aires, el hecho que cada nación tenía su ritmo y su toque, siendo particular el toque Banguela, por ejemplo. También se mencionan las 'calundas', o fiestas de los negros, es decir, rituales caracterizados por la percusión de tambores sagrados y la comunicación con los espíritus.[13]

En el sentido 'africano', las naciones indicaban muy probablemente la expresión de ciertas modalidades rituales vinculadas con el culto de los ancestros y de los espíritus ancestrales, pero estas prácticas estaban integradas en el sistema de cofradías. En qué medida los negros más integrados trataron de separarse de estos tambores, según un proceso de 'blanqueamiento' es algo que sólo podemos vislumbrar a través de ciertos documentos que denuncian y prohiben la obscenidad de estas manifestaciones. Tales conflictos reflejan la voluntad de separar la 'barbarie' negra (populachera, obscena) de la civilización. Es interesante destacar que en los testamentos de mujeres morenas de comienzos del siglo XIX, la hermandad a la cual pertenecen juega un papel fundamental en la transmisión de los bienes. Todas ellas piden ser enterradas en la iglesia a la cual pertenecen sus cofradías respectivas. Santo Domingo y la cofradía del Rosario aparecen como la referencia de aquellas mujeres originarias 'de Guinea' o de 'nación Banguela'. La tierra de origen desde donde fueron 'conducidas' es mencionada, siendo la iglesia y la hermandad la patria de adopción.[14]

12   Daniel Schavelzon, *Arqueología de Buenos Aires* (Buenos Aires, 1999), pp. 178–81. En una de las excavaciones efectuadas en el parque de Palermo se encontró un muñeco vodu tallado en madera con una espina de hueso atravesada en el corazón. Otros indicios son mas recientes y pueden ser fechados en torno a 1870.

13   Roger Bastide, *Les religions africaines au Brésil* (Paris, 1960), pp. 287–8; Stefania Capone, *La quête de l'Afrique dans le candomblé. Pouvoir et tradition au Brésil* (Paris, 1999), pp. 91–2.

14   AGN–A, Registro 5 (1806–1807), Thomas Boyso, fol. 204; (1808–1811), Thomas Boyso, fol. 125; Registro 3 (1813), Thomas Boyso, fols. 241v–242 ; fols. 239v–240 ; fol. 301 v.

Nación como pertenencia colectiva

Hemos mencionado los argumentos esgrimidos por los cofrades de La Piedad en favor de la creación de una nueva hermandad, a saber, los servicios hechos a la Corona y la participación de todos ellos en las batallas contra los extranjeros, en ese caso, los portugueses. Con la instauración tardía del virreinato del Río de la Plata, un nuevo significado de la 'nación' como entidad colectiva comparable a 'reino', 'pueblo' o 'estado grande sujeto a un mismo príncipe o gobierno' tendió a superponerse a la definición étnica clásica. Más aún, esta definición incluyente fue de gran utilidad para los esclavos y negros libres porque les permitía en cierto modo contrarrestar el poder de los amos. La personalidad de Pedro de Cevallos, que luchó contra los portugueses de la Banda Oriental y se apoderó de Colonia de Sacramento, facilita esa identificación. Personaje de gran popularidad, como lo muestran las numerosas odas compuestas en su honor, tanto en España como en América, Pedro Cevallos recibe efectivamente una acogida triunfal en Buenos Aires en 1777, y en las festividades del caso se destacan los negros de la 'nación Conga'.

La popularidad del virrey Cevallos entre la gente de color puede medirse por el incremento de las solicitudes presentadas por los esclavos ante el Defensor de Pobres. Estas son mucho más numerosas durante ese período que en los años posteriores pero sobre todo, el tono de los documentos es más libre y más audaz. Para los esclavos, el virrey, sustituto del monarca, pero legitimado por sus acciones militares y por ser el primero en gobernar el nuevo virreinato del Río de la Plata, es el 'amparo de pobres desvalidos'.[15] Después del triunfo de su Excelencia, los esclavos piden (sin éxito) que el tribunal de primera instancia les rebaje el valor — es decir, el precio en el cual pueden ser vendidos por el amo — para que puedan comprar la libertad o cambiar de dominio fácilmente y ser adquiridos por un amo más humano, ambas posibilidades que las *Siete Partidas* permitían. Para dar al virrey pruebas de su fidelidad, los esclavos prometen por escrito sacrificar la vida al servicio de Su Majestad y ratifican solemnemente su lealtad hacia las instituciones. En cierto modo, y este punto de vista será modificado posteriormente, la tiranía está encarnada por el amo y la justicia, por autoridades, cuyo mediador es el Defensor de Pobres.

En la mayoría de los casos, los esclavos pagaban a un abogado para que defendiera su causa. En Buenos Aires, a comienzos de la época virreinal, que coincidió con el apogeo del pensamiento ilustrado, el Defensor de Pobres redactaba las solicitudes y las dirigía al virrey, 'padre de pobres esclavos y director de ricos', que podía deliberar directamente — por ejem-

---

15   AGN–A, IX–13–1–5, Gobierno, Solicitudes de esclavos: 'Francisco del Rosario y todos los siervos de esta república'.

plo, bajo la forma de una apostilla: 'Désele papel de venta para que este pobre esclavo pueda pasar a otro dueño que le trate con más humanidad' — o bien remitir el pleito al alcalde de primer o de segundo voto, para que efectuaran una encuesta más detallada y administraran. El Defensor de Pobres, en el último tercio del siglo XVIII, desempeñó un papel consider-able en la propagación de las ideas liberales hostiles a la esclavitud o por lo menos, a los abusos de la institución. Es posible que en Buenos Aires, ciu-dad periférica en expansión y abierta a las ideas europeas, la influencia de esos abogados ilustrados fuera mayor que en otros virreinatos, o en todo caso más temprana. Carlos Aguirre nos brinda numerosas causas empren-didas por el 'Defensor de Menores' en Lima, después de la Independencia, pero éstas son más tardías — primera mitad del siglo XIX — y se sitúan en una corriente abolicionista.[16]

De la documentación reunida en los fondos 'Solicitudes de esclavos' de finales de la época colonial en el Río de la Plata, surgen reivindicaciones sorprendentes. Por ejemplo, la de 'Francisco del Rosario, postrado a las plantas de Vuestra Excelencia, y todos los siervos de esta república', solic-itud que indica una toma de conciencia general, o inducida por el Defensor. Estos esclavos felicitan a Cevallos por su campaña victoriosa, y bendicen el triunfo 'que bien podemos decir con el profeta Zacarías, Bendito sea el Señor Dios de Israel que envió nueva redención a su pueblo'. A continuación exponen las desdichas que sufren y piden que se les rebaje su valor en compensación por los años que han servido. Pero Cevallos, disgustado quizás por esas referencias mesiánicas, declara que no ha lugar.[17] Ese mismo año, en el proceso intentado por una mulata libre para rescatar a su hija esclava, aquélla produce un documento en nombre de 'Nosotros, los más humildes vasallos de Vuestra Majestad, inclusive todos los esclavos que al presente nos hallamos en esta ciudad de Buenos Aires', en el cual suplican que el rey les conceda 'algún alivio a nuestra opresa servidumbre'. Los esclavos expresan su fidelidad constante y piden que al cabo de diez años de servicio se les otorgue la posibilidad de adquirir la libertad a un precio bajo.[18]

Varios documentos presentan argumentos inspirados en el espíritu de las luces. Un esclavo pide papel de venta después de 17 años de servicio por malos tratos y porque 'jamás le trata como a racional, y no pudiendo ya el que representa tolerar semejante servidumbre'.[19] José Atanasio tiene sólo 17 años pero conoce los recursos que le brinda la ley y acude al Defensor de

16   Carlos Aguirre, *Agentes de su propia libertad. Los esclavos de Lima y la desintegración de la esclavitud, 1820–1854* (Lima, 1993).
17   AGN–A, IX–3–1–5, Gobierno, Solicitudes de esclavos (1777).
18   AGN–A, IX–36–5–3, Tribunales (1777), Autos de Maria Eulalia Valdivia, mulata libre, contra doña Manuela Sánchez Villavicencio'.
19   AGN–A, IX–3–1–5, Gobierno, Solicitudes de esclavos (abril 1778).

Pobres para obtener carta de libertad, diciendo 'mi amo, en que contra los sentimientos más íntimos del derecho natural se opone a que yo compre mi libertad y la adquiera por medio del dinero en que puedo ser vendido, cuando todos deben conspirar a abolir la esclavitud como repugnante a nuestra religión'.[20] Estos testimonios fueron inspirados probablemente por el Defensor, pero no puede excluirse tampoco que algunos esclavos se hayan familiarizado con temas políticos discutidos en las casas de los amos. Cabe recordar que una de las obras extranjeras que alcanzó mayor difusión en Hispanoamérica fue el *Contrato Social* de Jean-Jacques Rousseau, publicado en 1763 pero difundido en los años sucesivos en el continente.

La esfera institucional, el amparo que proporcionaban las leyes así como la posibilidad del recurso fueron cauces para la integración de la gente de color en un contexto más amplio que podemos llamar protonacional. La jurisprudencia fue un medio importante, a fines del siglo XVIII, para que un esclavo lograra (como lo estipulaban desde tiempos antiguos las *Siete Partidas* que aún regían las relaciones entre amos y esclavos) cambio de dominio, si se demostraba que había sido maltratado, o papel de venta a un precio razonable. La proximidad física entre los esclavos y los amos incitó a aquellos a amenazar a los señores con denuncias de toda índole: adulterio, malas costumbres y traición a la patria. Este tipo de conducta se acentuó en los momentos más tensos del virreinato, hasta volverse frecuente a partir de 1810.

Un interesante documento de 1795 muestra claramente este tipo de lealtades. Se trata de una causa contra varios franceses de Buenos Aires acusados de querer derribar al gobierno.[21] Recordemos que después de 1793 los franceses y sus ideas revolucionarias inspiraron gran desconfianza en el Río de la Plata, donde se temía la propagación de esas ideas subversivas. El asunto puede resumirse brevemente, aunque la documentación es sumamente extensa y merecería un estudio detallado. Varios amigos 'franceses de nación' acostumbraban a reunirse para comer y beber en casa de uno de ellos, llamado Luis Dumont. Uno de los esclavos que los atendía acusó a Dumont de conspirar contra el gobierno, organizando una rebelión que debía estallar el día de Viernes Santo. Otros esclavos se plegaron a esas acusaciones. Los franceses habían conversado con sus esclavos más de confianza para solicitar su ayuda en el levantamiento; les habían prometido que de triunfar, todos los negros de la ciudad serían liberados.

De hecho, a pesar de que un hombre de la estatura de Santiago Liniers se halló comprometido en el asunto, puesto que alguna reunión había tenido lugar en su casa, los principales reos eran gente plebeya, y el abo-

---

20   AGN–A, IX–56–12, 'Autos seguidos a instancia de Joseph Atanasio, esclavo de don Antonio Vélez sobre querer le de este su libertad,' Tribunales (1777), fol. 15.
21   AGN–A, IX–36–1–5, Tribunales, Exp. 60 (1795).

gado defensor utilizó ese argumento para quitarles importancia e influencia: 'el supuesto cabecilla (Luis Dumonte) no es más que un pobre panadero, sin el menor talento [...] Ninguno de ellos tiene armas, dinero, talento, ni son de aquellos hombres populares que se han adquirido reputación y partidos grandes en los pueblos, sobre cuya conducta debe velar el gobierno'. El abogado mencionó el odio que los esclavos sienten por el amo y el capataz, máxime si aquel era panadero, puesto que las panaderías eran pequeñas empresas que funcionaban con mano de obra engrillada muchas veces. Toda esa conjura había sido inventada para calumniar a los acusados. '¿Cómo podías los esclavos rebelarse contra el gobierno, ya que los escasos "movimientos" que han existido han sido dirigidos contra mayordomos crueles?' 'Una sedición popular, una revolución para trastornar el orden del gobierno en esta capital y adaptar las máximas que forman la detestable constitución de Francia, no es creíble [...] El pueblo todo está instruido en las miserias y horrores en que está sumergida aquella infeliz nación [saben] que en Francia el mayor delito es tener bienes'.[22]

Nación como patria

El servicio militar en las milicias, y posteriormente en los ejércitos coloniales reorganizados, constituyó para la gente de color durante todo el período colonial una posibilidad de integrarse a una entidad territorial y afectiva, la patria. A comienzos del siglo XIX existían dos compañías de Granaderos, una de morenos libres y la otra de pardos libres. Una tercer compañía de Granaderos negros fue creada en 1803. La compañía de artillería con 150 plazas estaba integrada principalmente por negros.[23] Los veteranos habían participado en las guerras contra los portugueses y algunos habían adquirido galones. Esto les daba prestigio. Esas milicias tenían también por misión el control del orden público en los tambos y candombes de la ciudad, y el apresar a los negros prófugos.

A raíz de las invasiones ingleses en 1806 y 1807, numerosos negros se alistaron y participaron a la defensa de la ciudad. Cuando las tropas inglesas invadieron Buenos Aires, Beresford promulgó un bando para sosegar a los amos, que temían una revuelta de esclavos. Esta actuación de los negros y pardos en las luchas contra los invasores extranjeros dio a la gente de color la ocasión de probar su fidelidad a la patria. Un moreno llamado José María formó un Cuerpo de Negros Esclavos y ofreció al cabildo el reunir a 4000 hombres de esa condición solicitando armas: chuzas, machetes y cuchillos, así como 500 lanzas que se hallaban en los depósitos del fuerte.[24] Otros desempeñaron

22 *Ibid.*, fol. 205–7.
23 Vicente Gesualdo, 'Los negros en Buenos Aires y el interior,' *Historia*, no. 5 (Buenos Aires, marzo–mayo 1982), pp. 26–49.
24 *Ibid.*, p. 39.

actos individuales de heroismo de los cuales atestiguaron sus amos. Esta actitud valiente de los hombres de color contradecía el criterio predominante entre la oficialidad castrense colonial sobre las compañías de gente de color que sólo servían 'para peones, guardar caballadas y otros precisos destinos'.[25]

Después de la victoria de Buenos Aires, el cabildo, en fecha de 22 de octubre de 1807, decidió recompensar 'el extraordinario entusiasmo con que la esclavatura de esta ciudad se dedicó a defenderla en los días 1 a 6 de julio', y otorgó la libertad a los que quedaron mutilados o inútiles para el servicio, asignándoles una pensión mensual de seis pesos. El cabildo propuso también libertar por sorteo a otros 25; después de efectuada la operación, el cabildo a su arbitrio, eligió a otros cinco esclavos y pagó el precio de su libertad a sus amos. El rey y vecinos particulares pagaron otros premios de libertad, y resultaron en todo 70.[26] La ceremonia del sorteo se realizó en la actual Plaza de Mayo, apiñada de gente. Después de la celebración oficial, hubo fuegos artificiales y música. Esta fue una de las primeras fiestas patrióticas.

La obtención de esa recompensa dio lugar a una serie de testimonios individuales que describen concretamente la actuación de esos esclavos. Don Martín José Medrano, capitán de la primera compañía del primer batallón de patricios, certificó 'que el moreno llamado Joaquín Alzaga, hallándome destinado en la azotea del Señor alcalde de primer voto don Martín de Alzaga, se me presentó ofreciendo todo auxilio para la gente que estaba a mis órdenes: asimismo me dijo que él tenía fusil y todo lo demás necesario para a mi lado hacer fuego en caso necesario'.[27] 'Ilario Armando, soldado de la compañía de pardos voluntarios de infantería y de la guarnición de esta plaza', sirvió en esas circunstancias con 'fidelidad y amor', puesto que procedió a la evacuación de las armas de la plaza, como él mismo lo afirmó: 'lleno del deseo de sacrificar primero la vida como aquellos muchos que hoy se ven mutilados con tanto honor y gloria, antes que sobrevivir a la desgracia de ver entregada la Patria a ajenada y enemiga dominación. Como el hombre no tuvo la suerte de ser sorteado y liberado, pidió certificado y lo obtuvo.[28] Otros esclavos aprovecharon esa coyuntura favorable, hicieron prueba de méritos y fueron manumitidos.

El viejo criterio de 'servir con amor a la patria', típico del pensamiento hispánico, aparece en estas solicitudes con toda nitidez. El tema del honor tampoco debe sorprender ya que desde la época del virreinato, las reivin-

25 Santiago-Gerardo Suárez, *Las milicias. Instituciones militares hispanoamericanas* (Caracas, 1984), p. 201.
26 José Luis Lanuza, *Morenada. Una historia de la raza africana en el Río de la Plata* (Buenos Aires, 1967), pp. 64–6.
27 AGN–A, Solicitudes de esclavos, Gobierno, IX–13.1.5., documento del 23 de agosto de 1808.
28 AGN–A, Solicitudes de esclavos, Gobierno, IX–13.1.5, documento del 5 de septiembre de 1808.

dicaciones de honra por parte de las clases bajas de pardos son frecuentes
en la documentación. Sin embargo, no siempre las promesas de libertad
hechas en el fragor de la batalla por los amos fueron cumplidas fácilmente.
Mariana Sosa habla en nombre de su hijo, esclavo, que participó con su
amo en la defensa de Buenos Aires. El amo le había dicho que 'para ser
libre dependía de que quedase con vida en la refriega, y si lo mataban, el
perdía gustoso su dinero'. La madre y el hijo aceptaron el acuerdo y
'después de haberse medio instruido con los demás en el cuerpo de su
clase, en el manejo de las armas' (incorporado en la tropa de las castas).
Pero el hijo fue gravemente herido en un brazo y tomado prisionero y llevado a Montevideo. Al fin, el amo le dio la libertad.[29]

La participación de los esclavos en la defensa de Buenos Aires durante
las invasiones inglesas (1807) tuvo como consecuencia inmediata la identificación de los negros y pardos con el pueblo. Los héroes de tez oscura
fueron ensalzados en el romance heroico de Pantaleón Rivarola, 'fiel vasal-
lo de SM y amante de la patria' en estos términos:

'No es posible aquí omitir para honor de nuestro suelo y de nuestro
Soberano las maravillas que hicieron, de religión y valor, los indios, pardos y
negros, todos todos a porfía [...] Los esclavos de las casas desamparan a sus
dueños y a la palestra de Marte van a porfía corriendo, sin que contenerlos
pueda, de sus amos el precepto ¡Qué prodigios de valor, qué heroicos hechos
no hicieron, estos valientes esclavos, a vista del mundo entero! '(el romance
cuenta cómo el comandante Juan Domingo Urien fué salvado por un negri-
to, a quien dijo, en señal de agradecimiento: 'búscame en mi casa, que eres
libre'). Pablo Jiménez, esclavo pardo, también es recordado por el bardo:
'Estas heroicas acciones, de su amo merecieron, la franqueza y libertad, que
le concedió al momento, brillando en amo y esclavo, honor de virtud y acuerdo'.[30] 'El Triunfo Heroico' de Vicente López y Planes, ensalza el valor del
pueblo de Buenos Aires, compuesto de todos sus habitantes: 'Qué tropa es
ésta', preguntarás, monarca muy benigno. 'Oh ínclito señor, ésta no es tropa,
Buenos Aires os muestra allí sus hijos: allí está el labrador, allí el letrado, el
comerciante, el artesano, el niño, el moreno y el pardo [...] Por todas calles
número infinito, de ilustre juventud a los cuarteles correr se ve, llevando tras
su brío, tras su heroico valor, tras su entusiasmo, al natural, al cuarterón, y al
hijo del tostado habitante de Etiopía'.[31]

Las circunstancias excepcionales que habían agitado la ciudad
favorecían esta visión romántica de las castas, constitutivas del nuevo
pueblo argentino. Esta idealización se prosiguió durante las luchas revolucionarias, donde los hombres de color desempeñaron un papel fundamental. Sin embargo la nueva era republicana, abocada a la consolidación de la

29   AGN–A, IX–13–1–5, febrero 1809.
30   *Antología de literatura virreinal* (Buenos Aires, 1967), pp. 74–7.
31   *Ibid.*, pp.101–06.

nación no resolvió sino tardíamente la cuestión de la esclavitud. Los negros integran el panteón de los próceres. Bajo las armas, los negros libres se convierten en 'ciudadanos'.

Por otra parte, para aumentar el número de soldados de los ejércitos de la patria, el gobierno ordenó, en mayo de 1813, el rescate de los esclavos de los extranjeros. Estos debían entregar a los esclavos excendentarios, que les serían indemnizados a un precio fijado y que giraba para un adulto en torno a los 200 pesos, valor más bajo que el de la tasa arbitraria que ponía el amo. Naturalmente, muchos dueños ocultaron o minimizaron el número de criados que poseían, para poder conservarlos. Pero los esclavos vieron en esta actividad militar la posibilidad de liberarse, y denunciaron a los amos recalcitrantes ante las autoridades, como lo hizo el moreno Manuel Juan, esclavo de don Diego Jackson, declarando ante la comisión de rescate que su amo tenía en realidad ocho esclavos, que cinco se le habían huído pero que aún le quedaban tres por presentar. Cabe notar la frecuencia de las denuncias hechas por los esclavos contra los amos que se negaban a entregarlos al servicio de la patria. Otro dato significativo es el de la frecuencia del apellido Patria a partir de 1810 entre los negros, libres o libertos.

Para conmemorar el año I de la Revolución de Mayo, el arquitecto Prilidiano Pueyrredón — el mismo que había tenido como maestro a un pintor pardo — concibió una pirámide de ladrillos cuya forma, instrumentos y materiales estaban inspirados en el simbolismo de la masonería. El artesano que construyó el monumento — el primero en todo el continente que materializó el triunfo de la libertad — fue el mulato Pedro Cañete. En 1815, para festejar el aniversario de la Revolución de Mayo, se colocaron en la Plaza de la Victoria cuatro estatuas que representaban las cuatro partes del mundo, y que llevaban las siguientes inscripciones alusivas: América libre, Europa admirada de esa libertad, Asia soportando aún cadenas y Africa redimida por la libertad de sus hijos de América: 'Africa hasta aquí lloró, a sus hijos en prisiones, que la crueldad aprobó. Su amargo llanto cesó, desde que el americano, con su libertad ufano, compasivo y generoso, prodiga este don precioso, al infeliz africano.'[32] La opresión de la esclavitud quedaba identificada con el régimen colonial.

Un decreto de diciembre de 1813 extensivo a toda la provincia, divide a los propietarios de esclavos en dos clases. 'La primera se compondrá de los que teniendo mas de un esclavo, dejaron de contribuir tanto con criados destinados al servicio doméstico como con los empleados en barracas, fábricas panaderías, y labranzas. Cada uno de los comprendidos deberá dar el nombre de un esclavo a la comisión de rescate, que hará se saquen a la suerte 15 por cada 100. La segunda clase de propietarios, los que tienen un excedente, deberán presentar el nombre de cada esclavo por cada exce-

---

32   Lanuza, *Morenada*, p. 70.

dente, los cuales se vacarán a razón de 30 por cada 100. Los esclavos enganchados se pagarán a sus amos bajo las mismas condiciones que los destacados para el primer batallón de libertos'. El 14 de enero de 1815, Carlos de Alvear decretó el rescate de esclavos para 'hacer una leva de todos los hombres de edad de 16 a 30 años' pertenecientes a europeos españoles que no tuvieran carta de ciudadanía, quedan destinados al servicio de las armas. Tienen la obligación de servir al ejército hasta un año después del fin de la guerra.

Las comisiones de ciudadanos debían examinar a los esclavos rescatados, descartando a los inútiles. A los amos se les daba un certificado, y el importe del esclavo debía serles pagado un año después. Toda ocultación por parte del amo le valía una multa de 500 pesos. Pero lo más importante era que los esclavos podían presentarse directamente a cualquier juez o jefe militar, para integrar los batallones de libertos.[33] Quedaban exceptuados del rescate los panaderos de la ciudad. Ello no impidió que en 1815, don José Guerra, del gremio de los panaderos, entregara ocho negros como tercera parte de los 24 que tenía para el trabajo de panadería. En 1817, 406 esclavos fueron rescatados para constituir el Batallón de Cazadores en virtud de una orden suprema de diciembre del año anterior. Pero la lista de los nuevos reclutas muestra que algunos de ellos fueron escogidos siendo menores de los 16 años previstos por la ley, siendo los mas jóvenes Miguel Pestana, de diez años, rescatado por 140 pesos, y Antonio Moslera, de ocho años, por el precio de 100 pesos. 'Aptos para el servicio de las armas', estos chiquillos fueron probablemente utilizados como tambores.[34]

A veces se desembarazaba el amo de un esclavo que le causaba problemas, como Antonio de Obligado que remitió a la disposición del comisario don Victorino de la Fuente, un esclavo de 35 años de nación angola, 'medio albañil, huidor y bastante ratero, a fin que se sirva destinarlo al servicio de la patria. O bien el amo se quita de encima a un enfermo, o a un borracho, o a un viejo 'no obstante que su natural vigor lo extraía de tal clase', como lo justifica ante las autoridades. Pero a pesar de las dificultades de ejecución del decreto de rescate, los negros esclavos o pardos libres formaron la mayoría de los regimientos de infantería de los ejércitos patriotas argentinos. En esa ocasión la participación fue masiva. Los batallones de cazadores 7 y 8 (el de Negros Libertos) del Ejército de los Andes lucharon valientemente en Chacabuco, Cancha Rayada y Maipú. Muchos murieron en la Cordillera. Samuel Haigh, que estuvo presente en la batalla de Maipu (1818), afirma que el ala izquierda del ejército patriota, bajo el mando del General Alvarado, estaba 'compuesta principalmente por negros', que dejaron en el campo de batalla 400 muertos y muchos heri-

---

33   AGN–A, X–43–6–7, Rescate de esclavos, 1813–17.
34   AGN–A, X–43–6–9, Policía, Libertos.

dos. Y cuando los patriotas llegan al Molino del Espejo con los prisioneros españoles, Haigh comenta: 'Nada podía exceder al furor salvaje de los negros del ejército patriota; habían llevado el choque de la acción contra el mejor regimiento español y perdido la mayor parte de sus efectivos; deleitábales la idea de fusilar los prisioneros. Vi un negro viejo realmente llorando de rabia cuando se apercibió que los oficiales protegían de su furor a los prisioneros.'[35] Los sobrevivientes constituyeron en el Perú el Regimiento del Río de la Plata.[36]

Los tiempos revolucionarios dieron también modelos negros, como lo habían hecho los santos hispanoamericanos a comienzos del siglo XVII. Desde luego, la hagiografía de estos personajes no implica la exactitud de los hechos, pero lo que nos importa aquí es el reconocimiento público de los méritos de esos negros patriotas. Antonio Ruiz, alias Falucho — apodo que se daba a los soldados negros — fué, para los porteños, el héroe de aquellos tiempos. Este moreno, veterano de Chacabuco y Maipu, se resistió, en Lima, a saludar a la bandera realista, que los veteranos impagos y descontentos hicieron flamear. El soldado fue fusilado y cayó al grito de 'Viva Buenos Aires'.[37]

Algunos nombres de estos heroicos soldados de San Martín han sido rescatados del olvido. No todos fueron criollos y hallamos también africanos, es decir, antiguos bozales integrados a la nueva patria. Uno de ellos fue Andrés Ibáñez, del batallón octavo, que había nacido en Africa y había sido vendido en Buenos Aires a la edad de 16 años. Ibáñez alcanzó el grado de capitán y ganó cinco medallas. Después de las Guerras de Independencia, el moreno se instaló en Buenos Aires donde adquirió una pulpería. Manuel Macedonio Barbarin, de nación Calivali, llegó a Buenos Aires a fines del siglo XVIII y fue probablemente esclavo del francés Juan Barbarin, uno de los reos de la causa de los franceses. Como tantos otros esclavos, intervino en la defensa de la ciudad contra los ingleses, fue liberado por sorteo y, en 1810, alcanzó el grado de capitán de milicias. Posteriormente, Barbarin tomó parte en las luchas independentistas, y cuando murió, en 1836, la *Gaceta Mercantil* publicó una 'canción fúnebre' para deplorar 'La pérdida funesta e irreparable de un militar valiente y memorable'.[38] Estos dos ejemplos, que no son únicos, muestran que el

35 S. Haigh, *Bosquejos de Buenos Aires, Chile y Perú* (Buenos Aires, 1920), cap. X, pp. 111, 113 y 116.
36 Gesualdo, 'Los negros en Buenos Aires,' p. 39.
37 Lanuza, *Morenada*, p. 8–9.
38 Marcos Estrada, *Argentinos de origen africano* (Buenos Aires, 1979), pp. 79–84. Es interesante comparar la participación militar de los hombres de color hispanoamericanos con la de sus congéneres de los Estados Unidos. Paul Gilroy (*The Black Atlantic*, p. 25) en su semblanza de Martin Robinson Delany, señala que 'Delany was commissioned as a major in the Union army, proudly assuming the regalia of the first black field officer in the history of the United States'. En el Río de la Plata había sargentos mayores negros desde la época de Pedro Cevallos.

ejército constituyó para los libertos un instrumento poderoso de ascenso social, ya que en la época colonial era difícil para las castas obtener galones militares, ya que 'para cabos y aún para ascender a sargento, se atienda a los soldados de nacimiento con preferencia a los demás, como tengan las circunstancias de aptitud, conducta y demás'.[39]

Por último cabe destacar la figura legendaria del negro Ventura, que denunció en 1812, ante el alcalde de Barracas, la conspiración de Martín de Alzaga contra la Junta Revolucionaria, que tenía dispuesto 'que no habían de quedar en ella criollos, mulatos, indios ni negros, sino solamente españoles. Que todos habían de ser enviados a España para que sirviesen a los franceses'. Ventura hizo la denuncia porque temió que Alzaga los matara a todos. Alzaga fue detenido y ejecutado pocas horas después. El gobierno pagó la libertad del negro y le obsequió un uniforme y un estipendio vitalicio de soldado, así como un escudo de honor con la leyenda: 'Por fiel a la patria'.[40]

¿Las 'naciones' o la nación?

En Buenos Aires las circunstancias excepcionales provocadas por las invasiones inglesas y por las luchas de la independencia convirtieron al negro en un personaje emblemático. Pero esta afirmación necesita ser moderada ya que el panteón de los próceres individualiza a ciertos hombres sin que ello redunde en la abolición definitiva de la esclavitud, que tuvo lugar tardíamente, en 1853, después de la caída de Rosas. A partir de 1812 se había prohibido el tráfico de esclavos en las Provincias Unidas. Un año después del Decreto de 1813 sobre la Libertad de Vientres, se permitió nuevamente la introducción de esclavos africanos que acompañaban a extranjeros en calidad de criados, pero éstos no podían ser vendidos. La libre enajenación fue permitida en 1831, bajo la gobernación de Rosas, y se desconoce el número de negros que ingresaron en esa época en el Río de la Plata.[41]

A partir de los años 1820, el gobierno de Rivadavia otorgó a los negros de Buenos Aires la autorización de constituirse en sociedades, que fueron llamadas 'africanas', y que ya no tenían, como las cofradías, un marco religioso. Estas sociedades tenían por objetivo libertar con sus fondos a 'aquellos socios que se hagan dignos de ello por su moral e industria', educar a los niños, auxiliar a los miembros brindándoles instrumentos para trabajar, velar por la conducta moral de la nación, conmemorar a los difuntos e impedir las escisiones en nuevas asociaciones.[42] Rivadavia las dotó de

39   AGN–A, BN 261, fol. 19, 1770.
40   Estrada, *Argentinos de origen africano*, pp. 64–6
41   Martha Goldberg, 'La población negra y mulata de la ciudad de Buenos Aires, 1810–1840,' *Desarrollo Económico*, no. 79, vol. 20 (1976), pp. 81–94.
42   AGN–A, X–31–11–5, Policía, no. 1 (Reglamento para las sociedades africanas).

estatutos, que debían ser aprobados por la policía. El objetivo era fomentar la ayuda entre los ex esclavos y facilitar los rescates. Quizás el modelo lejano fue el de las sociedades mutualistas de negros de Filadelfia, que se desarrollaron principalmente entre 1802 y 1812.[43] La creación de estas asociaciones es un aspecto del movimiento asociativo intenso que caracteriza la ciudad de Buenos Aires en la primera mitad del siglo XIX y que ha sido analizado en forma exhaustiva por Pilar González Bernaldo.[44] Es posible también, como lo piensa esta autora, que la fragmentación de la gente de color en pequeños grupos muy restrictivos en cuanto a la admisión de nuevos miembros — éstos debían pertenecer a la misma 'nación' — permitió un mejor control de la plebe urbana.

En el transcurso de 1822 fueron firmados cuatro decretos prohibiendo a los negros que bailaran en la calle, y arrestando a aquellos que lo hacían fuera de los lugares conocidos como 'casas de tango'.[45] Durante el primer gobierno de Rivadavia fueron creadas siete sociedades que corresponden a las naciones que encontramos en los documentos coloniales que se refieren a las cofradías y a los bailes, como las de los Congas, Cambundas, Benguelas y Minas, por sólo citar las más importantes. Las sociedades promovieron una cierta identificación étnica, expresada en los reglamentos que no admitían gente exterior a la nación. Pero de hecho la relación entre 'sociedades' y danzas pareciera confirmar nuestras hipótesis sobre el carácter religioso de estas asociaciones. Durante su presidencia, entre 1826 y 1829, Rivadavia organizó cinco sociedades más (Mozambique, Lubola, Angola, Huombe, Carabari).

A partir del gobierno de Rosas, las sociedades africanas proliferaron, e integraron nuevos esclavos venidos del Brasil, así como libres, pero la lista de 31 nuevos grupos que brinda la documentación es el producto de fisiones y de fragmentaciones de naciones más antiguas. Más de la mitad de esas sociedades de la época de Rosas (19) surgen en 1842, año marcado por el terror de la Mazorca y por el bloqueo francés. Junto con las ya existentes, esas asociaciones expresaron por escrito su apoyo al dictador en las páginas de la *Gaceta Mercantil*. A partir de esa fecha, aunque todavía hubo algunas creaciones, las asociaciones africanas declinaron, y las dos últimas fueron autorizadas en 1860.

43 Gary Nash, *Forging Freedom. The Formation of Philadelphia's Black Community, 1720–1840* (Cambridge, MA, 1991), p. 210. Este autor menciona igualmente las logias masónicas de negros que surgieron en esa ciudad en la primera mitad del siglo XIX. Si bien tenemos indicios de la importancia de la masonería en Buenos Aires y de la participación de hombres de color, los datos son demasiado fragmentarios todavía.

44 Pilar González Bernaldo, *La création d'une nation. Histoire politique des nouvelles appartenances culturelles de la ville de Buenos Aires entre 1829 et 1862* (Paris, 1992), 3 tomes.

45 *Ibid.*, tomo 1, p. 189.

Otra circunstancia particular dio a la población negra una cierta importancia bajo la dictadura de Rosas. A partir de 1835, con la instauración del gobierno rosista, los negros gozaron de la confianza del tirano. Muchos de ellos fueron reclutados como libertos en las tropas de Rosas para luchar contra los indios de la frontera, y muchos perecieron en los combates. Los criados y sirvientes desempeñaron un papel importante ya que su inserción en la casa de sus amos les permitía controlar las conversaciones y denunciar a los opositores. La fidelidad de los negros a la causa federal facilitó la integración de estos a la nación. La nación Loango, reunida en asociación, envió una carta en septiembre de 1846 fechada según el calendario revolucionario, del 'año 37 de la libertad, año 31 de la independencia y año 17 de la Confederación Argentina'.

Los negros fueron durante toda esa época glorificados por los periodistas a sueldo de Rosas. En los candombes se cantaban estribillos en los que se ensalzaba la causa federal. Estas coplas, estudiadas por Ricardo Rodríguez Molas, utilizan la jerigonza de los negros y la ingenuidad de la letra da más fuerza a la propaganda federal, cuyo programa resulta 'evidente' para las clases populares. A los adversarios a la causa de Rosas, los estribillos negros acusaban de traidores a la patria, utilizando referencias a viejos prejuicios racistas, como por ejemplo:

> Esi no tiene opinió
> Esi tiene mucha maña;
> Esi e moro y e judío
> Y trabaja para España[46]

En 1843, según la *Gaceta Mercantil*, 'Los pardos o los mulatos en nada desmerecen por serlo; al contrario son atendidos y considerados por el general Rosas, lo mismo que los negros, los africanos y morenos, como hijos del país, valientes defensores de la libertad que han conquistado gloria y fama en cien batallas […] El general Rosas aprecia tanto a los mulatos y morenos, que no tiene inconveniente en sentarlos en su mesa y comer con ellos, por lo que ha pretendido burlarse *El Nacional* (un periódico unitario de Montevideo) reprochándole que su hija, la señorita doña Manuelita de Rosas y Ezcurra, no tenga reparo en bailar en ciertas ocasiones con los mulatos, pardos y morenos honrados y laboriosos'.[47] El pintor Martín L. Boneo inmortalizó a la familia del dictador asistiendo a una fiesta organizada en los locales de la nación Angunga. El óleo muestra una pareja de negros que bailan al ritmo del tambor, ante un público encantado del

---

46 Rodríguez Molas, 'Negros libres rioplatenses,' *Revista de Humanidades* 1 (Buenos Aires, September 1961), pp. 99–126, p. 108.
47 George Reid Andrews, *The Afro-Argentines of Buenos Aires, 1800-1900* (Madison, 1980), p. 117.

espectáculo. Para conmemorar el 25 de mayo de 1845, aniversario de la revolución, Rosas invitó a los negros a bailar en la plaza de la Victoria, lo que le valió las críticas de la oposición unitaria, que se escandalizó al ver que 'bandas africanas de viles esclavos, por calles y plazas discurriendo van, su bárbara grita, su danza salvaje, es en este día meditado ultraje del nuevo Caribe que el Sud abortó', según escribe Juan Cruz Varela.[48]

Con el paso del tiempo los conflictos entre los miembros de cada sociedad se agravaron y el individualismo pudo mas que el sentimiento de pertenencia a la colectividad. Las nuevas generaciones ya nada querían saber de los 'negros viejos', como ocurrió en 1856 entre los de Mina Meji.[49] En vano la sociedad Huombé pidió ser representada por una persona que velara por los intereses de la nación y restableciera 'el honor que nos legaron nuestros antepasados', es decir, la participación al rescate de los esclavos.[50] Los negros viejos morían y las casonas de las sociedades, como sus dueños, caían en ruinas y se transformaban en 'taperas', es decir, en chozas miserables de indios. Otras sociedades estaban más próximas de los gremios que de los grupos étnicos, como la Sociedad de los Peluqueros Franceses de Buenos Aires, que eran en 1858 134, y que pretendían reagrupar a todos los que ejercían este oficio.[51]

El vocabulario utilizados por los miembros de estos grupos es significativo de la pérdida de referencias étnicas. Pocos emplean el vocablo de 'nación', que cae en desuso. Otros términos aparecen, como 'gremio', fraternidad, congregación, sociedad de ayuda mutua, sociedad filantrópica de beneficencia e inclusive 'club', réplica plebeya de las agrupaciones de la burguesía. Es así como se define la sociedad de 'Morenos criollos', autorizada por la policía en 1860, varios años después de la abolición de la esclavitud. Ya no se utiliza el calificativo de 'africano' sino la categoría más amplia de 'criollo' (que incluye no sólo a los pardos, sino a los mestizos indígenas y a los americanos blancos). El club está patrocinado por la Virgen de Luján, protectora del pueblo argentino. Otros ejemplos como el que ofrece la 'Sociedad Protectora Brasileira', fundada en 1856, muestran la pérdida de las raíces étnicas y la apertura de la admisión a estos 'clubes' a amigos y vecinos.[52] Las reivindicaciones étnicas, que aún existían en tiempos de Rosas, no resisten a la irrupción de la modernidad. En vano la 'Sociedad Africana Conga', probablemente la más tradicional y en todo caso la más antigua, recordaba en 1857 que no se debían admitir nuevos socios extranjeros al grupo. Pues si los fundadores habían muerto, sus

48   Andrews, p. 120; Rodríguez Molas, 106.
49   AGN–A, X–31–11–5, Policía, no. 32
50   AGN–A, X–31–11–5, Policía, no. 8.
51   AGN–A, X–31–11–5, Policía, no. 24.
52   AGN–A, X–31–11–5, Policía, no. 36 y 22.

descendientes debían conservar la casa que los reunía y el nombre de su nación para celebrar todos los años 'las cenizas de sus padres' en el 'cuarto de ánimas' para esas ocasiones.[53] Son éstos, quizás, los últimos vestigios del culto a los antepasados tan arraigado entre los pueblos africanos.

53   AGN–A X–31–11–5, Policía, no. 18 y 20.

CHAPTER 4

Blacks and the Forging of National Identity in the Caribbean, 1840–1900

Franklin W. Knight

The quest for an identity is an old one, especially among the transplanted and newly engendered populations throughout the Americas. This manifestation is universal. All across the American continent, however, one notable consequence of the erratic creation of European colonies after 1492 was the slow development of a general self-consciousness among the newly established overseas group that constituted, in some cases, but by no means universally, a manifest precondition for political independence. The complex and non-linear ways in which this process of self-consciousness evolved has been traced by a number of historians. A sample of these viewpoints can be gleaned in the excellent essays collected and published under the title, *Colonial Identity in the Atlantic World* by Nicholas Canny and Anthony Pagden in 1987.[1] Yet there never existed a uniform identity — political or otherwise — that could be detected across the region irrespective of time, place and local circumstances. Rather there existed several forms of identities — political, cultural, ethnic, religious, linguistic and racial — that had to be constantly created, mediated and negotiated in order to maintain a stable community.[2] For the Caribbean and the Americas as a whole these identities had to be worked out within the larger political context of the competing European empires and the inescapable underlying tensions between each metropolis and its geographical periphery. Moreover, such identities had to be articulated using the political discourse of those European languages formally disseminated throughout the region. This made international considerations an integral part of the process of establishing a local political identity. Pagden and Canny point out in their perceptive concluding essay:

---

1   Nicholas Canny and Anthony Pagden (eds.), *Colonial Identity in the Atlantic World, 1500–1800* (Princeton, 1987).

2   See, for example, Mieko Nishida, 'Identity and Slavery: Ethnicity, Gender, and Race in Salvador, Brazil, 1808–1888,' unpublished manuscript. I want to thank Professor Nishida for allowing me to read and cite her extremely interesting case study of the dynamism of various forms of identity among the African and Afro-Brazilian population of Salvador.

It was not our immediate assumption that self-perception or the acqui-
sition of a cultural identity, however conceived, is necessarily part of
the process by which colonies make themselves into nations. But the
questions of the relationship, necessary or contingent, between identity and independence cannot be easily avoided ... *By the middle of the nineteenth century the nation-state had become the only acceptable frame of reference for
the ambitions of colonized peoples, whatever origins those ambitions might have had.
Self-perception had become a question of nationhood and of very little else.* Cultural,
political, religious and even racial (or at least tribal) characteristics were all
perceived in national terms.[3]

Nevertheless, the Caribbean territories of the British, Spanish, French and
Dutch did not all fit neatly into the above pattern of subordinating all
other forms of identity to that of the imagined nation-state — at least not
during the nineteenth century. However valid the generalisation of Canny
and Pagden may be for the larger mainland units of the Americas, it is hard
to find any Caribbean example beside the well-known example of Haiti to
substantiate the assertion that the nationhood was the focus of Caribbean
colonial peoples. Haiti was in many respects singularly exceptional. The
slaves of French Saint Domingue who eventually created the independent
State of Haiti and then forged a nation began merely by seeking their collective liberty from slavery.

Haiti aside, nationalism was of enormous importance in the Caribbean
in the nineteenth century but it was not always identical with the quest of a
new State. Indeed, it may be argued that the construction of both State and
nation were tortuous and conflicted operations that were never necessarily
parallel or simultaneous operations. In some cases colonists worked out their
national identities along with the establishment of a new State. In other cases
national identities were resolved concurrently and compatibly with the con-
tinuation of the colonial status, as the Cuban example makes clear.

The period between 1840 and 1900 represented an important formative period in the history of the Caribbean region. Two simultaneous
processes permeated the populations of the region. The first was the
quest, especially in Cuba, Puerto Rico and the Dominican Republic, to
constitute a politically independent State, continuing the fashionable tradition of the neighbouring mainland from the United States to Argentina.[4]

---

3   Canny and Pagden (eds.) *Colonial Identity in the Atlantic World*, pp. 270–71 (emphasis
         added).
4   Nationalism and national identities developed widely and sequentially during the
         nineteenth century, promoted by fundamental structural and ideological social
         changes throughout Europe, Asia and the Americas creating a special political dis-
         course. See the insightful essay by Benedict Anderson, 'Nationalism,' in Joel Krieger
         (ed.), *The Oxford Companion of Politics of the World* (New York, 1993), pp. 614–19.

This process of state formation-cum-nation-building manifested itself most clearly in French Saint Domingue where, against formidable odds, the slaves successfully asserted their individual freedom and then declared their State politically free in 1804. By giving the new State a pre-European name, the leaders sent a message not only that they were independent of Europe but that they had also wished to give themselves a new identity not previously associated with their colonial status. Haitians thereby pioneered the simultaneous construction of a nation along with a State in the Americas. This was the most thorough case of revolution anywhere in the world. In about ten years of almost incessant fighting the Haitians shattered the entire social, political and economic structure of the pluralistically divided French colony and created a novel situation in which all citizens were free and equal before the law. The creation of the free egalitarian State of Haiti did much to accentuate black consciousness throughout the Americas.[5]

Sectors of the societies in Cuba, Puerto Rico and the Dominican Republic also pursued state formation, albeit in different ways and under quite varied circumstances.[6] In these cases the State often included concepts of some form of national identity. In Cuba the manifestation of a national identity, an incipient *conciencia de sí*, though apparent in the writings of Saco and others, was seldom explicitly articulated before the middle of the nineteenth century. Nevertheless, race formed an integral part of the national creation myth of the Cuban State from an early period, based on the centrifugal role of the virgin of Charity of El Cobre.[7] In 1868 some black as well as white Cubans opted for a free State with the *Grito de Yara* and began a thirty-year war that eventually culminated in a qualified form of political independence.[8] The issues of slavery, race and ethnicity were intimately connected with the political issues of the war and haunted the

5   See, Franklin W. Knight, 'The Haitian Revolution,' in *The American Historical Review*, vol. 105, no.1 (February 2000), pp. 103–15.
6   The literature on this period for these territories is quite extensive. Developments may be followed in María del Carmen Barcia, Gloria García and Eduardo Torres Cuevas (eds.), *Historia de Cuba. Las luchas por la independencia nacional y las transformaciones estructurales 1868–1898* (Havana, 1996); Emelio Betances, *State and Society in the Dominican Republic* (Boulder, 1995); Teresita Martínez Vergne, *Shaping the Discourse on Space. Charity and its Wards in Nineteenth Century San Juan, Puerto Rico* (Austin, 1999); and Franklin W. Knight, *The Caribbean. The Genesis of a Fragmented Nationalism*, 2nd edition (New York, 1990); Aline Helg, *Our Rightful Share. The Afro-Cuban Struggle for Equality, 1886–1912* (Chapel Hill, 1995); Christopher Schmidt-Nowara, *Empire and Antislavery: Spain, Cuba, and Puerto Rico, 1833–1874* (Pittsburgh, 1999); Ada Ferrer, *Insurgent Cuba. Race, Nation and Revolution, 1868–1898* (Chapel Hill, 1999); Patrick Bryan, *The Jamaican People 1880–1902* (London, 1991, new edition, University of the West Indies Press, 2000).
7   Olga Portuondo Zúñiga, *La virgen de la Caridad del Cobre: símbolo de Cubanía* (Santiago de Cuba, 1995).
8   On the Ten Years War see Franklin W. Knight, *Slave Society in Cuba during the Nineteenth Century* (Madison, 1970), pp. 154–78.

uneasy peace that followed the Pact of Zanjón in 1878. In Puerto Rico the *Grito de Lares* designed to achieve a similar goal of political independence quickly fizzled out. Puerto Ricans then cleverly worked out a form of dominion status within the Spanish sphere, only to revert to a modified form of colonialism after the US occupation in 1898. Race may not have been an important aspect of the early political machinations of the Puerto Ricans but it certainly became so after they entered the North American sphere in 1898.[9] The Dominican Republic spent much of the century developing a curious national identity based less on some positive ideal than on the fact of not being Haitian. But it is probably no exaggeration to state that both the State and the nation were weak concepts in the Dominican Republic in the nineteenth century. Rafael Trujillo and his intellectual supporters merely repackaged and refined that concept after the 1930s.[10]

The second process, more widespread among the colonial territories of recently emancipated populations at mid-century such as the English, French and Dutch Caribbean, involved the quest for an ethnic identity as a precondition to sharing the territorial political space in which identities could be constructed and articulated.[11] In the colonial territories, therefore, the pursuit of group identity generally preceded the desire to capture the State apparatus as in the case of Cuba.

The forging of a black national identity throughout the Caribbean demonstrated little uniformity across linguistic or imperial boundaries during the course of the nineteenth century. Given the contested history of the region and the long experience of the slave society that would have been impossible. Rather the way in which black national identity was constructed varied according to time, place and circumstances. Nevertheless, the construction of this black identity responded everywhere to some common forces of social change and alterations in local political power structures — the penetration of capitalism, mass production and marketing, as well as changes in colonialism and imperialism — that had prevailed across the Atlantic World since the middle of the eighteenth century. Black people throughout the Caribbean responded to the general influences of religion, mass education, mass communications and atavistic creational

9   On the issue of race and the impact of the United States, see Jay Kinsbruner, *Not of Pure Blood. The Free People of Color and Racial Prejudice in Nineteenth Century Puerto Rico* (Durham, 1996); Fernando Picó, *La guerra después de la guerra* (San Juan, 1987); and Raymond Carr, *Puerto Rico. A Colonial Experiment* (New York, 1984), esp. pp. 333–334.

10   Michiel Baud, '"Constitutionally White": The Forging of a National Identity in the Dominican Republic,' in Gert Oostindie (ed.), *Ethnicity in the Caribbean* (London, 1966), pp. 129–44

11   See Arlene Torres and Norman E. Whitten, Jr., 'To Forge the Future in the Fires of the Past: An Interpretive Essay on Racism, Domination, Resistance, and Liberation,' in Arlene Torres and Norman E. Whitten, Jr. (eds.), *Blackness in Latin America and the Caribbean*, vol. II (Bloomington, 1998), pp. 3–33.

myths of directorial elites but they had to demonstrate more than political sensibility, they had to prove everywhere that they were not inherently handicapped by race and colour. So throughout the Caribbean the quest for black national identity was inescapably and intimately connected with the quest for collective self-respect and social recognition.[12] Blacks throughout the region were not only confronted with the questions of who they were, but also with the indelible legacy of slavery and the plantation society and the custom of centuries in which they were presented consistently in a negative light.

Power and the Post-Slavery Social Structure

The progressive disintegration of the slave society across the Caribbean took an inordinately long time, with a lingering demise that lasted almost a hundred years from 1792 until 1886 — that is, from the early abolition in French Saint Domingue to the final abolition in Cuba. The complex forces that culminated in the abolition of the slave trade and slavery lie outside the scope of this chapter but can be readily examined elsewhere.[13] Except for Cuba, Puerto Rico and the Dominican Republic the majority of the populations everywhere were non-white. This had some inescapable social as well as psychological consequences. After 1792, and especially after 1804, whites throughout the region lived in what Anthony Maingot has described as a 'terrified consciousness'.[14] They had some reason for their mental state, given the generally brutally coercive structure they had supported under the slave system. Wherever the slave system had dominated the local societies throughout the Caribbean, Africans and their descendants constituted either the majority or a significant minority of the population. Regardless of their proportion in the local communities they were virtually excluded from political, social and economic power everywhere except in Haiti. Although not all Afro-Caribbean people were descendants of slaves, the existence of slavery resulted in their social subordination, with the consequent pejorative appreciation and damning den-

---

12   The point is well made in O. Nigel Bolland, *On the March. Labour Rebellions in the British Caribbean, 1934–39* (London, 1995) and in a longer forthcoming work.

13   See, for example, Franklin W. Knight, 'The Disintegration of the Caribbean Slave Systems, 1772–1886,' in Franklin W. Knight (ed.), *General History of the Caribbean. Volume III. The Slave Societies of the Caribbean* (London and Basingstoke, 1997), pp. 322–45, and Francisco Scarano, 'Slavery and Emancipation in Caribbean History,' in B.W. Higman (ed.) *General History of the Caribbean. Volume VI Methodology and Historiography of the Caribbean* (London and Basingstoke, 1999), pp. 233–82.

14   See Anthony P. Maingot, 'Haiti and the Terrified Consciousness of the Caribbean,' in Oostindie (ed.) *Ethnicity in the Caribbean*, pp. 53–80. The phrase is probably taken from Kenneth Ramchand, *The West Indian Novel and its Background* (London, 1970), p. 223. It is the title of his chapter.

igration of all blacks. During the nineteenth century the foremost intellectual ideas supported the hierarchical structure of society that invested
white people with all the desirable social ideals. History left the whites with
uncontested economic and political power but that was insufficient to support the unqualified dominance of all white ideals, especially in the cultural sphere. Even where non-whites constituted a minority their cultural
impact on the entire society tended to be enormous.

Indeed, the Caribbean was a major melting pot for various cultures. What
eventually constituted a Caribbean culture resulted from the Creolised cre-
ative amalgam derived from African, European and Asian, as well as the
indigenous cultures of the Americas. Regional elites may have adopted the
ideas, discourse and languages of Europe but they were forced to reconcile
them, however inconveniently, to their local realities — and these realities
were intrinsically Africanised. Black people could be dismissed in speech but
not in reality. Nowhere is the contradiction between language and reality better illustrated than in the astonishing observation of that aristocratic
Habanera, Doña María de las Mercedes Santa Cruz y Cárdenas, Montalvo y
O'Farrill, the Countess of Merlin in 1842. In her book on the city of Havana
she remarked: '*No hay pueblo en la La Habana, solamente hay amos y esclavos.*'
['Havana has no lower class, only masters and slaves.']¹⁵

Despite her statement, Havana did have a varied population in 1842,
divided into an overlapping structure of castes and classes. According to
data provided by Kenneth Kiple, at the time Santa Cruz wrote her account
in 1841, Havana had about 388,000 inhabitants, and whites were not even
a majority.¹⁶ Of the urban population more than 238,000 or approximately 61 per cent were non-white. The number of free persons of colour
amounted to more than 49,000 or approximately 13 per cent, and some
were respectable property holders within the city. By dividing the population simply into masters and slaves, Santa Cruz 'disappeared' or made
invisible more than one out of every eight urban inhabitants. Nor was the
opinion of Mercedes Santa Cruz unusual at the time. Her more politically
involved compatriot, José Antonio Saco, wrote somewhat later:

> *La nacionalidad cubana de que hablé, y la única que debe ocuparse todo hombre
> sensato, es la formada por la raza blanca, que sólo se eleva a poco más de 400,000
> individuous.*¹⁷

[The Cuban nationality of which I spoke, and the only type that could
occur to any intelligent person, is that represented by the white race,
that by themselves amount to a little more than 400,000 individuals.]

15   Mercedes. Santa Cruz, Condesa de Merlin, *La Habana*, translated from the original
      French by Amalia Barcardi (Madrid, 1981 [1842]), p. 121.
16   Kenneth Kiple, *Blacks in Colonial Cuba, 1770–1899* (Gainesville, 1976), p. 89.
17   Quoted in Eduardo Torres Cuevas, *La pólemica de la esclavitud: José Antonio Saco*
      (Havana, 1984), p.82.

Santa Cruz 'disappeared' only about 12 per cent of the population of Havana. Saco would have 'disappeared' more than half the population of the island. In Cuba, as elsewhere, forging an identity also meant that blacks had to make themselves visible — although that was hardly a sufficient requirement, and they knew it.[18]

The case of Cuba is especially interesting in the Caribbean. Throughout the nineteenth century Afro-Cubans approximated some 33 per cent of the island population, meaning that they were a minority, but a significant minority. Cuban whites were self-consciously assertive and had the critical mass to behave like a cohesive society, much as in the United States of America. As Saco and Santa Cruz illustrated, Cuban national ideology supported the superordinacy of the European segment, with due recognition for what they called a *raza de color*, meaning blacks.[19] Cuban whites savagely attacked and murdered a large number of blacks after the Escalera conspiracy of 1844; and again in 1912 when some blacks led by Evaristo Estenoz and Pedro Ivonnet formed a political party based on race. Nevertheless, Afro-Cubans enthusiastically supported the long struggle to gain political independence for the island, and, before 1886 many also supported the abolition of slavery. Afro-Cubans might have been denied equal rights before 1900 (when Cuba adopted universal male suffrage) but a substantial proportion whose identity with slavery was distant and largely inconsequential, considered themselves to be thoroughly Cuban. Moreover, in the long military campaign for independence between 1868 and 1898 blacks like Antonio Maceo and Máximo Gómez attained the status of unimpeachable national heroes. José Martí also did much during the 1880s and early 1890s to preach an all-inclusive nationalism in which every sector of Cuban society would find a redemptive justice. Many Cubans saw no contradiction in being both black and Cuban although many whites obviously felt uneasy about the assertion of a black identity.

Throughout Latin America and the Caribbean — as well as in North America and elsewhere — the forging of a national identity could not be separated from considerations of race and colour. As Michiel Baud points out the dominant social classes across the region absorbed the prevailing social Darwinist ideas emanating from Europe that declared the absolute superiority of Europe in the world and whites in their local spheres.[20] Most often they presumed that their views included those of the lesser orders of society. That was the sentiment reflected above in the statement by Saco, and

18   The ongoing saga of race and politics in Cuba may be followed in Aviva Chomsky, '"Barbados or Canada?" Race, Immigration, and Nation in Early-Twentieth-Century Cuba,' in *Hispanic American Historical Review*, vol. 80, no. 3 (August 2000), pp. 415–62.
19   The best study of the Cuban racial attitude in the nineteenth century is Aline Helg, *Our Rightful Share*.
20   Baud, 'Constitutionally White,' pp. 121–51.

the idea prevailed where whites constituted a critical mass that resembled an organic social segment. Yet because whites could not impose their views totally across their local communities, some pragmatic moderation of the most extreme views of race, colour and hierarchy took place everywhere. Whites could not be entirely oblivious of their pluralistic racial reality.

In the British Caribbean colonies this moderation in the fixed categories of race and colour began before the abolition of slavery in 1838. Throughout the British Caribbean the steadily declining numbers of white immigrants combined with their lower population growth rate resulted in two necessary social adjustments. The first was that an increasing number of free coloureds penetrated the previously restricted occupations open only to whites. The second was that the whites lost the self-confidence to establish and maintain the cultural norms of their community. In many islands whites did not form a sufficiently viable critical mass to fill the various occupations needed by the community. Viability demanded flexibility, and non-whites were gradually accepted into professions or social situations from which law and custom often excluded them. Gradually, too, free coloureds gained access to wealth and independence and challenged the political and social hegemony of the whites. By the early 1830s all legal discrimination based on colour ceased in Jamaica, Barbados, Dominica and Tobago. By the 1840s non-whites could aspire and achieve political representation in those island assemblies such as Jamaica, Antigua, St Kitts, Montserrat, Grenada, St Vincent and Barbados that enjoyed restricted male franchises. Except Barbados, all those territories would lose their political autonomy toward the end of the nineteenth century. Nevertheless, black political participation remained important in shaping the political futures of those territories and nowhere in the Caribbean was there any experience comparable to the vicious separatism that characterised the United States under Reconstruction.[21]

21   For Jamaica see Swithin Wilmot, "'A Stake in the Soil": Land and Creole Politics in Free Jamaica,' paper presented at a symposium on *Local Histories and Rural Economic Development in Cuba and the Caribbean*, The Library of Congress, Washington DC, 14–15 April 2000; Philip D. Curtin, *Two Jamaicas. The Role of Ideas in a Tropical Colony, 1830–1865* (New York, 1970[1955]); Patrick Bryan, *The Jamaican People*, Tomas Holt, *The Problem of Freedom. Race, Labor, and Politics in Jamaica and Britain, 1832–1938* (Baltimore, 1992); H.P. Jacobs, *Sixty Years of Change, 1806–1866* (Kingston, 1973). For Barbados, see Hilary Beckles, *A History of Barbados from Amerindian settlement to Nation State* (Cambridge, 1990), pp. 103–135. For Trinidad see, Bridget Brereton, *A History of Modern Trinidad, 1783–1962* (Kingston, 1998), pp. 76–156; and Bridget Brereton, *Race Relations In Colonial Trinidad, 1870–1900* (Cambridge, 1979). For British Guiana, see Walter Rodney, *A History of the Guyanese Working People, 1881–1905* (Baltimore, 1981).

Concepts of Self, State and Nation

For the variegated black masses after 1838 in the British Caribbean the problem of identity required the methodical working out of the concepts of self, State and nation — not necessarily sequentially. It was not easy. Freedom had to be redefined and defended against the planting classes and the local government. Priorities had to be reestablished not just for individuals and families but also for the entire community. In the initial period the governor of Trinidad, Lord Harris, declared in 1848 that 'A race has been freed but a society has not been formed'.[22] Harris clearly meant that the recently freed had not been fully accepted as enfranchised citizens of the colonial society. Nor was he of the inclination that non-whites should form part of the elected structure of local government. According to Juanita de Barros, in the late 1880s the British Foreign Office was still reluctant to accept black political participation, partly as a result of the racist writings of English travellers to the West Indies such as Anthony Trollope and James Froude.[23]

It was difficult to forge a coherent society under the auspices of the sugar plantation slave society, so it should not have been surprising if no such thing existed immediately after abolition. The typical plantation colony in the British Caribbean — at least after 1650 — was engineered more to achieve productive efficiency in export staples than to recreate microcosms of the metropolitan society. As such they were colonies of economic (and human) exploitation rather than true settlement colonies. The minority dominant whites luxuriated in their self-declared importance but maintained a psychologically ambivalent posture of perpetual transients. Beside that, in most cases they simply failed to convey to the non-whites — often the demographic majority — any exemplary models of local national identity.[24] By the early nineteenth century the sugar economy was undergoing recurrent crises and non-whites from the middle and lower orders of society moved into property holding by buying up bankrupt or auctioned estates. A visitor to Jamaica in 1830 reported that:

> The collared inhabitants, although borne down and disdained, are by no means so poor, helpless and uninfluential as is generally supposed.

---

22 Quoted among other places, in Eric Williams, *A History of the People of Trinidad and Tobago* (Port-of-Spain, 1962), p. 97.

23 See Juanita De Barros, '"Race" and Culture in the Writings of J. J. Thomas,' *The Journal of Caribbean History*, vol. 27, no. 1 (1993), pp. 36–53. See also, Anthony Trollope, *The West Indies and the Spanish Main* (London, 1869), and James Anthony Froude, *The English in the West Indies, or the Bow of Ulysses* (London, 1888).

24 This does not deny that Edward Long writing in the late eighteenth century came very close to the depiction of a Jamaican nationalist. See Edward Long, *The History of Jamaica*, 3 vols. (London, 1774).

In Jamaica alone they are in possession of wealth, which on a moderate computation has been estimated at not less than three million sterling. All the pimento plantations, with the exception of one only, are in their hands and they are the owners of several coffee estates, besides having the property of numerous houses in the various towns of the island.[25]

After full emancipation the free village movement expanded remarkably, reaching impressive limits wherever land was available either for purchase or for squatting.[26] The establishment of the so-called free villages was a deliberate act, assisted by the stipendiary magistrates sent out from England to oversee the reconstitution of the new societies and to provide legal assistance to the ex-slaves against the powerful opposition of the planter-dominated local assemblies. The long-term success of the free village structure depended on the peculiarities of geography, on managerial personnel, as well as the fortuitous nature of local politics.

In larger territories like Guiana, Jamaica and Trinidad, where there was ample available uncultivated land, the industrious example of the maroon communities had acted as a powerful magnet for the servile thousands working on the nearby sugar estates. With emancipation a number of these ex-slaves settled in the free villages and formed the foundation of an agricultural peasantry, sometimes acting symbiotically with the neighbouring plantations.[27] In Jamaica black freeholders increased from 2,014 in 1838 to approximately 7,800 in 1840, to more than 20,000 in 1845 and about 50,000 by 1859. In St. Vincent some 8,209 persons built their own houses between 1838 and 1857 and brought under cultivation more than 12,000 acres of land. In Antigua 67 free villages with more than 5,187 houses and 15,644 inhabitants were established between 1833 and 1858. In Guiana the situation was even more spectacular. Ex-slaves bought more than 7,000 acres of prime coastal land valued at more than $100,000 by 1842 and by 1848 had purchased more than 400 estates and built more than 10,000 houses.

By the later nineteenth century the black population had, despite official obstruction, effectively created two overlapping economies — a vibrant internal economy based on the free markets and the regular export economy that they helped revitalise.[28] With economic expansion came a greater diversification of the various strata of wealth and the evolution of a complex class structure. Patrick Bryan described the class situation for Jamaica in the following way:

---

25   Quoted in F.R. Augier, S.C. Gordon, D.G. Hall and M. Reckord, *The Making of the West Indies* (London, 1960), p. 164.

26   On the free village movement in Jamaica, see Audley G. Reid, *Community Formation. A Study of the 'Village' in Postemancipation Jamaica* (Mona, 2000).

27   In places like Puerto Rico and the Dominican Republic, free non-white peasants appeared long before the collapse of the sugar estates.

28   Bryan, *The Jamaican People*, pp. 131–60.

Occupational status and the possession of European cultural attributes were important variables in definitions of class but the status associated with an occupation could, in the Jamaican milieu, be modified by race and colour divisions. It is always difficult to draw rigid lines of division between classes given that there is an almost infinite gradation associated with material well being, place and type of residence, cultural attainments and occupation. At the same time it is not only that occupation determines class, but that class determines occupation ... the factor of race was an important division within this middle class.[29]

Economic activities created a number of new groups that shared a common interest, and perhaps had common aspirations with presumably a common consciousness. Throughout the British Caribbean this common consciousness was reinforced by a common elementary educational system. By 1870 there was a virtual mini-revolution in public education throughout the Caribbean, spearheaded by the black and collared populations. Nevertheless, the degree of literacy achieved should not be overestimated. A Royal Commission discovered in 1883 that only 22,000 of the 250,000 adults in Jamaica could read.[30] The educational system therefore bore fruits only in the twentieth century. But the foundation was laid in the nineteenth century. The system of religious and public elementary and secondary schools in the various territories provided training as well as politicisation for the masses. Based on the British system — even to the use of British textbooks and the sitting of tests written in Britain and for a long time invigilated by English expatriate examiners, the system was never modified to reflect Caribbean circumstances. The Trinidadian, C.L.R. James (1901–89), captures the point brilliantly in his outstanding book, *Beyond a Boundary*. He wrote, 'When I left school I was an educated person, but I had educated myself into a member of the British middle class with literary gifts ... '[31] His fellow countryman and contemporary, Eric Williams (1911–81), the celebrated intellectual and prime minister of Trinidad and Tobago, had the same reaction:

> The purpose of the secondary school in Trinidad was to ensure the Anglicanisation of the colony. It consciously took the English public schools as its model. ... The secondary curriculum was indistinguishable from that of an English public school ... Queen's Royal College and St Mary's College were not only English grammar schools in the tropics, they were also excellent grammar schools.[32]

---

29   *Ibid.*, p. 216.
30   Cited in Ramchand, *The West Indian Novel*, p. 23.
31   C.L.R. James, *Beyond a Boundary*, new edition (Durham, 1993 [1963]), p. 32.
32   Eric Williams, *Inward Hunger. The Education of a Prime Minister* (Chicago, 1969), p. 23.

Regardless of the biases and shortcomings of the British Caribbean educational system of the nineteenth century, it produced a cadre of leaders
throughout the region whose strong sense of local identity and acute
knowledge of English political institutions would serve the region well
during the twentieth century. West Indians like James and Williams, however, despite their English-slanted education, never escaped the indelible
sensibility of race and colour.

The education system produced two types of leaders in the British
West Indies. The first group closely identified with the British system —
especially with the Fabian Society of radical thinkers within the newly
formed British Labour Party. These leaders would support reformist politics — individuals like Sandy Cox and J.A.G. Smith in Jamaica, T. Albert
Marryshow in Grenada, D.M. Hutson in British Guiana, or A.A. Cipriani
in Trinidad. In their early careers they did not depend on the masses for
political support but they knew well how to incorporate the masses in their
determination to reduce the privileges of the old planter classes and to
bring some measure of social justice to the political system.

The second group was more overtly populist and less respectful of British
traditions and British institutions. They drew their inspiration from the long
tradition of racial nationalism that had been a part of the scene since the
early part of the century, and from a sort of religious millennial African spir-
itual atavism. This group included John J. Thomas (ca 1840–89), the articu-
late sociolinguist and formidable literary opponent of James Anthony
Froude; Claude MacKay (1890–1948), H.S. Williams (b. 1869), the founder of
the Pan-African Association in London in 1897; George Padmore, born
Malcolm Nurse around 1910 and later the grey eminence of Kwame
Nkrumah of Ghana; Richard B. Moore (1893–1978); W.A. Domingo; and
Marcus Mosiah Garvey (1887–1940), founder of the Universal Negro
Improvement Association in Jamaica (1914), and later Harlem (1916) and the
Atlantic World. Thomas, Williams and Padmore came from Trinidad —
although the latter two were sons of Barbadian immigrants. MacKay, Garvey
and Domingo came from Jamaica; and Moore from Barbados.

Racial nationalism did not become as highly developed in the British
Caribbean as in Haiti or the Dominican Republic. Patrick Bryan thinks that
the reason lies with the development of a class-consciousness that saw
'racism as the major hindrance to patriotism and a sense of community'.[33]
But it could also be that unlike Cuba with its civil wars, Puerto Rico with
its United States occupation, Haiti with its hostile international neighbours
or the Dominican Republic with its anti-Haiti sensitivity, the British West
Indian blacks were not forced to confront directly the issue of race. Their
middle class leaders accepted the misleading ideals inculcated through their

---

33   Bryan, *Jamaican People*, p. 262.

educational system and settled for being good Afro-Saxons in the tropics. This inevitably meant some ambivalence about self, social position and place, indicated by the character quoted in Patrick Bryan's *The Jamaican People*.

The 'Black' position was perhaps best stated by [John] Henderson's Black medical practitioner who described himself as 'an Imperialist, a Protectionist [who] believed in God and Jamaica and the Negro race'.[34]

Conclusion

The black population of the British Caribbean only came into the exercise of civil rights during the nineteenth century, and that only partially. Legally excluded from the professions and denied the opportunity to express themselves — denied even an elementary education — they left their record of their thoughts mostly through their actions. For the vast majority of non-whites the best opportunities for upward social and economic mobility were in military service. But military service inculcated the ideals of the larger empire and black units considered the entire British Empire their expected field of action — just as black military units in the French and Spanish empires fought bravely in those causes wherever their service was required. Loyalty to the metropolis held the expectation of material reward. But even military service reinforced the subordination of non-whites by placing all battalions under white officers, sometimes officers of limited experience and dubious merit. Black troops distinguished themselves in various theatres of war across the region from Florida to Saint Lucia. That black troops commanded by black officers could distinguish themselves militarily was patently illustrated in the case of Haiti.

Haiti was unique. As historian David Geggus described the situation:

> Having destroyed the wealthiest planter class in the New World and defeated the armies of France, Spain and England, the former slaves and free colours now went about making laws for themselves and erecting a state apparatus. In a world dominated by Europeans and where slavery and the slave trade were expanding, the new state was a symbol of black freedom and a demonstration of black accomplishments ... Haiti was a great experiment, a crucial test for the ideas about race, slavery and the future of the Caribbean.[35]

The political isolation of Haiti during the nineteenth century contributed to the development of a strong sense of identity and the healthy growth of a national consciousness. Other Caribbean blacks might have admired Haiti but they never had the experience of being the political masters of their own states.

34   *Ibid.*
35   David Geggus, 'The Haitian Revolution,' in Franklin W. Knight and Colin A. Palmer (eds.), *The Modern Caribbean* (Chapel Hill, 1989), p. 47.

With the staged abolition of slavery across the Caribbean the population of African descent were abandoned without the institutional support structure that white immigrants enjoyed. They fended for themselves and did very well where the opportunities presented themselves as indicated in the history of enthusiastic free village construction across the region. Blacks also created self-help associations that developed into the trades unions of the later period. But, at least among the whites of the economic exploitation zones local models for self-improvement and self-identity were hard to find. By and large local whites were not an exemplary lot both for demographic as well as circumstantial reasons. Apart from the few examples of settler societies like Spanish Santo Domingo, Cuba and Puerto Rico before the late eighteenth century, or Caribbean garrison towns like Havana and San Juan, the building of communities depended on black labour and sometimes black creativity.

Given this discouraging reality — a politically powerless and economically disadvantaged group in communities where they were a majority — it should not be surprising that some blacks throughout the Caribbean developed and manifested a strong local identity as well as a larger pan-African identity. In short, black people created multiple identities to suit their political situations, and these identities varied according to circumstances. Blacks in the Caribbean constituted a diaspora community long before the description became fashionable. Like most diaspora communities worldwide they experienced more mutually reinforcing social and occupational cleavages than crosscutting cleavages. They therefore had few opportunities such as the Wars for Independence in Cuba that would have created bonds with other groups or that would have minimised their abject political minority status. Their sense of community was, and remained, inescapably linked to the colour of their skin. That was the indelible facet of their identity whether it was individual, or communal or national. Yet a black national identity in the nineteenth century was not a viable option, nor was any assertion of a collective black consciousness.

The one hopeful mitigating factor at the end of the nineteenth century to the constraints of race and colour for the black population rested in the majority status and the determination of a number of them to exploit their limited political opportunities for structural changes in their societies. In the case of Cuba under the Partido Independiente de Color the attempt came to premature disaster in 1912 when the government brutally massacred some 3,000 Afro-Cubans members in Santiago and destroyed the hopes of a black political party. Meaningful black political participation would not come about until well into the twentieth century. Nevertheless, by the end of the First World War it was already clear to increasing numbers of the black population across the Caribbean that they had more in common than the colour of their skin. But if fundamental change were to take place they would have to do it by themselves by working within the system.

CHAPTER 5

Race, Gender, and National Identity in Nineteenth-Century Cuba. Mariana Grajales and the Revolutionary Free Browns of Cuba*

Jean Stubbs

ariana Grajales Cuello is a legendary figure in Cuba. Born in the
eastern city of Santiago de Cuba in the early nineteenth century,
the daughter of free brown émigrés from Santo Domingo, she is
best known as the 'glorious mother of the Maceos' — the most famous
were Antonio and José, epic brown generals in Cuba's 19th nineteenth-
century liberation army. She had four children by her first marriage to
Cuban free brown Fructuoso Regueiferos, who died in 1840, and nine subsequently with Venezuelan-born free brown émigré Marcos Maceo.
Mariana lost her husband Marcos, as well as Antonio, José and seven others of her 13 children, to Cuba's independence struggles.

The family has gone down in Cuban history as the 'heroic tribe' of a
valiant, self-sacrificing mother, who was instrumental in cultivating a sense
of justice and moral fortitude. Memoires and campaign diaries of Cuba's
first War of Independence, 1868–78, testify to how Mariana (by then in
her 60s), her two daughters Baldomera and Dominga, and Antonio's wife
María Cabrales, spent the whole Ten Years' War running Antonio's mobile

* A first version was presented on the centenary of the death in Jamaica of Mariana
Grajales Cuello to the Engendering Caribbean History Symposium, at the University
of the West Indies, Mona, Jamaica, in November 1993. It is dedicated to her memo-
ry, in the hope that it might stimulate further research on her, and other women like
her, in Cuban history. It is also dedicated to Mary Turner, who first opened my eyes
to Cuba being part of the Caribbean as much as, if not more than, Latin America. I
am indebted to the University of North London for giving me a sabbatical Autumn
1993 semester and to the Centers for Latin American Studies and African Studies at
the University of Florida, Gainesville, for having me as a Rockefeller Scholar to
undertake the research and preliminary writing. I would like to thank Richard Phillips,
Latin American and Caribbean librarian at the University of Florida, for his help in
locating material in the extensive Cuba holdings; Pedro Pérez Sarduy, Barry
Chevannes, Helen Safa, Olabiyi Yai, David Geggus, Nina Menéndez and Ofelia
Schutte for our many stimulating discussions; Louis Pérez, Lynne Stoner and Judith
Bettelheim for their thoughtful comments on the first paper. This paper is one of two
works derived from that initial paper and should be read in conjunction with its com-
panion article: Jean Stubbs 'Social and Political Motherhood of Cuba: Mariana
Grajales Cuello,' in Verene Shepherd, Bridget Brereton and Barbara Bailey (eds.)
Engendering History: Caribbean Women in Historical Perspective (Kingston, 1995). I am especially indebted to Olga Portuondo for new material and insights since.

base camps, tending the wounded and seeing to the provision of food and clothing. With a husband and son dead, and Antonio mortally wounded, she turned to a younger son and sent him off to fight.

Mariana Grajales Cuello was an extraordinary woman in her own right — though not so extraordinary in terms of what she represented in her time. Her life spanned virtually the whole of Cuba's turbulent nineteenth century and had ramifications in and beyond her native eastern Cuba. She was born into a demographically and economically strong free coloured stratum in eastern Cuba — the only one in which women outnumbered men, since the white settler and slave populations were more predominantly male. Her parents had a small farm in El Cristo, near Santiago, and Regueiferos and Maceo were of the small farming and merchant class. Mariana and Marcos consolidated three farm properties and a town house in Santiago de Cuba, and were well-connected among the white and free brown middle propertied classes in the more racially fluid Santiago society. Mariana's formative years, however, saw the rapid expansion of sugar and slavery, a growing 'fear of the black' on the part of the white planter class and a relative erosion of the position of free people of colour.

Mariana and her family were catapulted to the heart of the dual struggle in late nineteenth century Cuba for independence from Spanish rule and emancipation from African slavery. It would take 30 years of intermittent war (1868–78, 1879–80 and 1895–98) to break the slave regime (emancipation became inevitable in the 1880s) and achieve independence from Spain (in 1898, though on the back of the first US military occupation of 1898–1902). War broke out in the less wealthy, more creole and free coloured east and culminated in an 'invasion' of the west led by General Antonio Maceo, among others. While dogged by racial fear and difference, the struggle brought together the races and for many the old regime came to be as much a social as political anathema (social being a euphemism for race).

From the 1870s onwards fugitives and émigrés were fleeing eastern Cuba to nearby Jamaica, which is where the Maceo family went in 1878. Antonio Maceo headed the Baraguá Protest against capitulation to Spain under the Zanjón Truce that year, and only accepted leaving Cuba with his family when entrusted by the revolutionary government to muster much-needed support for the cause among Cuban communities abroad. The Maceo family was given a Spanish amnesty and escort to sail from Santiago to Kingston, where they had a small town house, and also a small farm on the outskirts. They were part of a substantial Cuban émigré community that became one of the organisational centres for the renewed Cuban independence effort.

From 1878 up until his return to Cuba to fight in the 1895–98 War, Antonio was in and out of Jamaica, constantly on the move in North and Central America and the Caribbean. He travelled to Haiti, Santo Domingo, Turks Island; to New York, New Orleans and Key West. He accepted a post with the Honduran army, had a subcontract with De Lessep's canal project in Panama, and founded a Cuban farming colony in Nicoya, Costa Rica. He collected and made substantial amounts of money, much of which went on failed expeditionary ventures. From his correspondence it is clear there were times when the family was in such straits that they had to turn to émigré friends for money.

Mariana and other family members remained in Jamaica into the 1890s, but we know little about those years. In April 1881 a liaison in Kingston between Antonio and a white woman, Amelia Marryatt, bore a son named Antonio Maceo. It is said that Mariana encouraged Antonio to make provision for this son, and that he did so with discretion and tact, since his wife María was in Kingston at the time (his small son and daughter by María had died of illness in the first year of the first war, and María seemingly dressed in black ever since). In 1884 Mariana approached the Spanish consul in Kingston for the release of José from a Spanish jail. In the event, José escaped, and years later, in 1894, in Nicoya, Costa Rica, he married white Jamaica-born Elena González y Nuñez. The next year, when José set sail to fight in Cuba, she returned to Jamaica where she gave birth to their son, also named José. Generals Antonio and José Maceo were both killed in battle in Cuba in 1896. They had outlived their mother by only three years.

Mariana Grajales Cuello died in 1893, aged 85, in Kingston, and was buried in the St Andrews Roman Catholic Cemetery. Her remains were ceremonially exhumed in 1923 and returned to Cuba, where they were laid to rest, alongside others of her family, in Santiago's Santa Efigenia Cemetery.

Myth and the Mythmakers

The story of Mariana Grajales Cuello has become a myth that is both inseparable from and as significant as reality. It is a myth that has been moulded to dominant gendered notions of history, in the same way that the Maceo-Grajales story has all too often been subsumed in a version of history that denies race.

The centenary of Antonio Maceo's birth witnessed a spate of biographical studies.[1] The Cuban Society of Historical and International Studies,

---

1   Emeterio S. Santovenia, *Raíz y altura de Antonio Maceo* (Havana, 1943); Rafael Marquina, *Antonio Maceo, héroe epónimo* (Havana, 1943); G. Rodríguez Morejón, *Maceo héroe y caudillo* (Havana, 1943); Leopoldo Horrego Estuch, *Maceo, héroe y carácter*, 2nd extended edition (Havana, 1944); Luis Rolando Cabrera, *El centenario de Maceo, 1845–14 de Junio 1945* (Havana, 1945); Herminio Portel Vilá, *Breve biografía de Antonio Maceo* (Havana, 1945); María Julia de Lara Mena, *La familia Maceo, carta a Elena* (Havana, 1945); Emilio Roig de Leuchsenring, *Revolución y República en Maceo* (Havana, 1945), and *Antonio Maceo* (Havana, 1946); Julián Martínez Castells (ed.) *Antonio Maceo: Documentos para su vida* (Havana, 1945); Fermín Peraza Sarausa, *Infancia ejemplar en la vida heroica de Maceo* (Havana, 1945); Octavio R. Costa, *Antonio Maceo, el héroe* (Havana, 1947). Other publications include *Antonio Maceo, documentos para su vida* (Havana, 1945).

set up in 1940, grouped together progressive historians in response to the more mainstream Academy of History. A major concern of the group was to conduct and publish scholarly historical research on the roots of Cuban nationalism. Maceo was seen as a key figure in forging the Cuban nation on two counts. First, he displayed great military genius in both the 1868–78 and 1895–98 wars. Moreover, as a free brown during slavery, he symbolised the coming together of the races in the nation, fighting for freedom. There had been earlier studies of Antonio, two of which were key: one in 1922 by a nephew of his wife María and another in 1930 by a former aide de camp.[2] Other biographies and studies followed in the years leading up to and after the 1959 Revolution.[3] The most recent was in 1998.[4]

In contrast to the voluminous accounts of Antonio, there have only been two — one in 1943 and another in 1973 — of his brother José, also a general but seen as the lesser hero of the two.[5] On the centenary of the death of Mariana, there was tantalisingly little on her: a 1942 study; two short monographs, one published in 1957 and one in 1977; and one substantial biography in 1975.[6] Only of Antonio do we have a handful of studies in English.[7]

2   Gonzalo Cabrales (ed.), *Epistolario de héroes, cartas y documentos históricos* (Havana, 1922); and Eusebio Hernández, *Maceo: dos conferencias históricas* (1913 y 1930) (Havana, 1968). Other publications include Gregorio Bustamante y Maceo, *Biografía de los Maceo* (San Salvador, 1938); and 'Hijo del Mayor General Antonio Maceo,' *El Mundo*, 30 May 1937.
3   José Luciano Franco, *Antonio Maceo, apuntes para una historia de su vida (1951–57)*, 3 vols. (Havana, 1975); *Ruta de Antonio Maceo en el Caribe* (Havana, 1961); *La vida heroica y ejemplar de Antonio Maceo* (Havana, 1963); also L. Griñan Peralta, *Maceo: Análisis carácterológico* (Havana, 1953); Rafael Esténger, *El hombre de las montañas* (Havana, 1953); José Antonio Portuondo (ed.) *El pensamiento vivo de Maceo* (Havana, 1963); Raúl Aparicio, *Hombradía de Antonio Maceo* (Havana, 1966). See also Sociedad Cubana de Estudios Históricos e Internacionales, *Antonio Maceo, ideología política, cartas y otros documentos*, 2 vols. (Havana, 1950–52).
4   Olga Portuondo, *Visión múltiple de Antonio Maceo* (Santiago de Cuba, 1998).
5   Manuel Ferrer Cuevas, *José Maceo: El léon de oriente* (Santiago de Cuba, 1996 [1943]); Abelardo Padrón Valdés, *El General José. Apuntes biográficos* (Havana, 1973).
6   Longinos Alonso Castillo, *Mariana Grajales, viuda de Maceo. Labor patriótica* (Santiago de Cuba, 1942). Aída Rodríguez Sarabia, *Mariana Grajales: Madre de Cuba* (Havana, 1957); Nydia Sarabia *Historia de una familia mambisa: Mariana Grajales* (Havana, 1975); Matilde Danger and Delfina Rodríguez, *Mariana Grajales* (Santiago de Cuba, 1977). There is also a compilation of articles, including José Guadalupe Castellanos, 'Madre de todos los cubanos' in *Mariana Grajales* (Santiago de Cuba, 1954). See also José Luciano Franco, 'Mariana Grajales, madre y revolucionaria,' *Revolución y Cultura*, no. 27 (November 1974), translated and included in 'Mariana and Maceo,' in Pedro Pérez Sarduy and Jean Stubbs (eds.), *AFROCUBA: An Anthology of Cuban Writing on Race, Politics and Culture* (Melbourne, New York and London, 1993).
7   Frank R.E. Woodward, *With Maceo in Cuba* (Minneapolis, 1896); Arthur Schomburg, 'General Antonio Maceo,' *The Crisis*, vol. 38 (May 1931); Laurence R. Nichols, 'The "Bronze Titan", The Mulatto Hero of Cuban Independence, Antonio Maceo', PhD dissertation, Duke University (1954); Philip Foner, *Antonio Maceo: The 'Bronze Titan' of Cuba's Struggle for Independence* (New York and London, 1977); Magdalen M. Pando, *Cuba's Freedom Fighter, Antonio Maceo: 1845–1896* (Gainesville, 1980).

Symptomatically, the Maceo biographers have all been male; the Grajales biographers, female. Their biographies are strikingly similar in the image they portray of Mariana as the self-sacrificing mother. They differ, logically, in the extent to which they focus on Mariana Grajales in her own right, but also in the emphasis and meanings they attach to her life and her various actions. Broadly speaking, the earlier biographies of Antonio bolster the political and military aspects of his life, in which race and religion are for the most part peripheral, but the mother is always formative in the making of the hero. The 1950s accounts display a striking polarisation, ranging from an attempt to redeem the race[8] to an almost whitened Catholic religiosity, which is at its most extreme in shoring up the Mariana mother figure.[9] The post 1959 studies tend to play down race and religion, seeking out the revolutionary in the male Maceos and their mother Mariana.

To date, there is reference to only one written document of Mariana, in the form of a letter to Antonio, and there is some dispute as to whether she even wrote it. We therefore have no direct account of her thinking. With some notable exceptions, much of our knowledge of her is mediated through white male references and perceptions.[10]

What follows is an attempt, culled from published collections of Maceo documents and correspondence, Maceo-Grajales biographies and studies, journalistic articles and Cuban historiography, including patriotic Cuban women's history,[11] to rethink the significance of Mariana and her life as a revolutionary free brown woman of Cuba in the forging of a national identity. I first outline the major relevant socioeconomic and political trends and events in Cuba, and subsequently trace the changing composition and position of free coloureds during Grajales's lifetime. It is important to note that the Cuban census category of free coloured (*color libre*) included free brown (*pardo*, later *mulato*) and free black (*moreno*, later *negro*), and much of the historiography uses the term indiscriminately for both brown and black, and only brown. To avoid confusion here, I use the term 'free coloured' in the broader sense when referring to Cuban census material, but wherever possible differentiate free brown, which is, of course, a nomenclature more common to the Anglophone Caribbean. Controversially, perhaps, I have chosen to use free brown, rather than

8   Franco, *Antonio Maceo, apuntes para una historia; Ruta de Antonio Maceo;* and *La vida heroica.*
9   Rodríguez Sarabia, *Mariana Grajales.*
10 Padrón Valdés, *El General José,* and Sarabia, *Historia de una familia mambisa,* are exceptional in this regard, in that they use oral history and testimony from female descendants, giving the reader extraordinary, and at the same time ordinary, altogether human accounts of the 'hero' and 'heroine'.
11 Examples are 'Mariana Grajales' in *Souvenir, centenario del natalicio del Lugarteniente General Antonio Maceo Grajales* (Santiago de Cuba, 1945); and *La mujer cubana en los cien años de lucha 1868–1968* (Havana, 1969).

mulatto, precisely to highlight Cuba in a Caribbean, as well as Latin American, context. I go on to consider elements in the life story of Mariana Grajales Cuello that are suggestive of the centrality of the position of free brown women — for whom Mariana serves as icon — to our very understanding of Cuban nationhood.

The Politics of Race and Nation

One significant trend in nineteenth century Cuban historiography has been to trace the emergence of nationalism and a national identity. Up to and including the eighteenth century, *criollismo* is seen to be subordinate to Hispanic hegemonic culture. The foundations of Cuban nationalism, it is argued, were laid in the first half of the nineteenth century, and cemented during the 30-year struggle for independence of the late nineteenth century. That struggle encompassed a conflictive yet ultimately integrationist process, out of which emerged a new creole ideology that lay at the heart of Cuban nationhood.[12] Among historians and anthropologists there are unresolved differences as to the interpretation of that creole culture, particularly concerning the extent to which the dominant Hispanic culture became Africanised as opposed to the African culture becoming Hispanicised;[13] how far the process was one of transculturation,[14] dissimulation versus syncretism,[15] or an ethnogenetic process of cultural transfer.[16] Moreover, there are significant lacunae and unresolved ambiguities about the role of free browns, which, I suggest here, may be more central to the emergent national identity than hitherto considered.

The process of national integration is considered to begin when neighbouring Saint Domingue was eliminated as an economic rival after the 1791–1804 Revolution. Cuba became the world's leading sugar-producing

12   This is perhaps best articulated in Jorge Ibarra, *Ideología mambisa* (Havana, 1967). See also, by the same author, *Nación y cultura nacional* (Havana, 1978), and the more recent 'Cultura e identidad nacional en el Caribe hispánico: el caso puertorriqueño y el cubano,' in Consuelo Naranjo Orovio, Miguel A. Puig-Samper and Luis Miguel Garca Mora (eds.), *La nacion soñada: Cuba Puerto Rico y Filipinas ante el 98* (Madrid, 1996).

13   Walterio Carbonell, *Cómo surgió la cultura nacional* (Havana, 1961), adopts a more Africanist approach. Rogelio Martínez-Furé, *Diálogos imaginarios* (Havana, 1979), adopts a more integrationist approach.

14   See Fernando Ortiz, *Cuban Counterpoint: Tobacco and Sugar* (Philadelphia, 1995 [1940]).

15   On dissimulation versus syncretism, see Raúl Canizares, *Walking the Night: The Afro-Cuban World of Santería* (Rochester, Vermont, 1993). This position is endorsed in Philip Howard, 'The Spanish Colonial Government's Responses to the Pan-Nationalist Agenda of the Afro-Cuban Mutual Aid Societies, 1868–1895,' *Revista/Review Interamericana*, vol. 22, nos. 1–2 (1992).

16   An excellent overview of the debate can be found in Stephan Palmié, 'Ethnogenetic Processes and Cultural Transfer in Caribbean Slave Populations,' in Wolfgang Binder (ed.), *Slavery in the Americas* (Wurzburg, 1993).

country, the prize possession of Spain's dwindling empire. Primacy, however, lay with western Cuba. The 1840s were something of a watershed in furthering a sense of nation, with the rapid expansion of railways, coastal shipping and telegraph services. Yet, in the 1860s 80 per cent of the wealthy lived in Havana, Matanzas and Cárdenas (if not Paris, Barcelona and New York), their fortunes tied to the great sugar plantations of the west. The east grew only 20 per cent of the island's sugar, and on smaller, less technologically developed plantations, with fewer slaves (ten per cent of the island's total). The economy was primarily livestock and subsistence farming, with enclaves of coffee and tobacco, and a relatively slow growing population. The east had 70 per cent of the land, 35 per cent of the population, 22 per cent of the national wealth and ten per cent of the island's trade; per capita income was less than half that of the west; and there were more white and coloured Cubans, fewer Spaniards (*peninsulares*) and fewer African *bozales*.[17]

There has until recently been far greater acceptance of the economic and political implications of the nationalist challenge gravitating from the east than there has been of the race implications. It is hard to see how a national culture and nation could have been forged at a time when over one third of the population was estimated to be first-generation African slaves incarcerated on plantations and the island was run by Spanish *peninsulares*. Haunted as they were by the spectre of Haiti, and finding the African influence on the language, music and dance movements of even high Cuban society cause for lament, western Hispanic elites strove to rationalise and protect their privileged whiteness through theories of their own racial superiority designed to undercut the more liberal aspects of Spanish slave society.

Free browns, who were seen as either parasitic or uppity and ambitious, as either a containable third force or a threat,[18] were increasingly the target of measures designed to demarcate them from the free black, slave and

---

17 The east-west divide was graphically illustrated in the landmark essay Juan Pérez de la Riva, 'Una isla con dos historias,' in *El barracón y otros ensayos* (Havana, 1975).

18 Francisco Dionisio Vives, the Spanish captain general (1823–32), feared the existence of free blacks and mulattoes as 'an example that will be very prejudicial some day, if effective measures are not taken in order to prevent their (the slaves) constant and natural tendency toward emancipation'. Vives would have liked to see the expulsion of the entire free coloured class, and felt it was 'not permissible to promote reform without stumbling into injustices that would awaken discontent and produce unfailingly the ruin of the country' (quoted in Robert L. Paquette, *Sugar is Made with Blood*, Middletown, Conn, 1988, p. 105) Even reputable artisans, good family men with urban estates and slaves might be dragged along by the torrent; and it was recommended that criminals be sent to Spain's African prisons whence they wouldn't return.

white populations.[19] Such measures were far removed from the favourable comments of contemporary travelogues as to the 'genealogical confusion' of the Cuban people as a hope for the future — and from the aspirations of people themselves, not least the free coloureds, especially in the east.

It would take plots, conspiracies, insurrection and ultimately war throughout the nineteenth century to break the 'criollismo' which defined only whites as Cuban. Each new defeat or victory brought its backlash, and each had its free coloured heroes: free brown Nicolás Morales in 1796,[20] free black José Aponte in 1812[21] and free brown Plácido in the Escalera Conspiracy of 1844, Year of the Lash.[22] We can only speculate as to how

19   Free and slave Africans of the same nation were allowed to group together in a *cabildo* (which could collectively buy slave members' freedom). For an informative and nuanced account of the agency of the nineteenth century *cabildos*, see Philip Howard, *Changing History: Afro-Cuban Cabildos and Societies of Color in the Nineteenth Century* (Baton Rouge, 1998). Brown and black militia battalions were differentiated in uniform, decoration and pay. There were brown, black and white mutual aid societies. Free blacks and browns were to be kept from the plantations and contact with slaves; from dances, avenues and theatres for whites; from being out at night, carrying arms or marrying white. In the mid-century free coloureds without a trade, property or known source of living were deemed vagrants; strict watch was kept over black and brown farmers, individuals of colour needed special permission to hold any meetings and were not to be employed in pharmacies for fear they would poison whites.

20   In 1795, Charles IV had granted persons of part-Negro blood the right to buy legal whiteness ('gracias al sacar'). By paying a fee to the Spanish Crown, browns could gain all the legal privileges of whites: marriage with whites, entry to the clergy, university education, etc. When the lieutenant governor of Bayamo failed to publish the decree, Nicolás Morales, a free brown farmer characterised as having been influenced by the revolution in Saint Domingue, plotted for reform. Denounced by a member of the free-coloured militia, Morales was hanged.

21   In 1812 José Antonio Aponte, a woodworker belonging to the black militia battalion of Havana and a member of the Yoruba *cabildo*, was hanged for planning field slave uprisings. He was betrayed by two slaves in Puerto Principe and hanged, along with five other free coloureds and three slaves. See José Luciano Franco, *Las conspiraciones de 1810 y 1812* (Havana, 1977).

22   Paquette details how La Escalera smashed the nascent brown and black petite bourgeoisie and intelligentsia as potential economic rivals and ideologues of antislavery. Of the 1,800 estimated to have been executed, deported or imprisoned, 1,200 were free coloured. The Spanish captain-general, Leopoldo O'Donnell gave all male adult foreign-born free coloureds 15 days to leave Cuba. Half of the 38 free coloureds executed were browns. Many prominent free coloureds lost their property. The black and brown militias were dissolved. (See also Pedro Deschamps Chapeaux, *El negro en la economía habanera del siglo XIX* (Havana, 1970). Carbonell highlights a growing separation between browns and blacks and rejects their leadership in La Escalera. The Spanish government acknowledged division between more moderate browns and a larger group of more radical blacks, but conceded that there was a brown-black alliance. At the baptism of Antonio Maceo in 1845, his maternal grandparents don José and doña Teresa were entered as 'de esta naturaleza' (of this land). This is thought to have been a deliberate falsification because of post-Escalera deportations.

far the decimation of Cuba's free coloured leadership after La Escalera contributed to a 20-year period of relative calm. But the Escalera martyrs and Plácido's poetry lived on; and the tensions and contradictions of 1844 would resurface in the 1860s. In an attempt to neutralise the middle-ground, white reformists — concerned by the racial mixing of the popular classes — sought but failed to secure certain rights for free blacks and browns of middle standing (but not free Africans).

In the Ten Years War of 1868–78 the rebel camp was pitted with regional, political, military and racial divisions. By the end of the war, only the eastern brown and black military — Antonio Maceo in the lead — were refusing to capitulate and sign the Zanjón Treaty. Theirs was the 1878 Protest of Baraguá. They were the protagonists of the 1879–80 Little War; and the 1895–98 Liberation Army is characterised as having been primarily soldiered (estimates of up to 85 per cent) and significantly commanded (40 per cent of commissioned officers) by browns and blacks: men like Jesús Rabí, Flor Crombet, Quintín Banderas, Guillermón Moncada, Antonio and José Maceo.

The first war left the east in ruins, making a mockery of Zanjón. Without abolition and independence, eastern generals questioned why they had been fighting. Punitive expropriation and ousting of separatist sympathisers, debt, rising taxes and unemployment swelled in the wake of 1880s abolition, left Cuba as a whole in crisis and helped turn political separatism into revolutionary populism.[23] Significantly, for our purposes here, the multiracial vision contained in that populism led key civilian and military leaders of the 1895–98 war — José Martí and Antonio Maceo are prime cases in point — to deny the very existence of race. And if, in the rest of Ibero-America, definitions of the nation rested more on notions of biological and cultural mixing, in Cuba national unity was cast as the product of joint political action by armed blacks, mulattoes and whites fighting an anti-colonial war. The nation was not so much imagined as cultural union but as the product of revolutionary cross-racial alliance. That Cubans should be speaking of the raceless society was all the more remarkable in an age when ascendant racism was one of the principal ideological currents of the late-nineteenth-century western world and a regressive, divisive force in its northern neighbour, the United States.[24]   In   order   to

---

23   This is a theme running through the prolific work of Louis Pérez: See, *On Becoming Cuban* (Chapel Hill, NC, 1999); *Slaves, Sugar and Colonial Society: Travel Accounts of Cuba, 1801–1899* (Wilmington, 1992); *Cuba: Between Reform and Revolution* (New York and Oxford, 1988); *Cuba Between Empires, 1878–1902* (Pittsburgh, 1983).

24   These points are conveyed forcefully in Ada Ferrer, *Insurgent Cuba: Race, Nation, and Revolution, 1868–1898* (Chapel Hill, NC, 1999). The themes of agency in the struggle for cross-racial alliance in turn-of-the-century post-emancipation Cuban society underpin the work of Ferrer's mentor Rebecca Scott, 'Raza, clase y acción colectiva en Cuba, 1895–1902: la formacion de alianzas interraciales en el mundo de la cana,' op. cit., Universidad de Puerto Rico, Centro de Investigaciones Históricas, no. 9 (1997); '"The

understand the rise of eastern free browns (such as Mariana and her family) to prominence among the revolutionary ranks, let us turn to the free
brown population of nineteenth-century Cuba in greater detail.

The Free Browns of Cuba

Among the slave societies of the Americas, Cuba ranked high among those
with significant numbers of free coloureds in similar periods of economic
development. Comparisons might be made with French Saint Domingue,
Spanish Lousiana and Florida during the late eighteenth century.[25] In the
nineteenth century only the Dutch and French islands and Brazil had higher proportions: in comparison with Cuba's 26 per cent of the population in
1841, and 33 per cent in the 1880s, Brazil had over 50 per cent in some
provinces in the 1870s, Curaçao 43 per cent in the 1830s and Martinique 32
per cent in the 1840s. In the Anglophone Caribbean, the figure was ten per
cent in Jamaica, seven per cent in Barbados, in the 1830s.[26]

And yet, Cuban studies of slavery deal with the free coloureds only
peripherally, as do many political histories. Other sources tend to be
descriptive or biographical. In addition to the studies of the brown inde-

lower Class of Whites" and "the Negro Element": Race, Social Identity, and Politics
in Central Cuba, 1899–1909,' in Naranjo Orovio, Puig-Samper and Garca Mora (eds.),
*La nación soñada, '*The Boundaries of Freedom: Postemancipation Society in Cuba,
Louisiana and Brazil,' in Hilary Beckles (ed.), *Inside Slavery: Process and Legacy in the
Caribbean Experience* (Kingston, Jamaica, 1996); *Slave Emancipation in Cuba: The
Transition to Free Labor, 1860–1899* (Princeton, NJ, 1985).

25   See John D. Garrigus, 'Catalyst or Catastrophe? Saint-Dominque's Free Men of Color
and the Battle of Savannah, 1779–1782,' *Revista/Review Interamericana*, vol. 22, no. 1–2
(1992), pp. 109–25, and 'Color and Class on the Eve of the Haitian Revolution,' paper
to the 26th Annual Conference of the Association of Caribbean Historians,
Interamerican University, San Germán, Puerto Rico, March 1994; Gwendolyn Midlo
Hall, *Africans in Colonial Louisiana: The Development of Afro-Creole Culture in the Eighteenth
Century* (Baton Rouge, 1992); Kimberly S. Hanger, 'Protecting Property, Family, and
Self: The *Mujeres Libres* of Colonial New Orleans,' *Revista/Review Interamericana*, vol.
22, no. 1–2 (1992), pp. 126–50, and 'Patronage, Property and Persistence: The
Emergence of a Free Black Elite in Spanish New Orleans,' paper to the 26th ACH
Conference; Paul Lachance, 'Free Persons of Color in Antebellum New Orleans:
How "Privileged" were they?,' paper to the 26th ACH Conference; Jane Landers,
'Gracias Real de Santa Teresa de Mose: A Free Black Town in Spanish Colonial
Florida,' *American Historical Review*, vol. 95 (February 1990), and 'Economic Activity
and Free Black Property Ownership in Spanish Florida, 1784–1821,' paper to the 26th
ACH Conference; Loren Schweninger 'Antebellum Free Persons of Color in
Postbellum Louisiana,' *Louisiana History*, vol. 30, no. 4 (1989). See also for the USA,
Ira Berlin, *Slaves without Masters: The Free Negro in the Antebellum South* (New York,
1974), and James Oliver Horton, *Free People of Color: Inside the African American
Community* (Washington and London, 1993).

26   David W. Cohen and Jack P. Greene (eds.), *Neither Slave nor Free: The Freedmen of African
Descent in the Slave Societies of the New World* ('Introduction') (Baltimore and London, 1972).

pendence fighters, there is work on other key figures such as the mid-nineteenth century brown poet Gabriel de la Concepción Valdés, alias Plácido,[27] and the late-nineteenth century brown politicians Martín Morúa Delgado and Juan Gualberto Gómez.[28] The classic nineteenth century anti-slavery novel, *Cecilia*,[29] revolving around the life of a free brown woman of Havana, provides a window onto west Cuban society (though there is nothing of its kind for Santiago and the east) and has occasioned some excellent literary analysis.[30] There have also been signal attempts to reconstruct the lives of ordinary people of colour.[31] The most complete studies of the free coloured population, however, have been undertaken by non-Cuban scholars in demographic and political history[32] and historical anthropology and sociocultural history,[33] from the late 1960s on.

Viewed as a whole, the studies point to the numerical and economic strength of free browns, especially in the urban crafts and trades, and small farming; and the complexities of social and political relations with, and within, this stratum.[34] Evidence is mustered to support benevolent inter-

27   Plácido was the illegitimate and orphaned son of a Spanish dancer and brown ('pardo') hairdresser. He had a black ('morena') wife, who was the sister-in-law of a black militiaman. His poetry spoke loudly to free coloureds who, after struggling long and hard, found themselves under attack. He was executed in La Escalera. Plácido remains a controversial figure: courageous precursor or sacrificial lamb?

28   Martín Morúa Delgado and Juan Gualberto Gúmez were prominent free brown politicians of the late nineteenth century. See Raquel Mendieta Costa, *Cultura: Lucha de clases y conflicto racial, 1878–1895* (Havana, 1989). Also, Angelina Edreira de Caballero, *Vida y obra de Juan Gualberto Gómez* (Havana, 1954); and Juan Gualberto Gómez, *Por Cuba libre* (Havana, 1954).

29   Cirilo Villaverde, *Cecilia Valdés or Angel's Hill* (1879) (New York, 1962).

30   Among the authors dealing with this are: Reynaldo González, *Contradanzas y latigazos* (Havana, 1983); and William Luis, *Literary Bondage: Slavery in Cuban Narrative* (Austin, 1990).

31   Pedro Deschamps Chapeaux and Juan Pérez de la Riva, *Contribución a la historia de la gente sin historia* (Havana, 1974).

32   Herbert S. Klein, *Slavery in the Americas: A Comparative Study of Virginia and Cuba* (Chicago, 1967); Franklin W. Knight, *Slave Society in Cuba during the Nineteenth Century Cuba* (Madison, Wisconsin, 1970), and 'Cuba,' in Cohen and Greene (eds.), *Neither Slave nor Free*; Gwendolyn Midlo Hall, *Social Control in Slave Plantation Societies: A Comparison of St Domingue and Cuba* (Baltimore, 1971); Kenneth F. Kiple, *Blacks in Colonial Cuba* (Gainesville, Fla, 1976); Paquette *Sugar is Made with Blood*.

33   Verena Martínez-Alier, *Marriage, Class and Colour in Nineteenth-Century Cuba* (Oxford, 1974); Vera M. Kutzinski, *Sugar's Secrets: Race and The Erotics of Cuban Nationalism* (Charlottesville, Virginia and London, 1994).

34   The Havana patrician José del Castillo reminisced that in the 1840s there were 'many blacks and mulattos, some of them with abundant wealth who in their lifestyle, in their dress and in their speech imitated those white gentlemen who still remained in Cuba, and among them no lack of people fond of reading serious books and even making verse'. An 1842 testimony in the Fourth Annual Report to the British and Foreign Anti-Slavery Committee stated that free people of colour 'treat [their slaves]

pretations of pre-nineteenth-century Spanish imperialism and evangelising Roman Catholicism, and a sharp nineteenth-century demarcation between the pre-plantation and plantation era, with its rise of pseudo-scientific racism. It is assumed that free coloureds occupied an ambiguous intermediate position, with lighter skin merging with white, but that there was a rapid deterioration of their physical, legal, social, economic and political conditions as a group, whereby they became the recipient of nineteenth-century racism in its most hostile manifestation. It might be argued that, of all groups on the island, they felt the greatest change. Increasingly excluded from owning property, for example, especially in the plantation west, they were forced to gravitate east.[35]

The nineteenth-century hardening of attitudes to free coloureds associated with Spanish officialdom and the Cuban white Creole oligarchy wrought multiple legally sanctioned colour distinctions and gradations (*cuarterón*, *octavón*, etc). This makes it increasingly difficult to make any broad-sweep delineation between brown and black — and a blurring with white, especially among the more popular classes — a point that holds as true for genetics as for ideology,[36] as well as demography. [37]

The rapid nineteenth-century growth in Cuba's coloured population can be seen in Graph 1. In Table 1, it is expressed in absolute and percentage terms, for the period 1774–1887, when the free coloured population increased from little more than 36,000 to over 500,000, a ninefold increase. Of the 54,000 in 1791, 34,000 were categorised as free brown: three out of every five. By 1841 the free coloured population had grown nearly threefold, but the proportion of free browns had fallen to about two in five. After 1841, the free brown element in the free coloured population stabilised at around 50 per cent. This distinction cannot be made after the 1860 census, when *pardo* and *moreno* were replaced by *gente de color*.

---

with the greatest kindness, they allow them the full Sunday and other holidays to work for themselves, provide them with decent clothes and give them three reales weekly; the slaves consider such masters as their fathers. The free Negroes who have acquired property frequently purchase the freedom of the whole family from the grandparents to the grandchildren, and afterwards that of their friends who have come from the same town or village in Africa. They are decidedly in favour of abolition of slavery.' (Paquette, *Sugar is Made with Blood*, p. 149)

35   Knight, 'Cuba,' p. 291.
36   Martínez-Alier, in her study of contested marriages, *Marriage, Class and Colour*, concluded that overall browns had more status than blacks, but that a wealthy black could have more than a poor brown.
37   I rely heavily on Kiple, *Blacks in Colonial Cuba*, for my demographic analysis.

Graph 1: The Population of Cuba 1774-1899

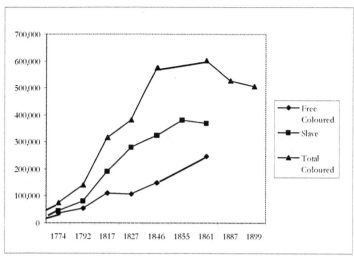

Source: Based on Cuban census figures. Taken from Kenneth F. Kiple *Blacks in Colonial Cuba* (Gainesville, 1976).

Table 1: Growth of the Free Coloured Population, 1774-1887

Year	Free coloured population	Percentage of total island population	Percentage of non-white population
1774	36,301	20.3	41.0
1792	54,154	19.0	45.6
1827	106.494	15.1	27.1
1841	154,546	15.1	25.9
1860	225,843	16.2	37.4
1877	272,478	20.0	55.7
1887	528,798	32.5	100.0

Source: Based on Cuban census figures. Taken from Franklin W. Knight, 'Cuba' in Cohen and Greene (eds.), *Neither Slave nor Free*, p. 284

The coloured population as a whole increased sharply at the end of the eighteenth century, after the 1789 free slave trade decree and the 1791–1804 Revolution in Saint Domingue. However, the slave and the free coloured populations were growing at a fairly similar rate. The late eigh-

teenth century was possibly the nearest there was to any notion of a
'haven' for free coloureds. The sugar revolution of the early nineteenth
century brought about a rapid increase in Cuba's slave population, in spite
of the first 1817 Anglo-Spanish anti-slave treaty ending the legal slave
trade. This possibly went with a curtailment of manumissions or *coartaciones*, and census data show a relative dropping back in numbers of the
free coloured population — and an absolute fall for a few short years.

It has long been argued that the Anglo-Spanish Treaties were ineffec-
tive in stopping the slave flow, which continued until the North American
Civil War, which brought a halt to Cuba's contraband slave trade and signalled the beginning of the end of slavery in the hemisphere. However, the
declining growth rate after the 1830s suggests that the second 1835 Treaty
had some effect, and that growth ceased completely by the mid-1850s, not
the mid-1860s.

From the 1850s there was a renewed growth of the free coloured population, which was when manumission became a matter of public record
and when Chinese indentured workers were brought in their thousands. By
the early 1860s, however, the total coloured population peaked and then
fell sharply. The end of the slave trade was one factor; another was
increased mortality through war (some estimates run as high as 50,000 for
coloureds). The Moret Law of 1870 provided for gradual emancipation
and immediate freedom of 1) the newborn (*vientre libre*); 2) those over 65,
later 60; 3) those fighting for Spain; 4) slaves confiscated from rebels; 5)
contraband blacks (*emancipados*); and 6) slaves discovered not to have been
included in the 1867 census.[38] Under the law, an estimated 26,000 slaves
and 5,000 *emancipados* were freed by 1872, some 50,000 by 1875.

The 1880 Law abolished slavery, with an apprenticeship (*patronato*)
envisaged for eight, but lasting only six, years, blurring free/slave distinctions in the 1880s. However, the figures show a dramatic decline in the
coloured population in the years 1887–99. Adjusting for the Chinese (who
went from being included in to excluded from the white category) and
recent coloured immigration in the 1899 census, over the 38-year period
1861–99 an estimated 100,000 persons of colour were lost, some 16 per
cent of the 1861 population.

The Gender of Colour

No tally over the 30-year period of struggle is likely to be reliable, but the
figures are suggestive of two things: firstly, that the coloured population
bore the brunt of the fighting, and secondly, that the loss was overwhelming among males. The overall decline of the coloured population over

38   See Scott, *Slave Emancipation in Cuba.*

1861–77 was 12.3 per cent, of females 6.3 per cent and males 17.2 per cent, suggesting a high number of deaths among men of colour during the Ten Years War. Similarly, while the coloured population of 1887–99 declined as a whole by 4.9 per cent, males by 14.4 per cent, females actually increased by 5.4 per cent.

It is important to note fertility, mortality and sex-ratios in general throughout the nineteenth century. The free coloured population experienced a relative decline during the first half of the nineteenth century, from constituting 40 per cent of the non-white population in 1774 to 29 per cent in 1846. Moreover, this signified a small natural growth because much of the addition in numbers would seem to have come from *emancipados*, captured before delivery to Cuban owners and set free: in the mid 1860s, they alone numbered 25,000. Statistics before then are poor on *coartaciones*, although subsequent figures and more qualitative data suggest this avenue to freedom was later important.

One counter argument to the explanation for the 1817–27 decrease in terms of excessive mortality, with deaths far exceeding births, is that birth figures are likely to have been grossly underestimated since they were based on baptisms (for which there was a charge). Manumission figures for 1858–62 are 58 per cent women, in a slave population that was only 41 per cent female. The bulking of older men and younger women is commonly explained as planters, in the former case, relieving themselves of an economic burden, and, in the latter, rewarding services rendered. Brown slaves were estimated to be less than five per cent of the slave population in 1846, and to account for 23 per cent of manumissions in the years 1858–62.

The sex/age composition of the free coloured population would suggest high fertility in this group. Table 2 shows the high proportion of women in the free coloured class. Between 1827 and 1841 the increase in the free coloured population amounted to 43.5 per cent; and 45 per cent of all free males and 49 per cent of all free coloured females were in the fertile (16–40) age group. Table 3 gives the age-sex profile in 1861, when women of prime childbearing age (16–40) comprised almost 60 per cent, of this population group. In 1861, by comparison, white females of 16–40 comprised only 40 per cent of the white female population and slave females of 16–40 comprised 49 per cent of the slave population. There was a much lower proportion of women among the white and the slave populations; and estimates for the sex ratio of the nineteenth century slave trade to Cuba stand at 2–3 men for every woman.

Table 2: Sex Ratios for the Slave and Free Coloured Population of Cuba, 1774-1861 (males per 100 females)

Year	Free coloured	Slave
1774	109.2	184.9
1792	87.1	127.6
1817	93.7	166.1
1827	94.4	177.7
1841	97.4	181.3
1846	94.7	173.0
1861	95.8	144.0

Source: Based on Cuban census figures. Taken from Kenneth F. Kiple, *Blacks in Colonial Cuba.*

Table 3: Cuba's Free Coloured Population by Sex and Age, 1854

	Age				
	0–14	**15–40**	**41–60**	**Over 60**	**Total**
Male	34,723	31,510	12,593	4,292	83,118
Female	33,130	38,133	13,788	4,409	89,460
Total	67,853	69,643	26,381	8,701	172,584a

A = erroneous sum by additional 6
Source: 'Estado que demuestra el número de personas de color libres ...1857,' AHN, Ultramar, Leg 4655, No. 183. Taken from Kenneth F. Kiple, *Blacks in Colonial Cuba.*

Without exception, all the studies of free coloureds are skewed to Havana and urban, western Cuba. Comparatively, however, census figures show the east and the city of Santiago as areas of concentrations for free coloureds and especially free coloured women. To take Santiago alone, free coloureds, whites and slaves are in roughly equal proportions in 1774-1817, with the balance tipping to white in 1774 and '92, and free coloureds and slaves in 1817. Free coloureds outnumber whites in the period 1817–61. They are increasingly outnumbered by slaves in the period 1817–46, but by 1861 they outnumber slaves also. With the exception of 1817 and 1841, women always outnumber men. The number of Santiago free brown women shot from some 2,000 in 1774 to 11,000 in 1817, and 18,500 by 1861. From 1817 to 1861 free coloured women outnumbered white women, though in the earlier part of that period, 1817–46, the ratio of slave to free coloured women rose to 3:1. We see then that there was in Santiago a major stratum of free coloured women that was witnessing a relative erosion of position in precisely those years which were formative for Mariana Grajales Cuello.

Santiago's Maceo-Grajales Family

In 1803, when Napoleon Bonaparte sent an expedition against Saint Domingue, there was a veritable influx into eastern Cuba: 'the flotsam of this sad tide came in such numbers to Santiago de Cuba that the sleepy city saw its population increase by alarming proportions'.[39] Santiago was the closest port-city to Haiti, and, if the spectre of Haiti was to haunt the whole of Cuba, its effect on eastern Cuba was particularly strong, with both the fear and promise of race redemption. Santiago took in refugees from all walks of life, but with the Napoleonic invasion of Spain in 1808 xenophobia against them rose, occasioning an exodus to Louisiana. A census taken that year in Santiago showed 7,500 'French', 22 per cent of the total population. Of these, only 28 per cent were native of France. The remaining 72 per cent were of all colours, and, it is supposed, rapidly became Cubanised. In addition, there were those who came from Santo Domingo — some themselves of Haitian descent.

In 1808 in Santiago de Cuba a daughter, Mariana Grajales Cuello, was born to don José Grajales and doña Teresa Cuello, free brown émigrés from Santo Domingo. That is, in all accounts but two, according to one of which she was born in Santo Domingo[40] and to another of which, the most recent, she was actually born in 1815.[41] Whichever, her background can hardly be seen as insignificant. All the Maceo-Grajales biographers emphasise the hard-working peace and harmony of first the Grajales-Cuello and later the

---

39   Juan Pérez de la Riva, 'Una isla con dos historias,' p. 71.

40   There is no reason to doubt the Dominican connection. It is nonetheless interesting that in the late eighteenth century there were Graxales and Coellos moving between Cuba, Florida and Louisiana, the latter two also under Spanish rule at the time. The Grajales of Santo Domingo have links with both Santiago de Cuba and San Juan de Puerto Rico, and have a history of fighting against Haiti and against Spain. The Cuellos are in the main mulatto, though some are white, and Antonio Maceo is often linked to Leovigildo Cuello, whom he was to meet in person in 1880; both have a similar physiognomy. See Emilio Rodríguez Demorizi, *Maceo en Santo Domingo* (República Dominicana, 1945).

41   Olga Portuondo Zúñiga and Joel Mourlot, *Visión múltiple de Antonio Maceo* (Santiago de Cuba: 1999).

Maceo-Grajales households, with Mariana achieving a home with 'under-standing, virtue and moral rectitude ... mutual respect and consideration, where the seeds of freedom and solidarity found fertile ground',[42] leading a life around the home and possibly helping out in the fields. They draw on a quasi-idyllic picture of race relations, which shaped Mariana's humble family upbringing, and contrast this with the hardening race hatred, ill treatment of slaves, grief and death of patriots in Cuba. Near to the fam-ily home, it is said, stood the runaway slave depot, which made a lasting impression on Mariana.[43]

While studies coincide in signalling how the Maceo-Grajales family's growing desire for social justice became translated into patriotism, and how instrumental Mariana was in this, they differ with regard to whom they consider most repsonsible — the father Marcos, the son Antonio or the mother Mariana.

The story of Marcos is at present the most disputed. Long held to have been born in Venezuela, as a young man, it was said, he fought with the Spanish army, until Simón Bolívar and José San Martín expelled the Spanish forces from mainland Latin America; his grandfather was white French/Saint Domingue, Gabriel Matiu, who wound up in Venezuela; and there he entered into free union with a free black woman from Santo Domingo, recognising her children with a Spanish version of his name. Their daughter Clara had four sons with Manuel Alvarez de la Higuera, whose name none of them bore.

With the defeat of Spain Clara Maceo supposedly left with her two sons, Marcos and Doroteo, and two daughters, Bárbara and María de Rosario, for Santo Domingo in the 1820s. It was a time of great instability, and the Maceos soon left for Cuba — Spain's 'Ever Faithful Isle'. Despite a royal 'cédula' prohibiting the admission of coloured people into Cuba, the Maceos managed to evade the law and enter the port city of Santiago de Cuba. Doroteo joined the Spanish army in Oriente; Marcos started a small business in agricultural produce, which was destined to prosper.[44]

All of this is now challenged, as new documentation has been brought to light suggesting Marcos was born out of wedlock in Santiago de Cuba in 1808 to Clara Maceo and was the son of José Antonio Machuli Hernández. Both were free browns. Machuli was the son of Miguel Machuli, of Valencia, and free brown Teresa Hernández. Marcos was left

---

42   Danger and Rodríguez, *Mariana Grajales*, pp. 3–4.
43   Sarabia, *Historia de una familia mambisa*, p. 27. From 1807–1810 there was an annual average of 64 runaways taken to the depot in Santiago, 51 in Puerto Principe, 50 in Matanzas and 1,000 in Havana. See Gabino la Rosa Carzo, 'Cimarrones, apalencados y rancheadores en Puerto Principe,' *Del Caribe*, vol. 4, no. 8 (1987).
44   Olga Portuondo, 'El padre de Antonio Maceo: ¿venezolano?' *Del Caribe*, no 19 (1992), pp. 93–7.

an orphan at an early age and taken in by free brown María Josefa Amelo Hernández. Moreover, Doroteo, Bárbara and María de Rosario are now said not to be related.[45]

The circumstances surrounding the early relationship between Marcos and Mariana are unclear. The narrative is fairly straightforward for Mariana's first marriage to Fructuoso Regueiferos. Interestingly, one early account has her married with her first child at age 12 if born in 1808, only five if born in 1815![46] However, for the most part, she is said to have married in her early twenties, and to have had four sons — Felipe, Fermín, Manuel and Justo — all in the 1830s, and been left widowed at 32 with the death of her husband in 1840 (in one account 1838). The Regueiferos–Grajales couple are described as sharing ideals of justice and administering the home so well as to dress poverty in splendour.

Many accounts simply refer to her second marriage in 1843 to Marcos Maceo, with whom she had nine children, seven boys and two girls — Antonio, María Baldomera, José, Miguel, Dominga, Marcos, Tomás, Julio and Rafael. Only a few refer to the minor detail that theirs was initially a free union. Not until the 1972 biography of José do we learn that the first wife of Marcos Maceo was Amparo Tellez, with whom Marcos had six other children (one also named Antonio Maceo and all equally involved in the liberation struggle). It was in 1851, after the death of Amparo, that Marcos and Mariana were married and their children legitimised — by then Antonio, Baldomera and José had all been born. The last son is said to have been born in 1860, when Mariana would have been 52.

The Maceo-Grajales family business is said to have prospered. This is mostly implied as coming initially from Marcos' side, despite his humble origins, though buttressed with Mariana's thrift. Only the 1972 study of José suggests the money might have been on Mariana's side, and more from her marriage to Regueiferos. However, again more recent versions suggest these did not go to Mariana.[47] Three Farms were added to the spacious residence in Santiago: La Esperanza, La Delicia and El Piloto, in the rich agricultural area of Majaguabo, San Luis, in the foothills of the Sierra Maestra mountains. La Delicia is described as having nine *caballerías* of good land with a stone house and several buildings for tobacco, storage and stables. It produced an abundance of coffee, tobacco, bananas and a variety of staples that formed a part of the regular diet of Cuban families. It also supported a few beef cattle and horses.

As their farm business grew, the family was regarded as an important member of the local rural middle brown class — a fact often ignored or dis-

45   Olga Portuondo, 'Ascendencia paterna de Antonio Maceo,' *Del Caribe*, no. 35 (2001), pp. 88–93.
46   Hernández, *Maceo: dos conferencias históricas*, p. 33.
47   Portuondo, 'Ascendencia paterna'.

puted even in more recent accounts, which seem to equate brown with humble origin (*de origen humilde*). They are generally assumed not to have been
slaveholding. However there is reference to the sale of one creole slave:
'Mariana cannot forget what she has seen in her childhood and youth. As a
woman and mother, she insists that Marcos not hold in property another
man. In her veins runs African blood, something she would never forget.'[48]

The family had good connections with prominent whites and free
browns in the region, from among whom several of the Maceo-Grajales
children had godparents: the baptismal record of Antonio in Santo Tomás
Church names white Santiago lawyer don Ascencio Ascencio and doña
Salomé Hernández, both of whom are said to have taken an active interest in Antonio's upbringing. Interestingly, Ascencio is often accredited with
being a lawyer but more recently a lowlier clerk, and Hernández, in several accounts, is said to be Ascencio's wife, but more recently asserted to
have been free brown Maria Josefa Amelo Hernández.[49]

The growing family lived mostly at La Delicia, but the children received
some schooling in Santiago de Cuba.[50] At the age of 16, Antonio Maceo
is described as having the responsibility, along with his half-brother Justo,
for marketing the farm produce by mule. This took him regularly into the
countryside, giving him knowledge of the terrain of eastern Cuba, along
with skills in horsemanship, the handling of firearms and the use of the
Cuban machete, all of which would be useful in war. In 1866 Antonio married a light brown woman of the neighbourhood, María Magdalena
Cabrales y Fernández, described as the mirror image of his mother, and
they went to live at La Esperanza.

Santiago in the 1850s and 1860s was a tumultuous city, spawning pro-
independence posters, leaflets and couplets that occasioned the imprisonment and deportation of those responsible; a city as full of polemic as of
dance and music — the controversial and sensual *sompimpa* and *chupadera* were
all the rage. How attractive or how much of a contradiction this was to the
alleged moral austerity of the Maceo-Grajales household we can again only
speculate; but it was all soon to be truncated by war. Mariana is attributed
with laying the groundwork for the family's involvement, with stories of slave
rebellions, the Escalera Conspiracy, the death of Plácido and others, to win

48   Sarabia, *Historia de una familia mambisa*, p. 65. The point is never elaborated. Was this
      the only slave? Why was the slave sold and not given his freedom? These are not only
      unresolved but unformulated questions.
49   Portuondo, 'Ascendencia paterna'.
50   Accounts differ as to whether the young Maceos had some private schooling or
      attended elementary school (all that was allowed for their race). In the 1790s, there
      had been racially mixed schools, but nineteenth century law pressed for stricter seg-
      regation by colour. In the 1830s, elementary schools for people of colour were said
      to be the most numerous and better constituted.

over her husband Marcos and bring up her children loyal to the Cuban cause.[51] In 1864, we are told, don Ascencio had introduced Antonio to the Masonic Lodge of Santiago, out of which came later revolutionary conspirators. The same don Ascencio would keep Antonio and the family informed of events. However, it has more recently been suggested that don Ascencio, like Antonio Maceo, may well have been active in the cabildo *de nación*, as these originally African nation groupings broadened to embrace all those of African descent and subsequently whites, too.[52]

The story goes that when the Camagüey planter Carlos Manuel de Céspedes declared the outbreak of war in 1868 and freed his slaves on his estate La Demajagua, young Marcos Maceo was sent to the local store to pick up news. Coincidentally, Santiago captain Rondón, who was headed for the mountains with a rebel group, had stopped at the store. Rondón knew Marcos and Mariana, and recognised young Marcos. 'Tell your mother to prepare supper for us,' he was told.

After the meal Marcos Maceo was asked for a contribution and gave horses, four ounces of gold, a dozen good machetes, two revolvers, four shotguns, and a blunderbuss. The rebels also recruited three volunteers: Antonio, José and Justo. María Cabrales later wrote that Mariana, 'bursting with joy, went into her room, picked up a crucifix she had and said: "on your knees everyone, parents and children, before Christ, who was the first liberal man who came to the world, let us take an oath to liberate or die for our country"'.[53]

'True to Mariana'

The family left Majaguabo before the Spanish authorities arrived and burned down the family farm. They took prisoner 16-year old Rafael who had returned for some personal belongings. Marcos offered himself in his son's place, his son later escaped and Marcos himself was subsequently released through Mariana's invocation of help from Spanish friends. Mariana was the one who told her husband: 'And you, Marcos, get ready, this is war.'[54] Within the month, the whole family was installed deep in the rebel camp.

---

51   The three Mariana biographies all emphasise this. It should be noted that from 1795 to 1843, during Mariana's formative years and during plantation takeoff, there were 100 urban and rural rebellions, 60 after 1833. See Alain Yacou, 'El proyecto de las rebeliones esclavas de la Isla de Cuba en la primera mitad del siglo XIX,' *Del Caribe*, vol. 5, no. 13 (1989).
52   Portuondo, 'Ascendencia paterna'. This tallies with my own interpretation of the lodges and the *cabildos* (Stubbs, 'Mariana Grajales').
53   This is retold in all the accounts, albeit in varying form. This quote is from Franco (1963), pp. 72–4.
54   Sarabia (1975), *Historia de una familia mambisa*, p.79.

Already by then Céspedes in Camaguey was reputed to have an army of 12,000, a considerable part of them coloured, without uniform and most commonly armed with the machete. The rebel forces received opportune aid from a group of exiles from Santo Domingo led by Máximo Gómez, Luis Marcano and Modesto Díaz, with military experience, especially guerrilla tactics, in the Dominican wars against Spain. It was under Gómez that the Maceos rapidly ascended.

Organised into highly mobile small units, the insurrectional forces operated on the move. When not fighting, Maceo was reputed to operate from maroon settlements (*palenques*) — El Frijol, Bumba, Maluala — in the forest heart of the eastern mountains, inhospitable terrain untouched by the coloniser. From these settlements his troops set fire to estates, felled trees and plundered food in the stealth of the night. There, his troops' families had their living quarters.[55] There, Mariana and other women were instrumental in running hospitals, workshops and food stores. Maceo seemingly also made good use of the illicit traffic operating in the Caribbean to bring in medicines, salt, ammunition and other indispensable items from nearby Jamaica, Santo Domingo and Haiti. As a result, his forces were relatively well-fed, well-dressed and well-armed.

In May 1869 Marcos Maceo was killed in battle, fighting alongside Antonio. His dying words are recorded as: 'I've been true to Mariana'. Mariana Grajales had lost a son — Justo, who had been captured and executed trying to visit his wife's home — and a husband. A week later, attacking the sugar mill La Armonía, Antonio received the first of his many wounds, to be nursed back to health by his wife and mother. 'Out of here, skirts. This is no time for crying,' were Mariana's words to women around her at the time:

> Her unhappiness urged her in direct ratio to her pain to continue in the work of destroying the chains which kept Cuba bound. Mariana Grajales, living incarnation of Cuban patriotism, cried out to the youngest of her sons, still a little boy: 'And *you*, boy, it's time you were off fighting for your country.'[56]

55   A unique traveller's account is James O'Kelly, *Mambi-Land, Adventures of a Herald Correspondent in Cuba* (Philadelphia, 1874). From Santiago to Caney in Ti Arriba, 'these people were colored men and armed … they were evidently surprised to see a white man alone …' (p.112–3). O'Kelly wrote of 'El Silencio', a secret society or masonic brotherhood, and the voudou religious dance ceremony of the African blacks, claiming that most of the coloured people 'pretty freely characterised the people who took part in it as savages – barbaros' (p. 223) The fine line between *vodún*, freemasonry and the Afro-Cuban 'cabildos' is as yet little explored in Cuban historiography. However, the emphasis is more Afro-Cuban in Pedro Deschamps Chapeaux 'Presencia religiosa en las sublevaciones de esclavos,' *Del Caribe*, vol. 4, nos. 16–17 (1990); and Howard, 'The Spanish Colonial Government's Responses'.

56   Santovenia (1943), *Raiz y altura de Antonio Maceo*, quoted in Foner, *Antonio Maceo: The 'Bronze Titan'*, p. 28.

On 18 February 1878, with the rebel forces on the verge of capitulation at the end of the war, General Máximo Gómez wrote in his Campaign Diary:

> The 19th, wishing to see the General's family, set off for the settlement. The General sent his brother José to accompany us and we spent the night there. Being among those patriotic women, our comrades in the hills during that terrible ten-year struggle, in which we had all suffered so much, was one of the saddest nights for me.'[57]

The full story of the feats of the independence struggle up to and beyond Mariana's death, and the cleavages fast developing in the rebel ranks between planter procrastination and the tide of popular forces over the issue of slavery and tactics and strategy, are necessarily beyond our scope here; so too the 'black caudillo' fears over the legendary Antonio and José, and their response to the intrigue against them. However, in his defence, and probably sharing his mother's point of view, Antonio wrote:

> as a man who entered the revolution for no other reason than to shed his blood to see the slaves and his country free ... since I belong to the coloured race, without considering myself worthy more or less than other men, I cannot and must not consent to the continued growth of this ugly rumour ... Since I form a not unappreciable part of this democratic republic, which has for its base the fundamental principles of liberty, equality and fraternity, I must protest energetically, with all my strength, that neither now nor at any time am I to be regarded as an advocate of a Negro Republic or anything of that sort. This concept is a deadly thing.[58]

He declared in a proclamation calling for the support of Oriente in the Protest of Baraguá:

> ... the era of the whip and of Spanish cynicism has come to an end, and we ought to form a new Republic assimilated with our sisters Santo Domingo and Haiti. The great spirit of Washington, Lafayette and Bolívar, liberators of oppressed peoples, accompanies us and is one with us ...[59]

From Kingston in 1878 he issued a Manifesto:

> Slaves! The tyrant has denied you your liberty, and has condemned you to Martyrdom. The black man is as free as the white; the wickedness of your oppressor has you suffering ... You must remember at all times that your comrades who fought in the last war

57 Foner, *ibid.*
58 *Ibid.*
59 Portuondo, 'Ascendencia paterna,' p. 24.

achieved their liberty because they embraced the Cuban flag, which belongs to all Cubans alike. Get together under the same flag and you shall obtain freedom and your civil rights ...[60]

In Jamaica, as in Cuba and the United States, Maceo was accused of fomenting a black Haiti. When he was in Haiti, this was turned on its head when the Spanish spread the rumour he was a traitor to his race for staying within the same movement as white racists calling themselves revolutionary — and, one suspects, for being so elegant, eloquent, gracious and courteous. In 1880, he reiterated: 'I love all things and all men, because I see more of the essences than the accidents of life, for that reason I have above the interests of race, whatever that may be, the interest of Humanity.'[61]

Of the free brown Maceo–Grajales family, only Marcos, Tomás and Dominga survived the wars. Julio died in 1870 and Miguel in 1874 in Cuba. Rafael was deported to Spain and died in 1887. Baldomera died in Montecristo, Santo Domingo, a few months before Mariana herself died in Kingston, Jamaica, in 1893. José and Antonio died in battle in Cuba in 1896. In a last letter to María in March 1895, Antonio Maceo wrote: 'Honour before all else. The first time, we fought together. Now I must fight alone for us both. If I win, the glory will be yours.'[62]

Mariana never returned to Cuba; she lived to see abolition but not Independence. María returned and died in 1905, three years after the founding of the republic. For those like her, the glory was little and short-lived; they returned to a shadow of their former position. Before the decade was out, after two US occupations, class, race and gender lines were redrawn; and Oriente was the scenario of the 1912 Race War.[63]

Revolutionary Free Brown Woman

By the time of Mariana's death, a *cubanía revolucionaria* was being forged from disparate elements, with brown and black (male) revolutionary thinkers: Flor Crombet, Juan Gualberto Gómez, Martín Morúa Delgado, Rafael Serra and Antonio Maceo. Of them all, Antonio emerged as the great hero, spontaneously among the masses, calculatedly by politicians. His official image was transmuted from 'black caudillo' to 'Cuban', and only more recently resurrected as the 'bronze titan', symbolic of Cuba's browning (*mulatización*).

60   Franco, *Las conspiraciones de 1810 y 1812*, p. 209.
61   *Antonio Maceo* (1950–52).
62   Portuondo, 'Ascendencia paterna', p. 121.
63   This is told forcefully in Aline Helg, *Our Rightful Share: The Afro-Cuban Struggle for Equality, 1886–1912* (Chapel Hill, NC, 1995). See also 'Race in Argentina and Cuba, 1880–1930: Theory, Policies and Popular Reaction' in Richard Graham (ed.), *The Idea of Race in Latin America, 1870–1940* (Austin, Tex, 1990).

With the image of the mother's son went that of the son's mother. Monuments went up to Antonio and Mariana. In 1916 an equestrian statue of Antonio was erected in Havana, since described as one of the most striking in the Americas to a man of mixed blood. There are busts of Mariana in San Luis and Santiago. A monument of 1937 in the park of her name in Vedado, Havana, is a statue of her with a small son, her arm pointing, with the inscription: 'To Mariana Grajales, mother of the Maceos. The people of Cuba.'[64] The image is significant. It is how Cubans chose to interpret the meaning of Mariana's life. They recognised and celebrated the defiant and heroic mother-leader, whose loyalty was to causes beyond her own image and those of husband, father or son; whose social convictions placed love and justice over and above narrow race privilege, sentiments that forged revolutionary patriotic conviction.

Elsewhere, I analyse the shoring up of the 'Mariana the mother' image, and the dominant gendered assumptions behind the mythology surrounding it.[65] It is important to critique both the Catholic, marianist, quasi-fascist rendering in 1957, when Mariana was declared 'official mother of Cuba', and the secular revolutionary brown matriarch of post-1959 revolutionary times. There is an equally possible Afro-Cuban reading of the eastern war experience and the Maceo-Grajales family, and a more gendered reading of Mariana. Faced with the emasculation of slavery and racism, the gender ideals of the middle brown stratum cantered around women charged with fertility and respectability, with raising the next generation for the good of the race — preaching the value of hard work, responsibility, strength and self-reliance. Mariana could become a strong revolutionary Cuban icon because she symbolised the spirit power of Afro-Cuban women to lead and commune with the orishas to redress imbalance through ritual and action: to exhort to kill and to die is within the power and right of a strong nurturer-warrior woman.[66]

It is also necessary to draw attention to how the life story of Mariana Grajales Cuello and her family challenges pervasive assumptions about free browns. Characterisations of 19th century Cuban free browns have ranged from 'the integrated ... colored community as an essential economic ... component of Cuban society ... a natural and accepted part of

---

64   See Aristides Sosa de Quesada, *Martí, Maceo, Agramonte a través de sus reliquias* (Havana, 1944); and Estuch, *Maceo, héroe y carácter.*
65   Stubbs in Shepherd et al., *Engendering History.*
66   In this I concur in singling out qualities that have been central to the Africanist-Feminist approach to black woman cross-culturally. See Rosalind Terborg Penn, 'Black Women in Resistance: A Cross-Cultural Perspective,' in Gary Y. Okihiro (ed.), *In Resistance* (Amherst, 1986). I am also grateful to K. Lynn Stoner and Judith Bettleheim for their insightful comments. See also K. Lynn Stoner, *From the House to the Streets: The Cuban Woman's Movement for Legal Reform, 1898–1940* (Durham, NC and London, 1991); and Judith Bettleheim (ed.), *Cuban Festivals: An Anthology with Glossaries* (New York, 1993).

that society'[67] to one in which the plantation culture 'militated against incorporation of free persons of color into the society. Rather than fostering an
integrated community, the plantation engendered racial and social hostility.'[68]

There has also been a more homogeneous interpretation: that the free
coloured community was not revolutionary. Thus:

> ... precisely the possibility and the existence of racial mixture provided a
> safety valve for the system by creating an intermediate group, the mulattos,
> whose allegiance to the blacks' cause was often minimal. It was the blacks
> that were frequently the most rebellious; whereas among those that pursued
> fugitive slaves, for instance, one could find many mulattos.[69]

Also:

> The free colored community was certainly less revolutionary than the cre-
> ole whites, who sought political independence from Spain, or the slaves,
> who sought their liberty. But it was also weaker numerically and was in a
> much more precarious position than either of the other groups. The divi-
> sion between free blacks and free mulattoes may also have vitiated group
> solidarity ... The two groups did not face a common threat, as was the
> case with the gens de couleur of Saint Domingue after 1789. The absence
> of this common threat in the face of possible chaos seems to have pre-
> disposed the free coloured community in Cuba to make individual deci-
> sions about politics and society rather than resort to group action.[70]

The question we are left with is: did Mariana Grajales Cuello and her family act individually or as representative of eastern free browns, Cuban free
browns or a grouping that transcended the boundaries of race?

The prevalent view of free browns in the Americas sees their middle
ground position in terms of culture, appearance, wealth and status as essentially one of ambiguity and compromise. They have been described as a
'buffer' group, a position all too often assumed to be disenabling, aspiring to
white, distancing the horrors of slavery.[71] The men sometimes led rebellions,
but also participated in their repression. The women were stereotyped as the
moral stalwarts of upwardly mobile families but also sensual and licentious.[72]
Individually they might have commanded respect from the dominant society,
but collectively they were often viewed with fear and contempt.

67   'The Freedman as an Indicator of Assimilation – An Integrated Community: The
      Free Colored in Cuba,' in Klein, *Slavery in the Americas*.
68   Knight 'Cuba,' p. 305.
69   Martínez-Alier, *Marriage, Class and Colour*, p. 39.
70   Knight 'Cuba,' p. 307.
71   This is especially argued for Jamaica. See Mavis C. Campbell, *The Dynamics of Change
      in a Slave Society: A Sociopolitical History of the Free Coloreds of Jamaica, 1800–1865*
      (London, 1976). An opposing argument is formulated in Gad Heuman, *Between Black
      and White: Race, Politics, and the Free Coloreds in Jamaica, 1792–1865* (Oxford, 1981).
72   This is explored in depth for the nineteenth century in Vera Kutzinski, *Sugar's Secrets*.

Mariana Grajales Cuello during her exile in Kingston, Jamaica, 1879.

The historical Mariana would seem a not unusual representative of the light-skinned, rural middle class of the Caribbean: the moderately prosperous farming background, the very large number of children, the early ones born outside marriage, church baptism and later marriage affording respectability as a weapon to combat white racism. The apparent early exclusion from commercial activity and confinement to the domestic sphere might be a specifically Hispanic element. Her mythic motherhood combines with political rectitude, and her intermediary status as a brown icon serves the function of reconciling and uniting disparate elements in the nation, in a way that was less needed for more predominantly black or white societies. Interestingly, Brazil, like Cuba, has the ultra-sensuous *mulata*. But neither Brazil nor Saint Domingue, which experienced a similarly bitter and divisive war of independence, would seem to have a comparable female icon to Mariana.[73] This makes her all the more remarkable.

73   I owe the finer honing of these points to David Geggus, 'Slave and Free Colored Women in Saint Domingue,' in David Barry Gaspar and Darlene Hine (eds.), *More Than Chattel: Black Women and Slavery in the Americas* (Bloomington, 1996). The nearest we have to a strong female icon is the legendary warrior Nanny of the Maroons a century earlier in Jamaica. The fact that Mariana should have lived her latter years and died in Jamaica, and be almost forgotten there today, rendered all the more emotive the commemoration of the centenary of her death with this study.

And yet, attempts to explore the ambiguities and ambivalence of free coloureds in the Americas do suggest that the group, and key individuals within that group, could play a sometimes pivotal role in their society and times. Consciously and unconsciously, free browns and free blacks offered the seeds of revolt or threatened revolt to the unfree blacks. Their alliances with the slaves were especially strong where progressive, anti-colonialist movements included not only slaves and free coloureds but also abolitionist whites as well.[74]

Mariana Grajales Cuello was a free brown woman who did not compromise herself or her family, was not disenabled, was proud of her colour and gave up an established position for political and social, not economic, reasons: to fight against slavery and Spanish colonialism and for a vision of a politically and racially free Cuba. In the context of contemporary Cuba's defence of socialism and non-capitulation to US neocolonialism, symbolised as today's Baraguá, Mariana's is a life story we would do well to remember.

---

74   Cohen and Green (eds.), *Neither Slave nor Free*, 'Introduction'.

CHAPTER 6

Catalysts in the Crucible: Kidnapped Caribbeans, Free Black British Subjects and Migrant British Machinists in the Failed Cuban Revolution of 1843

Jonathan Curry-Machado

On 26 March 1843, the enslaved workers on five neighbouring sugar plantations in the Bemba (Jovellanos) and Cimarrones districts, near Matanzas, simultaneously rebelled, setting fire to crops and buildings on the estates, and causing damage to the railway line running from Matanzas to Júcaro. Though their number was estimated at 950, they were quickly suppressed by the rapid mobilisation of troops from both Matanzas and Havana. By the end of the day, more than half had been slaughtered — either shot down or, according to some accounts, having taken their own lives rather than be returned to servitude. That night 'the woods [were] filled with hanging victims'.[1]

A few days previously Joseph Tucker Crawford, the British consul general in Havana, received an unexpected visitor. 'I was called upon by a Coloured man of some respectability', he later wrote to his superiors in London. To Crawford's great surprise, Juan Rodríguez had come to enquire about the arms and munitions that the consul's predecessor, David Turnbull, had allegedly offered to supply in the event of an uprising on the island. This would seem to have been the first he had heard of such a conspiracy, and certainly of any British complicity in the forthcoming insurrection:

> I think I was able to convince this man of the madness of any such attempt in their circumstances: I told him that emancipation is to be brought about without violence or an open and disastrous war of castes, but he expressed very great doubts whether the delegates from other parts of the Island now here, would be persuaded to abandon or could induce their people to give up the project, as it was the general opinion amongst them, that if they were all sacrificed it would be preferable to their present state of existence.[2]

---

1   Public Record Office, London (PRO), FO 72/634 — Letter no. 15 of 1843 from Joseph T. Crawford, British consul general in Havana, to Earl of Aberdeen (Foreign Office), Havana, 18 April 1843.
2   PRO, FO 72/634 — Letter no. 16 of 1843 from Joseph T. Crawford to Earl of Aberdeen (Foreign Office), Havana, 18 April 1843.

Their aim was little short of a revolution that would simultaneously bring an end to slavery in Cuba and give the island independence from Spain. As it turned out (and despite Crawford's warnings) the events near Bemba proved to be just the start of what was to be a tense and, in the end, very bloody twelve months. Intermittent uprisings occurred throughout the principal sugar-producing areas of Havana and Matanzas. An army of self-liberated slaves, led by José Dolores, carried out guerrilla-style attacks on plantations and sought to free those who had been imprisoned in the earlier rebellions.[3] Even when no open confrontation occurred, slave owners were reporting that throughout 1843 even the more trusted house slaves were showing increasing levels of insubordination; and the uprisings reached a climax in November, when the *dotación* on the 'Triunvirato' estate rose up and took their rebellion to several plantations and mills in the Sabanilla district.[4] This coincided with the arrival of Leopoldo O'Donnell as the new captain general of Cuba, and the beginning of a brutal repression not just against the slaves who had the temerity to break their shackles, but also — and particularly — against those free coloureds who, like Juan Rodríguez, had been involved in the conspiracy to organise a general rebellion.

Though much remains hidden as to the true extent of the underground organisation of the attempted uprising, the response of the government left little doubt as to the seriousness with which O'Donnell treated the threat. Theodore Phinney, a British landowner who later complained of the death and injury of many of his own slaves as a result of the extremity of the persecution, described the method of torture used that gave this failed revolution its subsequent name: 'La Escalera' (Ladder):

> Stripped naked and lashed to a ladder on the ground with a rope round each wrist so tight that the blood could scarsely [sic] circulate, and the whole arm drawn above the head till the shoulder joints fairly cracked, while the ropes were secured to the top of the ladder, the feet and legs stretched in the same manner, and fastened to the lower part with a double turn round the loins and back, binding the whole trunk of the body immoveably to the rounds of the ladder ... in this position, the poor negro was thought to be ready to commence his declaration! Every limb trembling with affright, and every cord and muscle quivering in expectation of the lash, knotted and thicker than a man's thumb! Good God! Is it in the nineteenth century that we live? Or the palmy days of the Inquisition once more returned?[5]

3   Robert L Paquette, *Sugar is Made with Blood: The Conspiracy of La Escalera and the Conflict between Empires over Slavery in Cuba* (Middletown, Conn., 1988), pp. 177–9
4   *Ibid.*, pp. 209–10
5   PRO, FO 72/664 — Copy of letter from Theodore Phinney to Joseph T. Crawford, 29 June 1844, contained in Dispatch no. 19 of 1844 from Crawford to Earl of Aberdeen (8 July 1844).

Although Crawford appears to have been unaware of any British involvement in the conspiracy until his meeting with Rodríguez, the fact that the conspirators were prepared to take him into their confidence bears witness to the support they expected, or had been led to expect, from the British government. Unfortunately for them, Turnbull — who had dedicated his brief time as consul largely to the furtherance of the abolition campaign in Cuba — had been expelled from the island in 1842.[6] A few months later he was captured having re-entered Cuba at Gibara, near Holguín, and after several weeks imprisonment in Havana was again removed, to continue agitating from the safety of neighbouring islands.[7]

It has been the role played by Turnbull and other representatives of the British State and abolition movement that has received most attention in the discussions around the possible existence (or non-existence) of an organised plot to bring independence to Cuba and an end to slavery. There were, however, three groups of British subjects living and working in Cuba at this time who played a part, which, while hidden, may have been at least as important in the development of events in the 1840s. There were Caribbeans, mostly from Jamaica or the Bahamas, who had been kidnapped into slavery; there were free black British subjects forming a part of the growing free coloured population of Cuba; and there were numbers of skilled British workers, machinists who migrated to Cuba to operate and maintain the steam technology that was being imported in those years. None of these groups was particularly numerous in itself, and until now they have been relegated to the footnotes of Cuban history. However, their insignificance in numbers was more than made up for by the role they played in events such as those surrounding the Escalera conspiracy. They were, in their different ways, catalysts both for the attempted uprising and, in the longer term, for the emergence and consolidation of a multiracial and multinational Cuban working class.

Kidnapped Caribbeans

In 1842 a young Jamaican known as Wellington finally found himself returning home to Kingston from Santiago de Cuba. Seven years previously he, along with a number of other young Jamaican men and boys, had been kidnapped by a small-time slave trader, Captain Francis James. Despite the international outlawing of the slave trade, James took

6   For a detailed account of the role played by British abolition agents such as David Turnbull and Francis Ross Cocking in the undermining of Cuban slavery in this period, see Rodolfo Sarracino, *Inglaterra: sus dos caras en la lucha cubana por la abolición* (Havana, 1989); also Paquette, *Sugar is Made with Blood*, pp.131–82.

7   PRO, FO 72/634 — Letter no. 18 from Joseph T. Crawford to Earl of Aberdeen (Foreign Office) (Havana, 4 May 1843).

Wellington and his companions to a remote part of the Cuban coast near Manzanillo, in the east of the island, and there sold them to the owner of the 'Guamá' plantation. Six weeks later Wellington was taken to Santiago de Cuba, where he was sold again. Passing through several owners, all attempts on the part of the British authorities in Cuba and Jamaica to locate him and restore him to liberty appeared to have been in vain. Finally, in 1841, two of those who had been captured with him, and previously freed, were brought back to Cuba to help in the search. Despite attempts by his captors and the local authorities to hide his true identity, he was found. Although the British consul in Havana, David Turnbull, referred to him as 'the unfortunate Wellington', he was, no doubt, more fortunate than many in being freed and returned to his home and family.[8]

The scale of the problem of kidnapped Caribbeans is not clear. Despite the official outlawing of the slave trade through the treaty signed between Britain and Spain in 1817, little if anything was being done in Cuba to bring the trade to an end. Despite the presence in Havana of one of the mixed courts set up by the two countries to monitor the implementation of the treaty — and to bring freedom to those who had been taken into slavery illegally — the 1830s saw more slaves than ever being introduced into the island — more than 18,000 a year.[9] In 1846, some 36 per cent of the total population of Cuba were slaves.[10] It was therefore relatively easy to hide individuals who had been smuggled in from neighbouring islands. This was particularly so, since on arrival they would frequently have their name changed, and would even be re-baptised, to make them appear to be other than they were. This is what made difficult the discovery of William Jones, also kidnapped from Jamaica during the 1830s. When he was finally found, he was registered as 'Julian Carabalí No. 42'.[11] Even when an individual was found, it was by no means a straightforward process to achieve his or her liberty. Not only was it necessary to contend with the obstructions of the slave owners, but also in many cases those of the Spanish authorities. For example, Henry Shirley was kidnapped and brought into Cuba in 1830. In 1840 the British consul laid claim to him, only to be informed by the lieutenant governor of the province where Shirley was found that he was in fact dead. On investigation it was revealed that he was actually in prison, at the behest of the same official.[12]

8   Archivo Nacional de Cuba, Havana (ANC), Fondo Gobierno Superior Civil (FGSC), 844/28360.
9   David Eltis, *Economic Growth and the Ending of the Transatlantic Slave Trade* (New York, 1987), p. 249; and Christopher Schmidt-Nowara, *Empire and Antislavery: Spain, Cuba, and Puerto Rico, 1833–1874* (Pittsburgh, 1999), p. 4.
10   Louis A. Pérez, Jr, *Cuba: Between Reform and Revolution* (New York, 1988), p. 86.
11   ANC, FGSC, 843/28293 — Letter from Charles Tolmé, British consul in Havana, to the captain general of Cuba, 21 September 1840.
12   ANC, FGSC, 844/28360.

It was not only through being snatched from their home islands by unscrupulous traders that the black inhabitants of British colonies might find themselves as slaves in Cuba. With the abolition of slavery in the British West Indies in 1833 a number of slave owners in those islands decided to relocate themselves, together with much of their workforce. This was the case with William Forbes of New Providence, who came to Cárdenas with 120 slaves who would otherwise have been freed, and there established the 'Santa María' coffee plantation. Though Forbes had died, the slaves continued to be held in servitude by his heirs.[13] Such was the scale of this influx of British refugees from abolition that the area between Gibara and Holguín, in the eastern part of the island, became known as 'English Cuba', for the number of English-owned plantations that appeared from the 1830s, manned with slaves brought with the owners largely from the Bahamas.[14] It was by no means a coincidence that the latter region was where Turnbull was discovered on his covert re-entry into Cuba towards the end of 1842; nor that prior to his removal from the island — and while still consul — the authorities had been paying close attention to his movements in the vicinity of the Forbes plantation in Cárdenas.

It was, in part, this attention that they attracted from the British authorities and abolition agents that made these kidnapped Caribbeans important, despite the apparent insignificance of their numbers among the hundreds of thousands who were likewise enslaved in Cuba. Although Turnbull and his associates were happy to fight against slavery wherever it occurred, and whomever it might affect; the possession of slaves by British subjects on the island, at a time when the British government was so actively seeking abolition, was clearly something of an embarrassment. Slave ownership was cited by Charles Clarke, British consul in Santiago de Cuba, as the reason for his choice of Dr James Forbes as acting consul when he took a leave of absence in 1844:

> There are only three other British subjects resident in this place whose standing in society would warrant the consulate being entrusted to them — they are all three partners in the house of Wright Brooks and Company, and they are all three ineligible from the fact of their being large holders of slaves — added to which Mr Wright was a notorious slave trader in former years. Doctor Forbes assures me that he does not possess any slaves.[15]

Clarke's scruples were not shared by all British officials in Havana, however. Both of the British Judges on the Mixed Court for the Suppression of

---

13   ANC, FGSC, 845/28385; and Paquette, *Sugar is Made with Blood*, p. 152.
14   Paquette, *Sugar is Made with Blood*, p. 155.
15   PRO, FO 72/634 — Letter no. 25 of Charles Clarke to Earl of Aberdeen (Foreign Office), Santiago de Cuba, 12 December, 1843.

the Slave Trade — James Kennedy and Campbell James Dalrymple — were known to have hired, on terms similar to those of slaves, the very people they had themselves emancipated. The wife of Charles Tolmé — Turnbull's predecessor as consul — owned sugar plantations run by slaves, and the family had slaves as domestic servants,[16] as did George Canning Backhouse, judge on the mixed court in the 1850s.[17]

This might seem potentially to have discredited the abolition stance of the British. However, simple ownership of slaves in Cuba at this time was unlikely to have attracted much attention, other than from the staunchest of abolitionists.

> In Cuba everybody had slaves, from the most exalted peninsular monopoliser of commercial lines in the export and import market, to the neediest widow barely owner of a tiny living space known as an outhouse in any of the periferical quarters of Havana or Santiago de Cuba. Slaves were owned by the whites, the mulattos, the blacks and the Chinese. They were owned by artisans and peasants; laymen, clerics, freemasons and *abakuá*. Separatists, annexationists, autonomists and integrationists. Nobody escaped for the simple reason that in order to live within a slave society one had to have slaves.[18]

The British in Cuba were no exception to this. Such merchants and landowners of British descent as the Drakes in the west and the Brooks in the east certainly relied upon slave labour on their plantations, or in the copper mines, and made no apology for this. Middle class Britons such as Charles Bourlier, 'a British subject who died at Casa Blanca in the summer of 1834', likewise possessed slaves. The British consul provided a list of belongings that Bourlier left on his death:

> 512 pesos two reals in cash, four pairs of razors, two dozen penknives, one sailor watch and twenty slaves; all regarded as property by the laws of this country.[19]

Even working class British residents had slaves. In 1841 Mary Gallagher, a British washerwoman resident in Havana, was caught up in an official extortion scam concerning her young African slave, Enrique.[20] When George Decker, a carpenter from Jamaica, died in Santiago de Cuba in 1836, the little property he left, with a total value of just $311, included a slave.[21]

16   Paquette, *Sugar is Made with Blood*, pp. 144–5.
17   Luis Martínez-Fernández, *Fighting Slavery in the Caribbean: The Life and Times of a British Family in Nineteenth Century Havana* (New York, 1998).
18   Joel James Figarola, 'La Cuba profunda y la religiosidad popular,' in *La Gaceta de Cuba*, no. 5 (September–October 1998), p. 9 [current author's translation].
19   ANC, FGSC, 840/28245.
20   ANC, FGSC, 844/28326.
21   PRO, FO 72/888.

The importance of the kidnapped Caribbeans, however, was not so much that they were slaves but that they were technically British. As such, the British authorities could claim jurisdiction over them; and since slavery was now illegal in the British territories, they could declare their servitude in Cuba as likewise illegal and deserving of their attention. In the process, the spotlight was placed on the continued existence, under Spanish auspices, of slavery and the slave trade in Cuba. This gave an impetus to abolitionist tendencies in the peninsula and put pressure on the Spanish Government to correct at least the most exposed abuses.[22] Even if their representatives on the island were frequently unsympathetic to the plight of the kidnap victims, orders generally in the end came down from Madrid to secure the freedom of the individuals concerned, the investigation of how they came to be brought into Cuba and their safe return to their homelands.[23] In this sense the kidnapped Caribbeans were something of a weak link in the edifice of the slave system. Their presence provided a way in for those who, like David Turnbull, were intent on bringing the whole structure down.

Free Black British Subjects

In the hysteria that followed the Escalera conspiracy in 1844, Andrew J. Dodge, a free British subject 'of colour' born in Providence and educated as a dentist in London, came under suspicion of complicity. Dodge had been practising his profession for many years, first in Havana and subsequently in Matanzas, 'with notable success and fortune'. He was married to Gabriela Pimienta, sister of Santiago Pimienta, one of the free coloured leaders of the conspiracy. Naturally, considering the scenes of extreme violence that accompanied the investigation, Dodge denied any involvement, or knowledge, of the planned uprising, writing to the local authorities:

> If you believe ... that an honourable man, father of a family, who has in no way, directly or indirectly, taken part in what he has been accused of, which would go against his interests, purely for being coloured, cannot live in the island of Cuba, then I will board a ship and forever leave this country. You decide ...

Far from being allowed simply to leave, Dodge was arrested four days later, whipped until almost dead, but saved so that he could be shot a month later along with his brother-in-law and others accused.[24] He was sentenced to be shot in the back and have his head mutilated for being part of the

22 See Schmidt-Nowara, *Empire and Antislavery*.
23 This occurred, for example, in the protracted case of 'the unfortunate Wellington'. See ANC, FGSC, 844/28360.
24 Jorge Quintana, *Indice de extrangeros en el Ejército Libertador de Cuba (1895–1898)*, tomo I (Havana, 1953), pp. 190–92 [current author's translation].

organising junta of the uprising and designated ambassador 'without doubt for his knowledge of English and French, and good manners'.[25]

Although such rebellion as occurred in 1843 was largely limited to numerous slave uprisings, when it came to the repression of 1844 some 2,187 of the 3,066 processed by the Matanzas Military Commission were free coloureds.[26] Of course, many of the slaves involved would never have made it to even the pretence of a trial. Whether shot, summarily punished or even protected by owners keen to limit the financial damage suffered by them at a time of rising slave prices, they were far less likely to be brought formally before the authorities. Nevertheless, the extent of the attack made on the free coloured population is staggering, especially considering that the plans of the organisers for a general uprising never came to fruition and that they themselves continually postponed their implementation.[27] By 1844, though, rumours abounded concerning the imminence of the conspiracy. William Norwood, a North American visiting the Mount Vernon Estate near Matanzas, wrote in his diary about a plot to poison the white population with arsenic:

> An attempt was ... made to poison the whole garrison of 8000. The bread is all furnished them by one bakery and the Negroes who work in the establishment had poisoned it all. The fact was discovered just before the bread was to have been sent to the barracks ... Another attempt was made yesterday to poison one of the first families of the city by putting arsenic in their soup. The dose was so strong that it was tasted by the first of the family who tasted the soup and one mouthful made her sick.[28]

Apocryphal as this might sound, such gossip had a profound effect upon many, and helped generate a level of racial fear that found its outlet in the extremity of the punishments meted out to those who were thought to be implicated.

25   ANC, Fondo Asuntos Políticos, 140/26.
26   Paquette, *Sugar is Made with Blood*, p.229. The number of free coloureds accused of involvement is particularly striking considering that in 1841 there was a total of just 6,344 living in Matanzas province (Laird W. Bergad, *Cuban Rural Society in the Nineteenth Century: The Social and Economic History of Monoculture in Matanzas* (Princeton, NJ, 1990, p. 34). Although some of those processed came from outside the province, the majority didn't. Thus, as many as one in three free coloureds in Matanzas came under suspicion.
27   PRO, FO 72/634. The scale of the repression is all the more staggering considering the relatively small size of the free coloured population. In 1841, free coloureds represented just 4.3 per cent of the total population of Matanzas province — though almost half of them were concentrated in the city of Matanzas, where their presence would have been considerably more visible (15.9 per cent of the total population) (Bergad, *Cuban Rural Society*, p. 34).
28   William Norwood, diary, 9–14 April 1844, cited by Paquette, *Sugar is Made with Blood*, pp. 222–3.

There was, among the Cuban white elite, an almost instinctive fear of the black population. This was consciously exploited by the Spanish authorities, who saw this as a means of maintaining control of the island and preventing attempts at independence on the part of the whites. Far from feeling that the events of 1843 and 1844 demonstrated the necessity to reduce the proportion of blacks and mulattos in the population of Cuba — as was being argued by many white creoles[29] — Captain General O'Donnell felt that:

> The day that [whites] become more numerous than blacks and the balance between the castes is broken, the security of keeping the integrity of the territory [Cuba], and its dependence upon the metropolis, will end.[30]

Although the proportion of whites in the population was slowly increasing, in the 1840s it still stood at around just 47 per cent.[31] The Spanish used this effectively to create a racialised distance within the Cuban population. By characterising popular discontent as being specifically black, and throwing up the spectre of Haiti, they succeeded in depriving the nascent independence and abolition movements of a unity of purpose, sowing divisions that would lead to the collapse of such opposition. This was a strategy that continued to be used throughout the century, with particularly good effect during the Ten Years War (1868–78) and the Guerra Chiquita (1879–80), and with somewhat less success in the 1895–98 War of Independence.[32] In the case of the Escalera, although the conspiracy had originally been conceived as a cross-race movement that would combine both the abolition and the independence platforms, as 1843 progressed those influential whites, such as Domingo del Monte, who had been close to David Turnbull and possibly involved in the plot, turned against the plans.

It was not just a question of colour that generated the elite white fear of the free coloured population, but of the feared challenge to the power that was attached to colour. While slaves could be beaten into submission, free blacks and mulattos were coming to occupy important positions in society. At a time when the skilled trades were becoming increasingly crucial to the functioning of the Cuban economy, white Cubans appeared to be reluctant to enter such occupations, leading to a disproportionate number of free people of colour becoming carpenters, masons, blacksmiths,

---

29   See, in particular, the writings of José Antonio Saco and Domingo del Monte: prime promoters of white colonisation.
30   Leopoldo O'Donnell, 'Confidential Report to the Spanish State Secretary, 1845,' cited by Joan Casanovas, *Bread, or Bullets! Urban Labour and Spanish Colonialism, 1850–1898* (Pittsburgh, 1998), p. 50.
31   *Cuadro estadístico de la siempre fiel Isla de Cuba*, 1847.
32   See Ada Ferrer, *Insurgent Cuba: Race, Nation, and Revolution, 1868–1898* (Chapel Hill, 1999).

miners or mechanics.[33] This burgeoning black artisan class provoked fear amongst the white Cuban elite:

> [A]mong the enormous evils that this miserable race [the free coloureds] has brought to our land, one of them is that of having sep-arated our white population from the skilled trades.[34]

Attempts were made to prevent any possible independence of action on the part of such skilled workers and place them under white control, through such legal mechanisms as the apprentice system that forced indentureship upon many young workers.[35] However, the same methods that had sought to keep blacks and whites apart and prevent them from organising together also led to the emergence of underground, predominantly black societies, such as the Abakuá, that provided a potential organising ground for insur-rection. Among the measures taken by Captain General O'Donnell follow-ing the uncovering of the conspiracy in 1844 was the banning of such inde-pendent black organisations as the African cabildos, and even the disband-ing of the Free Coloured Militia (*batallones de pardos y morenos*) amid claims that these had been actively involved in the planned uprising.[36]

There was more than an element of settling accounts in the repression of the Escalera. Prominent free black intellectuals were particularly targeted. Gabriel de la Concepción Valdés — known, through his writing, as Plácido — was tried and executed as one of the leaders of the planned rebellion. Another free black writer, Juan Francisco Manzano, was likewise arrested, and was fortunate to escape with his life. Both writers had been part of the intellectual circle surrounding Domingo del Monte. Free coloured profes-sionals, like Andrew Dodge, were also regarded as especially suspect, though it may have been more than coincidence that white professionals were able to move into the gap that their elimination achieved.[37]

However much scapegoating might have gone on in 1844, it neverthe-less seems undeniable that there was a conspiracy afoot. It may be ques-tioned just how much of a threat this conspiracy really was and the extent to which those involved in the organising committees were genuinely con-trolling the outbursts of slave rebellion that were occurring. Yet they cer-tainly seem to have considered themselves to have been leaders of a forth-coming revolution, if the information given to the Crawford by Juan Rodríguez can be trusted:

> ... they reckon upon their inaccessibility, the approach of the rainy sea-son, consequent sickness amongst the troops from exposure in such a

33   Paquette, *Sugar is Made with Blood*, pp. 106–07.
34   José Antonio Saco, cited by Paquette, *Sugar is Made with Blood*, p. 119.
35   Joan Casanovas, *Bread, or Bullets!*, p. 58.
36   *Ibid.*, p. 48.
37   Paquette, *Sugar is Made with Blood*, p. 234.

climate and the impassable state of the inland roads as well as the distracted attention of the military to so many points, enabling them to hold out until sympathy shall bring them assistance from abroad.[38]

Though such help — promised as it had been by Turnbull — was never forthcoming, free coloureds with foreign links were prominent in the organisation of the conspiracy. According to Charles Clarke (British consul in Santiago de Cuba) only three people were arrested in that part of the island in connection with the planned uprising. Although none of them was British, all three were coloured and only one was native to Cuba. There was a dentist from the United States, a Spanish boot-maker implicated in earlier insurrections and a creole carpenter. The latter, although born in Cuba, was of French descent and appears to have been 'speaking chiefly that language'. All three were sent by the governor to Havana for trial.[39]

It is hard to discern exactly how many free black British subjects were resident in Cuba in the 1840s. The censuses of the time only made distinctions by national origin for whites: all blacks and coloureds being grouped together with only the distinction of whether free or slave being expressed in the official statistics.[40] It is unlikely, however, that there were many. Charles Clarke only knew of two or three in the whole of Santiago de Cuba and its environs — and they had been resident in Cuba for so long that he thought it doubtful that 'any of them would be considered as British subjects by the authorities'.[41] Although Crawford felt that 'from the whole Island there must be many'; he himself only knew of a few living in Havana, where the total free foreign black population did not exceed 100.[42] Nevertheless, as with the kidnapped Caribbeans amongst the slaves, their importance may be seen as lying not so much in their numerical strength as in their role as catalysts amongst the free blacks of Cuba. Partly this might have been through the introduction of ideas — whether revolutionary, liberal or anti-slavery — and the sharing of such ideas and experiences with those among whom they lived and worked. Certainly the authorities considered this to have been a threat, as Captain General O'Donnell expressed:

38   PRO, FO 72/634 — Confidential letter from Joseph T. Crawford to Earl of Aberdeen, Havana, 22 May 1843.
39   PRO, FO 72/662 — Memorandum sent by British consul Charles Clarke to the Foreign Office, 3 July 1844.
40   *Cuadro Estadístico de la siempre fiel Isla de Cuba*, 1847.
41   PRO, FO 72/662 — Memorandum sent by British consul Charles Clarke to the Foreign Office, 3 July 1844.
42   PRO, FO 72/664 — Letter no. 9 of Joseph T. Crawford to Earl of Aberdeen, 8 May 1844. There is a problem in accounting for free foreign blacks, since many who originated outside Cuba may have been considered naturalised due to their length of residency in the island.

> For the security of this island, it is necessary to bear in mind that a mul-
> titude of men, schooled in revolutions and many of them in crimes ...
> seek refuge and take shelter [here].[43]

Free black British subjects also played a more clearly active role in the
organisation of the conspiracy than just as members of a more general
milieu. In 1837 a military commission tried a coloured Briton 'on the suspicion of having diffused pernicious doctrines'.[44] In 1842 Joseph Mitchell
was arrested in the island 'having been employed in the dissemination of
discontent and insurrection amongst the slaves'. Initially sentenced to
death, he subsequently had this commuted 'to labour on the public works
... of this Island for life'. Although Mitchell originally claimed to be
Jamaican, it subsequently turned out that he was African by birth, and had
been the slave of the Mitchell family (where is not clear), from whom he
had purchased his freedom. He was clearly working as part of a network
of abolition agents and organisers of rebellion. Letters of three other
black British subjects were found on him upon his arrest. These individuals had returned to Jamaica in January 1842, with passports acquired in a
less than legal way by David Turnbull, only to re-enter Cuba surreptitiously later that year. It would seem that the letters found on Mitchell's person
were sufficiently incriminating to secure their arrest.[45]

   Whatever the real threat that such free black British represented, the perceived threat was sufficient to warrant Captain General O'Donnell passing a
law in 1844 that called for the expulsion of all 'male, adult, foreign-born, free
people of color' from Cuba.[46] Although many of them had been living fully
integrated lives in the island, they were given just 15 days to sell their property, make arrangements for their families and get out — or else face being
transported to the Isle of Pines.[47] Subsequent entry of free persons of
colour and emancipated slaves also became prohibited by a royal order.[48]

Migrant British Machinists

In 1857 James Mather of Montrose — a Scottish machinist in the 'El
Destino' sugar mill near Corralillo (Las Villas province) — was imprisoned
in Puerto Príncipe 'for having attempted ... to commit suicide'. This
occurred just after the conclusion of the sugar harvest when he would

43   Letter of Leopoldo O'Donnell to the Spanish secretary of state, 28 February 1844,
     cited in Paquette, *Sugar is Made with Blood*, p. 116.
44   *Diario de la Habana*, 25 July 1840, cited in Paquette, *Sugar is Made with Blood*, p. 126.
45   PRO, FO 72/634 — Letter no. 20 of Joseph T. Crawford to the Earl of Aberdeen
     (Foreign Office), Havana, 5 May 1843.
46   Paquette, *Sugar is Made with Blood*, p. 228.
47   ANC, FGSC, 850/28634.
48   Paquette, *Sugar is Made with Blood*, p. 228.

have been in a very good financial position. Indeed, it seems that he had just been paid around $800 for his work, and had more money saved. He also owned a gold watch and two gold chains.

> It appears that this unhappy man had on other occasions shown signs of dementia, despite being a well-ordered person and of good customs. It is not known what the motive for such an act might be since it is known from his colleagues and countrymen that this individual was living in good circumstances.[49]

On the consul's intervention, Mather was released and returned home to his family in Scotland.

Whatever led Mather to the extremity of seeking to take his own life, he was just one among many British machinists who took up residency in Cuba during the middle years of the nineteenth century. Most of these found themselves working in sugar mills that were being revolutionised by the introduction of steam machinery made by such British engineering companies as Fawcett Preston of Liverpool. Since at this time there was a severe lack of workers in Cuba possessing the necessary expertise to operate and maintain these engines and related machines, there was a need to promote the immigration of such artisans. In 1840, it was commented in the Sociedad Económica in Havana that:

> ... every mill, every steam ship, every locomotive on the railway has to have beside it an intelligent foreigner who directs and inspects the machine ... Little does it matter that they are foreigners ... on the contrary, it is of benefit for us to acquire individuals who augment ... our white population.[50]

With the production of the sugar plantations depending upon the efficient operation of the steam engines and machines, and with the lack, until later in the century, of Cubans with the necessary skills, the foreign machinists were greatly respected and did not suffer the same exploitation that other workers could expect. Following his visit to a plantation, the US artist and writer Samuel Hazard wrote:

> The 'maquinista', or engineer, is really the most important man upon the place, as upon him depend the grinding of the cane and the care of the mills and its machinery ... [51]

49   ANC, FGSC, 1032/35719.
50   *Memorias de la Sociedad Económica*, tomo IX (1840), p. 240 [current author's translation].
51   Samuel Hazard, *Cuba with Pen and Pencil* (Hartford, 1871), reproduced as an extract in Louis A. Pérez, *Slaves, Sugar and Colonial Society: Travel Accounts of Cuba, 1801–1899* (Wilmington, Delaware, 1992), p. 75.

They could expect to receive a special house and even a couple of slaves to look after their personal needs.[52] As for their salaries, these were extremely high:

> The salaries of engineers upon estates worked in the old-fashioned manner, average about one hundred and twenty dollars a month during the grinding season. But [the new] machinery is conducted by persons of superior capacity, who are tempted hither from Europe or America by the offer of permanent situations or much higher salaries. Four or five such persons must be maintained upon a large estate.[53]

This compares very favourably even with other migrant British workers in Cuba. For example, many of the Cornish miners working in the copper mines at El Cobre, near Santiago de Cuba, were earning as little as US$ 30 a month.[54]

The British population in Cuba, while never being numerically large, grew rapidly during the middle years of the nineteenth century. According to available censuses, from numbering just 327 in 1841, by 1846 there were some 605. By 1862 this figure had doubled again to 1,244 — the overwhelming majority of whom were living in the booming sugar districts of Havana and Matanzas.[55] Cuban immigration records giving details of foreigners seeking to domicile themselves in the island during the 1840s suggest that at least half of this growth in numbers was due to the arrival of machinists.[56]

When the Spanish authorities began to uncover the apparently extensive conspiracy for uprising in 1843 and 1844 a significant number of the 96 whites who came to be tried by the military commission in Matanzas were British.[57] Of these, the majority were machinists or engineers working in the sugar mills. Henry Elkins was the machinist on one plantation near Cárdenas. Following the discovery of a plot to rise up among the field slaves of the estate, he was implicated in the conspiracy as a result of evidence forced from one of those captured. Officials went to his home to seize him, and then searched the house for incriminating papers, even carrying out a body search of his wife. He was then taken to the prison in

52   Manuel Moreno Fraginals, *El ingenio*, tomo I (Havana, 1978), p. 306.
53   William Henry Hurlbert, *Gan-Eden; or Picture of Cuba* (Boston, 1854), reproduced as an extract in Pérez, *Slaves, Sugar and Colonial Society*, p. 57.
54   PRO, FO 72/634 — Letter of Charles Clarke to Joseph T. Crawford, Santiago de Cuba, 27 April 1843.
55   *Memorias de la Sociedad Económica*, 1844; *Cuadro Estadístico de la siempre fiel Isla de Cuba*, 1847; Armildez de Toledo, *Noticias estadísticas de la Isla de Cuba en 1862*. For a general history of British migration to Cuba in the nineteenth century, see Jonathan Curry-Machado, *Running from Albion: British Migrants in Nineteenth Century Cuba*, unpublished MRes thesis, University of North London (1999).
56   ANC, ML, 11910.
57   Paquette, *Sugar is Made with Blood*, pp. 224 and 229; also PRO, FO 72/664.

Cárdenas to await his transferral to Matanzas, where the Commission was meeting. Following his arrest, all the slaves of the engine house (who had previously not been implicated in the unrest) were imprisoned and crudely interrogated as to what other foreigners they had seen in the company of Elkins. It seems he had been regularly visited by other British machinists from neighbouring plantations, among them Daniel Downing and Robert Hiton. These too were arrested, and taken to Cárdenas where they were kept for several weeks bound by irons and in the stocks, in appalling conditions:

> ... the dimentions [sic] of their prison are so limited that no more than the one half can sleep at the same time, and this in a West India climate where the heat ranges 85 degrees and upwards, and with the addition of the animal effluvia that is exhaled from such a number of human bodys [sic], this appears to me only a second edition of the Black Hole of Calcutta. It may be more slow, but it is equally as certain as the English that suffered in the former place.[58]

In the end, they were all released, following vociferous complaints by the British government to the Spanish government in Madrid.[59]

It has been suggested that such men 'had the misfortune of being caught in the wrong place by the wrong person at the wrong time'.[60] It could be that they were just the victims of the Anglophobia that was sweeping Cuba, largely provoked by the abolitionist activities of Turnbull and his associates, and fed by threats such as 'that here one hundred thousand men have sworn to assassinate every living Englishman the moment England obtains a blank check in the business of our slavery'.[61] They might have also fallen victim to similar jealousies as those suffered by free blacks who were occupying skilled trades. That the sugar producers found themselves so dependent upon foreign machinists to keep production going, and enable it to expand, came to be seen as a cause for some concern by many of the white elite. In 1843 strong protests were made against foreign artisans who refused to train local apprentices.[62] Machinists in railway workshops and sugar mills were often contractually bound to pass on their skills, with a view to the island eventually becoming self-sufficient in such workers.

---

58 PRO, FO 72/664 — Copy of letter from William Sim to Joseph T. Crawford, Matanzas, 31 May 1844.
59 A large amount of the correspondence between the British consul general in Havana and the Foreign Office in 1844 related to the imprisonment of British subjects implicated in the Escalera, and includes statements made by the prisoners themselves (PRO, FO 72/664).
60 Paquette, *Sugar is Made with Blood*, p. 234.
61 Gaspar Betancourt Cisneros to Domingo del Monte, 30 March 1841, cited in Paquette, *Sugar is Made with Blood*, p. 140.
62 *Memorias de la Sociedad Económica*, tomo XVI (1843), p. 7 and pp. 228–9.

Nevertheless, there is some evidence of radical political attitudes, and even militancy, among many of the British working class migrants in Cuba. In 1841, James Joyce — an Englishman at that time engaged in logging near Cienfuegos — was arrested and charged with sedition. It appears that during a conversation in a bar one night he suggested that 'within four months … the whole of the island of Cuba was bound to be English, and that all the blacks would be free'.[63] In 1853, a British machinist on the San Lorenzo Estate found himself in prison on similar charges in Matanzas:

> Said Mr James Daykin, it appears, was present at the Baptism of the child of a carpenter his friend, who resides at Canasí, and when the parties were about to retire, somebody present called out 'viva el cura' upon which the said Daykin was arrested.

No doubt the cry had been mistaken for '*Viva Cuba*', or some such statement of Cuban nationalism, though it would seem peculiar to lay the blame upon an Englishman unless there existed some more substantial motive to suspect that he might have been in some way complicitous with such sentiments.[64] During 1843, at the height of the slave uprisings in the west, a group of British miners in El Cobre, near Santiago de Cuba, was thrown into prison for having gone on strike demanding higher wages. Though their dispute was with a British company (the Royal Santiago Mining Company), their action seems to have had an influence on miners throughout the district. It possibly represents one of the first instances of industrial militancy on the island.[65]

Catalysts in the Crucible

In the mid-nineteenth century Cuba was a highly race-polarised society. At the same time that they sought to maintain the numerical supremacy of the black and coloured population over the whites, the Spanish also sought to keep the races carefully segregated. Whites could not join black popular organisations, or vice versa. Even Cuban-born blacks were prevented from joining native African *cabildos* until much later in the century, and white Cubans found themselves excluded from *peninsular*-dominated associations.[66] If the Spanish limited the access to political power that elite white creoles might expect, these latter generally did all they could to prevent the encroachment on their space of the black and coloured population. Domingo del Monte might have counted the black writers Plácido and Manzano within his entourage, but they were accepted on white, rather

63   ANC, FGSC, 846/28418.
64   ANC, FGSC, 857/28958.
65   PRO, FO 72/634.
66   Casanovas, *Bread, or Bullets!*, p. 56.

than black, terms. Though del Monte was forced to leave Cuba following the uncovering of the Escalera conspiracy, he appears to have done all he could to separate himself from the planned uprising. Meanwhile, Manzano was imprisoned and Plácido executed.

Most people, if not everyone, living in such a racially-divided country as Cuba, in which a large proportion of the black population was enslaved, would be likely to have internalised much of the racism inherent in such a system. However, it was also a highly class-divided society. While much of this could be described along race lines (all the elite groups were white, while popular groups were disproportionately black), such a division was by no means absolute. White workers might have obtained some advantage from the colour of their skin, and some may have felt racial prejudice against blacks, but 'in a basically slave society the free worker tends not to remain as such'.[67] The reality of the situation in which most of these workers found themselves was such as to assist, despite the dominant culture, the formation of a class identity that went across racial barriers. White workers in city workshops could expect to be working alongside not just free blacks but also hired slaves and indentured labourers. This would have had the tendency of depressing wages, and hence leading to white working class abolitionism; but also of creating the basis for the development of a common understanding between whites and blacks. As was stated in an official report from Cienfuegos in 1860: 'the white proletariat treats the coloured class on a completely equal footing'.[68]

This process was one in which the three groups discussed here played an important, if somewhat invisible, part. Although they could all lay claim to being British subjects, and hence receive the support of the British authorities should they find themselves in trouble in Cuba, the link between them was not through a shared national identity. There was little immediately in common between a white machinist from Liverpool or Glasgow and a Jamaican ex-slave kidnapped from Montego Bay. However, through their inclusion in the melting pot of racial and ethnic identities that was the Cuban working class, they were important in helping to bridge the divides that existed between slaves and free workers, blacks and whites.

While the kidnapped Caribbeans certainly provided a justification for the abolitionist activities of Turnbull and others, to portray them in this light is to suggest that they were little more than victims, passively providing honourable white men with an excuse for combating slavery. Their importance, and the danger they represented to the Spanish authorities and Cuban elite, was somewhat greater than this. Though relatively few in number, their presence would have been provocative. Of course, no slave

---

67   Julio Le Riverend, *Economic History of Cuba* (Havana, 1967), p. 158; cited in Casanovas, *Bread, or Bullets!*, p. 56.

68   Cited in Casanovas, *Bread, or Bullets!*, p. 62.

was unaware of the servile condition in which they were being kept. While not all would have been prepared to rise up in violent rebellion, most were increasingly engaged in small, everyday acts of subversion of the system. This might range from managing to save sufficient money to be able to purchase their manumission, through carving out a space for themselves within the plantation or city in which — whether through growing their own crops or earning a small amount in wages — they could acquire this money; to acts of direct insubordination, rebellion or escape.[69] To have in their midst individuals who had been brought from neighbouring islands, where slave emancipation had occurred only recently and who had tasted the fruits of freedom, may well have acted as a catalyst. Certainly the kidnapped Caribbeans did not create the conditions whereby an open challenge would be made by slaves to the society and system that had enslaved them. Those conditions were already present in abundance; and their numbers were probably not sufficient to, in themselves, cause an uprising. Nevertheless, they could be seen as an important part of the spark that ignited the Cuban slaves in the events of 1843.[70]

In addition to this catalytic role they also helped to reveal that the division between slave and so-called free worker was not as categorical as has generally been assumed. They may have begun their life as slaves in, for example, Jamaica. They were then emancipated, a process which often involved passing through a period of semi-free labour, to subsequently become free workers or peasants. They were then captured and sold once more into slavery in Cuba. If they were fortunate, as the 'unfortunate' Wellington finally was, to be found, they might then be once again freed, and returned whence they came. For them, the boundary between slave and wage labour was clearly precarious. They were living evidence for Cuban slaves of how possible emancipation might be; but at the same time, their present condition reminded free blacks of how close they continued to be to that servile state they had supposedly escaped from.

As has been shown, free British blacks played a prominent part in the events surrounding the Escalera conspiracy and were in some instances directly implicated. They also helped to bridge something of the gap between the black and white populations. Some had been trained in professions in Britain, British colonies or North America — such as the dentists Andrew Dodge and Charles Blackley — and were therefore able to occupy positions that were more normally the preserve of whites. Excluded from providing services to the white elite, they would be in a position to provide some medical assistance to those who were otherwise

69   See Rebecca J. Scott, *Slave Emancipation in Cuba: The Transition to Free Labour, 1860–1895* (Princeton, 1985).

70   This hypothesis remains to be tested to see what correlation there was between presence of kidnapped Caribbeans on a particular plantation and the incidence there of rebellion or other acts of subversion and insubordination.

unable to obtain it. This would have been not just other blacks, but also working class whites. Many of the free black British were artisans and would have participated in the developing cross-race atmosphere of the urban workshops. At a time when white Cubans appear to have resisted participation in the mechanical trades, and white Spanish were largely unskilled in such occupations, with the resultant arrival of many foreign white workers, in particular from Britain and North America: as English-speakers, the free British blacks would have been in a position to help bridge such racial gap as existed.

Many of the migrant white workers, and in particular the machinists bound for the sugar plantations, came from the industrial cities of Britain at a time when the British working class was consolidating a militant class identity. The 1840s was the decade of the Chartist movement; and these were workers who were members of one of the most organised and politically conscious sections of the working class at that time. Abolitionism was not just a middle class preserve. There had for a long time been an awareness of a certain common cause between the African chattel slave and the European wage slave.[71] Machinists such as Daniel Downing and Robert Hiton had only arrived the previous year — 1843.[72] Even if they were not formally agents of the Anti-Slavery Society, and in fact innocent of the charges levelled against them in 1844, it would be surprising if they did not bring many of these deeply held attitudes with them, and come to play some kind of role in the emergence of oppositional movements in Cuba.

As was the case with both the kidnapped Caribbeans and the free black British subjects, it could be argued that, while never numerous, these British workers acted as a catalyst in the heated environment of the sugar plantations and cities of Havana and Matanzas in the early 1840s. As with the other two groups this would partly have been through the simple communication of alternative ideas and experiences. There also existed the likelihood of at least some of them having been in communication with David Turnbull, in particular when the latter was touring plantations ostensibly searching for those who were wrongfully held as slaves, while (if the accusations are to be believed) actually helping to organise an uprising. They were certainly accused of this by the military commission in 1844.[73]

However, their presence was catalytic in ways that were much further-reaching than simple participation in an aborted revolution. Their presence may well have played a crucial part in the overcoming of racial differences within the Cuban working class. The machinist in the engine house of a mill could not do all the work himself. As a result there would be a team of assistants, made up of white and free coloured wage work-

71 See Robin Blackburn, *The Overthrow of Colonial Slavery, 1776–1848* (London, 1988).
72 ANC, ML, 11910.
73 PRO, FO 72/664.

ers, as well as black slaves.[74] In many cases, even the latter could expect to be trained by the machinist. In the 1850s, the North American Richard Dana visited a sugar estate:

> [H]ere an intelligent negro has been taught enough to take charge of the engine when the engineer is off duty. This is the highest post a negro can reach in the mill, and this negro was mightily pleased when I addressed him as maquinista [machinist].[75]

That British (and other foreign) machinists were arrested, imprisoned and tried alongside the slaves in 1844 is perhaps, in the end, testament not so much to the hidden conspiracy that was threatening to overthrow both slavery and Spanish power as to the recognition that here there could be found a potentially dangerous combination. When Julia M. Woodruff visited Cuba in the 1870s, she described a plantation that she was shown around:

> [I]t is a little village within itself, containing church, dwellings, hospital, workshops, storehouses, water works and whatever is necessary to its daily economy. That of Santa Sofía numbers about four hundred souls, of whom not more than a dozen or fifteen are contained in white skins; a disproportion which seems to justify, in a measure, the firearms, whips, chains, locks, gratings, etc., which are so prominent a part of its system ...[76]

Clearly a lot of effort went into keeping the white skilled workers separated from the mass of enslaved blacks. It is to be questioned whether this was for their own protection or to prevent such potentially dangerous communication from occurring.

Whether they were, in the end, segregated — either physically or by virtue of the superior rewards received for their work — or supplanted by the training of indigenous workers, as was the case of the British machinists; expelled and excluded from the island, like the free British blacks; or found, released and returned whence they came, as happened to the kidnapped Caribbeans: the Spanish authorities, and the white Cuban elite, went to a lot of pains to remove the threat represented by these three groups. They received a level of attention at the time that belies their apparent numerical insignificance and reveals the importance that such historical footnotes can have within the wider history. Although not the creators of the social struggles and reality in which they found themselves as a result of their voluntary or forced migration, they were catalysts in the heated crucible that was mid-nineteenth-century Cuba.

74   Moreno Fraginals, *El ingenio*, tomo II, p. 37
75   Richard Henry Dana, Jr, *To Cuba and Back: A Vacation Voyage* (Boston, 1859), cited in Pérez, *Slaves, Sugar and Colonial Society*, p. 63.
76   W.M.L. Jay, *My Winter in Cuba* (New York, 1871), cited in Pérez, *Slaves, Sugar and Colonial Society*, p. 70.

CHAPTER 7

Antislavery and Abolitionism: Thinkers and Doers in Imperial Brazil

Nancy Priscilla Naro

razil was the last country in the Americas to abolish chattel slavery and enable some 700,000 captives to embrace freedom and citizenship. This chapter explores the process of the transition from slave to free labour, beginning with immediate post-Independence moves in favour of equality for all citizens. As the emancipation movement was advanced in official and in informal ways by antislavery proponents, abolitionists, sympathisers and by slaves themselves, it is argued that the ideal of equality for all citizens was compromised in the face of concerns on the part of the State to preserve national unity and to safeguard the monarchy. This chapter highlights the role of the Brazilian State in defining the trajectory from 'slave to citizen', drawing on comparisons with the transition processes in the United States and in Cuba. It is observed that Brazil avoided the United States-style civil war and the subsequent constitutional guarantees of basic rights of citizenship that were grounded in law but ignored in practice. Yet, despite similarities in the gradual nature of the Brazilian and Cuban transition processes, it is argued that the important link between national unity and antiracism that was so vital to the Cuban independence-cum-abolitionist struggles was not paralleled in the Brazilian case. The chapter concludes with considerations about citizenship in post-emancipation Brazil and finds that whereas a pro-slavery bargaining stance served the State as a means to assure national unity during the monarchy, the 1850s and subsequent legislation governed a transition to citizenship that was compromised in the rigid and exclusive social hierarchy that re-enforced inequality and racial exclusion.

Fledgling Unity, Conflicting Agendas: Independence and Beyond

Brazilian slavery provided a mainstay for a plantation complex that lasted more than three centuries without engulfing the country as a whole in a civil war, pervasive slave resistance or long-standing public antislavery debate.[1] At the time of Brazil's Independence, the slave population was

---

1   Antislavery views defined a 'generalized posture of opposition to slavery that did not necessarily look forward and fight for abolition'. Celia Marinho de Azevedo, *Abolitionism in the United States and Brazil. A Comparative Perspective* (New York, 1995), p. xxiv.

among the largest in the Americas, as was the population of freed slaves. The acclaimed father of Independence, José Bonifacio de Andrada e Silva, sub-divided the country's total population of approximately 4,000,000 people into the following categories: 843,000 white, 426,000 free people of colour and 159,500 free blacks, for a total of 1,687,900 free persons and 300,000 civilised Indians.[2] Bonifacio numbered the black slave population at 1,728,000 souls; to this figure he added 202,000 mulatto slaves that brought the total slave population to 1,930,000.[3]

Bonifacio's figures confirm the blend of many nations of Africa, indigenous peoples and European colonisers who forged Brazil's complex mixed racial and ethnic identity. Sixty three per cent of Brazil's population, or 2,515,500, was non-white at the time of Independence, a figure that is compatible with Cuba where, in 1827, the colonial free and slave non-white population totalled 393,440, or 56 per cent of a total population of 704,491.[4] The non-white population continued to exceed the white population for the rest of the century in the two societies and in that respect they provide a significant contrast to the United States where a white majority prevailed during and after the 1807 suspension of imports of captive African labour.[5]

In 1823 José Bonifacio warned leaders of Brazil's complex ethnic and racial legacy that, short of becoming a homogeneous nation, 'Brazil would never be truly free, respectable, and happy'.[6] According to Bonifacio, if Brazil's indigenous population was incorporated into society, the enslave-

2   José Bonifacio D'Andrada e Silva, *Memoir Addressed to the General, Constituent and Legislative Assembly of the Empire of Brazil*, translated from the Portuguese by William Walton (London, 1836), p.v. Some of José Bonifacio's data are missing or were misprinted: the correct total is 1,428,500. His figures for the indigenous population were incomplete, owing in part to the vast unexplored depths of territory where the size and distribution of the Indian population was unknown at the time.

3   Bonifacio, *Memoir*, p.v. The heaviest concentrations of slaves were in five of the 18 provinces — Maranhão, Pernambuco, Bahia, Minas Gerais and Rio de Janeiro, where the plantation complex concentrated production of sugarcane, coffee and tobacco. In Minas Gerais, mining of semi-precious minerals in addition to agriculture provided the bases for export and supply to internal markets. The figures in Leslie Bethell (ed.), *Brazil: Empire and Republic, 1822–1930* (Cambridge, 1989), pp. 45–6, are a total population of 4–5 million, of which slaves accounted for approximately one third, or 1,147,515; free non-whites for one third; Brazilian Indians for 800,000; and whites for the rest. Matthias Röhrig Assunção and Michael Zuske's population breakdown for 1817–18 are closer to Bonifacio's estimates: slaves represent 50.6 per cent; whites 27.3 per cent; free coloureds, 15.3 per cent; and Indians 6.8 per cent. '"Race", Ethnicity, and Social Structure in 19th Century Brazil and Cuba,' *Ibero-Amerikanisches Archiv. Zeitschrift für Sozialwissenschaften und Geschichte*, vol. 3–4 (1998), unnumbered table, p. 405.

4   Louis A. Pérez, Jr. *Cuba: Between Reform and Revolution* (New York, 1988), Table 9, 'Population (1817–62),' p. 86.

5   For the Cuban free coloured population in a later period, see Table III, 'Cuba's Free Coloured Population by Sex and Age, 1854,' in Jean Stubbs's essay in this collection.

6   Bonifacio, *Memoir*, p. 16

ment of Africans would be unnecessary. Bonifacio proposed improvements to the lives of slaves and envisioned progressive emancipation that would 'convert these immoral beings, as they now are, into useful, active, and moral citizens'.[7] A year later, Bonifacio publicly advocated the abolition of the transatlantic slave trade before the newly independent General, Constituent and Legislative Assembly. In 1825 Bonifacio re-issued his plea to end the transatlantic slave trade and to eventually abolish slavery: 'Generous citizens of Brazil and lovers of your *patria*, you realise that without the complete abolition of the African slave trade, and without the successive emancipation of the present captives, Brazil will never establish its national independence and secure and defend its liberal constitution.'[8] Although many of his views went unheeded after the Emperor Dom Pedro I's closure of the assembly, the measures affecting the transatlantic slave trade were drafted into the text of the Anglo-Brazilian Treaty of 1826.

Outstanding among the liberal principles upon which Brazil's fledgling constitutional monarchy in the tropics posited its political agenda for State formation were the right of citizenship and the right to hold property. Political leadership rested on a colonial legacy that upheld the 'good man' (*o homem bom*), a property-owning male whose suffrage and wealth endowed him with political prominence. Portuguese citizens who remained in Brazil enjoyed the right to be naturalised under the 1824 Constitution. Many vied for political office with Brazilian social elites, military officers and political counsellors, not a few of whom were educated at the University of Coimbra during the colonial period and were conversant with the extensive bureaucracy that included official church and military sectors.[9]

Restrictions on suffrage in the 1824 Constitution suggest that in this blueprint for State formation political rights would not be equally and uniformly enjoyed by all citizens. For Richard Graham the sizeable and growing population of free persons of colour, at least theoretically under the tenets of liberalism and individualism, represented would-be citizens. He argues that the maintenance of a rigid hierarchy based on social distinctions, the *condição* (social standing or condition), 'restrained the threat that freedmen might otherwise pose'.[10] Under the 1824 Constitution, citizens who were eligible for election were distinguished by income and property

---

7   *Ibid.*, p. 34.
8   José Bonifacio, cited in Joaquim Nabuco, *O abolicionismo* (Recife [1883], 1988), p. 45: 'Generosos cidadãos do Brazil, que amais a vossa Patria, sabei que sem a abolição total do infame trafico da escravatura Africana, e sem a emancipação successiva dos actuaes captivos, nunca o Brazil firmará a sua independencia nacional e segurará e defenderá a sua liberal constituição.' Cited in Nabuco, *O abolicionismo*.
9   See José Murilo de Carvalho, *O teatro de sombras: a política imperial* (Rio de Janeiro, 1988) for a detailed study of the Brazilian political elite. Also, Roderick Barman, *Brazil. The Forging of a Nation, 1798–1852* (Stanford, 1988).
10   Graham, 'Free African Brazilians,' pp. 33–4.

ownership from non-active citizens (those who did not meet income requirements to enable them to vote). Furthermore, free Brazilians who were descendants of slaves were eligible to vote in primary elections but not in the second-round elections to parliament. For Graham, 'the provision allowing freedmen to vote, but not to be voted for, publicly affirmed the differentiation between their rank and that of others'.[11]

Advocates for equal rights for freedmen were few and far between among the largely European and Europeanised political elites. Antonio Pereira Rebouças, a black politician from the north-east who rose to prominence as a specialist in civil law and a statesman, was a staunch defender of equal rights for all citizens.[12] Hardly a supporter of abolition in a country where ownership of human property was pervasive among rich, poor and among slaves themselves, Pereira Rebouças focused on the distinction between liberal ideals governing property and those governing freedom. For Pereira Rebouças, citizenship was premised on the free status of the individual and, whether born free or attaining freedom at some time, all citizens should enjoy rights on an equal basis.[13] Popular unrest and glaring economic disparities of a regional nature overshadowed the consideration or even the implementation of Pereira Rebouças's proposals. In the same year as the passage of the 1824 Constitution a six-month long secessionist movement named the Confederation of the Equator Movement engulfed the north-east. Centred in Pernambuco, the leaders protested the Constitution's centralisation of political authority in the imperial Court of Rio de Janeiro. In this and in subsequent demonstrations of popular political agency, underlying class and racial tensions surfaced in protests that challenged the legitimisation of the imperial government. Troop insurrections in the major ports of Salvador, Recife and Rio de Janeiro protested delays in payment, counterfeit coinage, enlistment of foreign mercenaries and Portuguese military command of battalions. For Graham conscription itself reflected a 'State policy based on racism' that disciplined the poor free population and targeted free African Brazilians for forced recruitment into the military.[14] For Hebe Mattos the conscripted free non-whites who made up the troops articulated a collective consciousness of their situation when they appropriated the forum of the streets to demand equality for 'all colours of citizens.'[15] She attributes to the popular protests the government's decision to disband the separate regiments that had previously distinguished whites and freedmen from other non-whites.[16]

11   *Ibid.*, p. 37.
12   On Pereira Rebouças's political ideals, see Hebe Maria Mattos, *Escravidão e cidadania no Brasil monárquico* (Rio de Janeiro, 2000), pp. 40–54. Also, Graham, 'Free African Brazilians,' pp. 42–3.
13   Mattos, *Escravidão*, 40–54, especially, p. 43.
14   Graham, 'Free African Brazilians,' pp. 34–6.
15   Mattos, *Escravidão*, p. 22.
16   *Ibid.*, p. 23; Graham, 'Free African Brazilians,' p. 25.

Slaves also demonstrated political agency through challenges to the 'peculiar institution'. Freedmen and free African Brazilians were strongly implicated as collaborators in such movements, yet the outcome of the struggles rarely engaged widespread popular support for emancipation. Slave rebellions were commonplace in the north-eastern province of Bahia in the 1820s and 1830s, and were met with the exemplary harsh punishment of the leaders and suspected participants in the aborted revolt of Haussá slaves in Salvador, Bahia in 1835.[17] These events heightened planters' concern over the potential disruption that slave revolts posed to the security of private property and the plantation complex and united otherwise disparate regional slave-owning elite factions in support of national regulatory measures to safeguard the property order. The Código de Proceso Criminal of 1832 detailed the legal conditions for repression of slave-motivated rebellion, conspiracy and revolt, the punishments and the sentences for collaborators.[18] Local and provincial elites at the helm of the government, the police, the national guard (created on the model of the French institution in 1831) and the local courts responded individually to government appeals for national unity but actively sought central government assurances to safeguard local autonomy, especially in matters concerning slaves and slavery. In practical terms, the State was acquiescent in a tacit arrangement that left the handling of slave matters to 'plantation justice', the private discretion of the slaveowner.

The size and diversity of Brazil's population and its extensive territory also posed difficulties to central government influence over provincial and local power struggles. Two social movements in the north began as inter-elite struggles that turned into popular warfare involving indigenous peoples and slaves. Before provincial authority was restored, 30,000 pro-government and rebel forces had been killed in the five-year-long Cabanagem movement in the northern province of Pará (1835–40). The second social movement was the Balaiada Civil War in the northern province of Maranhão (1838–41) in which non-white citizens demanded equal rights with white citizens. According to Matthias Röhrig D'Assunção, the movement addressed 'the exclusion of the free poor from political participation and discrimination against the coloured in general and their slave-like treatment in particular'.[19] Common to both movements was widespread popu-

---

17 João José Réis, *Slave Rebellion in Brazil. The Muslim Uprising of 1835 in Bahia* (Baltimore, c. 1993).

18 Murilo de Carvalho, *O teatro de sombras*, pp. 14–15.

19 Matthias Röhrig D'Assunção, 'Popular Culture and Regional Society in Nineteenth-Century Maranhão, Brazil,' *Bulletin of Latin American Research*, vol. 14, no. 3 (1995), p. 281; by the same author, 'Elite Politics and Popular Rebellion in the Construction of Post Colonial Order. The Case of Maranhão, Brazil (1820–1841),' *Journal of Latin American Studies*, vol. 31, no. 1 (1999); Assunção and Zeuske '"Race", Ethnicity, and Social Structure'; Murilo de Carvalho, *O teatro de sombras*, pp. 14–15.

lar furore over perceived Portuguese merchant monopolies over credit, loans, retail and wholesale commerce. Equally, rebels singled out landowners who claimed and controlled large landholdings. For their part, Conservative and Liberal Party members and adherents to local political factions that emerged during the movements blamed the central government for imposing political and judicial outsiders to execute imperial directives that were often at odds with local and regional political agendas. The awesome duration of the two social movements and the death tolls and casualties attest not only to the fragile social fabric but also to the tenuous political power of the State and the fractured commitment of local and regional elites to an ideal of national unity.

Antislave Pressures

Conflictive relations between the provinces and the central government lessened during the Second Empire under Dom Pedro II (1840–89) in the aftermath of liberal opposition movements in Minas Gerais and in São Paulo in 1842, and the *Praieira* Revolt in Pernambuco in 1848.[20] Less easily resolved were tensions surrounding Brazil's continued involvement in the transatlantic slave trade in breach of the 1826 treaty with England that established the termination of the trade within five years. Liberal discourse that fuelled antislavery debates in Great Britain and in France indirectly influenced 1840s British naval blockades of Brazilian ports, the seizure of suspected slave ships on the open seas and the prosecutions of the ships' captains. Leslie Bethell and, latterly, Jeffrey Needell support the view that Brazil's diplomatic relations with the British worsened as British pressures against the transatlantic slave trade became intertwined with British interests in the La Plata region and Britain's own attempt at mediating Brazil's frontier disputes with Uruguay and the Rosas government in Argentina.[21]

Whether it was a result of a diplomatic compromise with Great Britain, the consensus of Brazilian political elites or both of these factors, the official abolition of the transatlantic slave trade that became the Eusebio de Queirós Law on 5 September 1850 enabled the State to open the way towards eventual emancipation. The law was not the consequence of broad-based public consultation, nor did it serve to generate a widespread or immediate public debate over the future of slavery or the morality of

---

20   On the 1848 *Praieira* Revolt, see my 'Brazil's 1848: The *Praieira* Revolt in Pernambuco,' in Guy Thomson (ed.), *The European Revolutions of 1848 and the Americas* (London, 2002), pp. 100–24. Also, Barman, *The Forging of a Nation*, pp. 7, 170, 216f, 228–9, 232.

21   Leslie Bethell, *The Abolition of the Brazilian Slave Trade* (Cambridge, 1970); Jeffrey D. Needell, 'The Abolition of the Brazilian Slave Trade in 1850: Historiography, Slave Agency and Statesmanship,' *Journal of Latin American Studies*, vol. 33, no. 4 (2001), pp. 681–712. See Murilo de Carvalho's alternative view, *O teatro de sombras*, pp. 54–7 and 60.

slaveholding. The imposition of the State into the issue of slavery was largely effective although slave-owners and slave traders developed alternate inter-provincial slave-supply routes that transported slaves from regions of abundant free labour to the dynamic sugar and coffee-producing areas of the south-east. In the same year, the State also regulated land ownership through the passage of a land law. The 1850 law provided public lands for foreign colonisation projects but also made transfers of public land to private hands conditional upon purchase. Land was not only transformed into a marketable commodity, but infringed on the liberal right of citizens to own property and, in so doing, frustrated potential access of ex-slaves to ownership of small property.

Antislavery

In contrast to the United States where slavery's opponents organised support beyond the borders of the slave states, the two 1850s laws established the bases for the anti-slavery movements and debates that unfolded within Brazilian slave society.[22] Official positions towards slavery ranged at first from benevolent neglect to cautious and vague proposals, acted upon or not, regarding the treatment of slaves. The communiqué from the minister of justice to the president of the province of Rio de Janeiro is, at best illustrative. Urging judges to consider degrees of whipping relative to the age and strength of the slave delinquent, the communiqué fell short of defining precise guidelines or taking a moral stand on the institution. Its significance lay in the underlying expression of concern over arbitrary slave punishment. In May 1862 a hint of concern over the morality of the institution was signalled when Senator José Ignacio Silveira de Mota introduced a project to prohibit the separation of slave families. Seven years elapsed until congress endorsed the prohibition of public slave auctions, the separation of married slave couples and the separation of slave parents from their infants. The delay in the passage into law suggested that the moral responsibility of mothers to their families and their children, a moral ideal that was fashionable in England and the United States, had little resonance for slave families in Brazil.

Brazil's involvement in the War of the Triple Alliance (Paraguayan War, 1865–70) also played a part in the evolving process of transition. On the one hand, a government decree of November 1866 freed the 'slaves of the nation' who were designated for military service and offered compensation to citizens who freed slaves to serve in the army.[23] On the other hand, con-

---

22 The definition of anti-slavery, 'a generalised posture of opposition to slavery that did not look forward and fight for abolition' is taken from Marinho de Azevedo, *Abolitionism in the United States and Brazil.*, p. xxiv.

23 Murilo de Carvalho, *O teatro de sombras*, p. 63.

sional debates over the morality of slavery awaited the outcome of the
In May 1865 Acaiaba Antonio Pimenta Bueno proposed an agenda
he gradual emancipation of slaves to begin in January of the follow-
year. Only on 29 September 1871 did the so-named Rio Branco Law,
ularly known as the Law of the Free Womb, legislate the freedom of
newborns, conditional upon service until the age of eight with remu-
tion from the State to the master. The law gave slave masters the alter-
ve option of holding a slave child as an apprentice until the age of 21,
n freedom would be granted. Lacking any provision for retroactive
lementation, the law left more than a million children in an unchanged
dition of bondage, leading to criticisms of the law for failing to pro-
for the emancipation of the country's existing slave population. The
created a register of all slaves and an emancipation fund in addition to
authorising slaves to purchase their freedom through agreed-upon prices
and terms of payment with their masters under a personal liberation fund
(*pecúlio*) or through negotiations with a third party, usually a local magis-
trate. Conditional on the master's consent, the law also legitimised the
donation of gifts and the provision of legacies to slaves and also recognised the validity of a slave's personal thrift.

The state sponsorship of the gradual transition envisioned by the 1871
Rio Branco Law was similar to the Moret Law of 1870 in Cuba. The Moret
Law provided for, among other rights, some freedom to elderly and young
slaves who were born to slave mothers after 1868. Masters were expected
to provide for them and expected them to work in return. Slaves who were
coartados — slaves who made a downpayment of an agreed price (that
could not fluctuate) for their freedom — could not henceforth be sold
without their consent. From 1880 to 1886 the Cuban *Patronato* made further basic provisions for education for all *patrocinados*, and established a
monthly wage to further the transition from slave to citizen. An equivalent
Brazilian set of provisions was not forthcoming.

In his May 1867 speech from the throne Emperor Pedro II addressed
French emancipationist appeals, stating that: 'the freedom of slaves, a consequence of the abolition of the transatlantic trade, is only a matter of
form and of opportunity' that would be given primary attention at the
conclusion of the Paraguayan War.[24] Rio de Janeiro's influential daily newspaper, *Jornal do Comercio*, regularly reported on the state-directed empower-
ment of black citizens through the suffrage and the right to dispute pub-

---

24 'A emancipação dos escravos, consequência da abolição do tráfico, não é senão uma
    questão de forma e de oportunidade. Quando as circunstâncias penosas em que se
    encontra o país permitirem, o governo brasileiro considerará objeto da primeira
    importância a realização daquilo que o espírito do Cristianismo há muito reclama do
    mundo civilizado.' Cited in Lilia Moritz Schwarcz, *As barbas do imperador* (São Paulo,
    1998), p. 315. See also Murilo de Carvalho, *O teatro de sombras*, pp. 61 and 64.

lic office that the 13th, 14th and 15th amendments granted in the aftermath of the War of Secession. From the British Caribbean came additional reminders of post-emancipation limitations that colonial governments placed officially and informally upon former slaves as they sought full entitlement to citizenship in the British Caribbean. The emperor and his government needed no reminder of the heavy price that would be exacted if the country's unity were compromised by pro and anti-slave campaigns.

Abolitionism and Abolitionists

The pace of Brazil's trajectory to emancipation quickened in the 1870s after the emperor's tardy acknowledgment that slavery was a problem in need of a solution, in partial acquiescence of the growing indignation among the public over the arbitrary nature of 'plantation justice' and the stigma that slavery presented to the modernisation of the market. Six thousand Brazilian 'slaves of the nation', slaves of religious orders and privately owned slaves were following their service to the country during the War of the Triple Alliance. Some, like Dom Obá II d'Africa, the leader of a black battalion from the north-east of Brazil pressed the State for the lifetime pension that was bestowed on free servicemen in recognition of their duty to the *patria*.[25]

The political pendulum was shifting from antislavery towards abolitionism, a 'system of thought which had as its central focus the critique of slavery and which stressed the need to end slavery, whether gradually or immediately'.[26] For Robert E. Conrad, the new phase in the transition from slave to free labour was inaugurated when '[It] became clear that most children "freed" by the [1871] law remained *de facto* slaves, one of the law's key creations, the emancipation fund, was freeing few persons, and that otherwise the plan to end slavery gradually was not achieving great results'.[27]

Prominent statesmen, public speakers, free, freed and slave thinkers and doers also pressed the country's mood towards abolition. Congressman Joaquim Nabuco was a member of the white elite, born in Recife, Pernambuco in 1849 to sugar planter society and attended by slaves from early childhood. He must certainly have witnessed the arbitrary cruelty of 'plantation justice', the unbending rigidity of the hierarchical social structure and the high prices that slaves often paid for their freedom. Elected to the Chamber of Deputies in 1878, Nabuco became an official spokesman for slaves who 'lacked consciousness of their civic status or

25 Eduardo Silva, *Prince of the People. The Life and Times of a Brazilian Free Man of Colour* (New York, 1993), Appendix A, pp. 162–3.
26 Marinho de Azevedo, *Abolitionism*, p. xxiv.
27 Robert E. Conrad, *Children of God's Fire. A Documentary History of Black Slavery in Brazil* (Princeton, 1983), p. 302.

were unable to protest because of their lack of it'.[28] He valorised the African races for 'giving us a race' and for 'constructing the country' but his paternalism fell short of the promotion of equal rights for all citizens or the need for structural changes.[29] He advocated abolition on the basis of human dignity and the universal rights of man but was less willing to endorse a link between abolitionism and the advancing republican movement. Nabuco, like his predecessor, José Bonifacio, proposed the abolition of slavery to deter the potentially divisive impact that slavery held over the country's wellbeing. Whereas Bonifacio had projected the attainment of this ideal through stages that included the abolition of the slave trade and the incorporation of slaves and indigenous peoples into society, Nabuco viewed the institution of slavery itself as the principle deterrent to national unity: '"holding that race" in bondage diminished the meaning of citizenship for every Brazilian'.[30]

Nabuco held the imperial State accountable for the abolition of slavery. As Republican advocates challenged the powerful interventionist and centralised monarchy, Nabuco defended the monarchy as the central authority with the power to end slavery. Yet, just a decade after the 1871 Rio Branco Law was passed he admonished the State for failing to protect slaves from exceptional laws that left them open to personal and family abuses by masters under a harsh labour regime that offered no safeguards. Nabuco blamed the 'blind eye' concessions that the central government gave to slave-owners and the arbitrary nature of 'plantation justice': 'We, a humane and civilised nation, condemn more than a million persons, as so many others were condemned before them, to a condition alongside which imprisonment or the gallows seems better!'[31]

Nabuco directed his campaign to the official chambers of power but was also financed and endorsed by elite patrons to engage with other abolitionists in debates over abolitionism at the Sociedade Brasileira contra a Escravidão, founded in Rio de Janeiro in 1879, at secret abolitionist societies and clubs, and in *O Abolicionista* and other newspapers.

---

28 Lilia K. Moritz Schwarcz, 'Com Estado mas sem nação: a construção de um modelo imperial brasileiro de fazer política,' Paper presented to Oxford Brazil Centre, Oxford University, March 1999.

29 Nabuco, *O abolicionismo*, p. 21. 'Em primeiro lugar, a parte da população que descende de escravos é pelo menos tão numerosa como a parte que descende exclusivamente de senhores; isso quer dizer que a raça negra nos deu um povo. Em segundo lugar, o que existe até hoje sobre o vasto territorio que se chama Brazil foi levantado ou cultivado por aquella raça; isso quer dizer que foi ella que construiu o nosso paiz.'

30 Nabuco, *O abolicionismo*, p. 20. 'aceitámos esse mandato como homens políticos, por motivos políticos, e assim representamos os escravos e os *ingennos* na qualidade de Brazileiros que julgam o seu titulo de cidadão diminuido emquanto houver Brazileiros escravos, isto é, no interesse de todo o paiz e no nosso proprio interesse'.

31 Cited in Conrad, *Children of God's Fire*, p. 456.

Prominent non-white abolitionists who engaged the public through their appeals in newspapers, and their addresses to secret societies and public meetings, were the freedmen José do Patrocínio and Luiz Gama, and the engineer and businessman, André Rebouças, the son of Antonio Pereira Rebouças.[32] As a result of his detailed analyses of land, labour and agricultural production in Brazil, published in 1883, André Rebouças was uniquely positioned to project reforms beyond the act of emancipation of slaves. His proposals encouraged individual initiative: landowners would incorporate ex-slaves, landless farmers and immigrants into rural society through rental or sale of 50 acre plots of land that would include pastures and forests to allow for the production and rotation of export crops. Harvested crops would be sold to the former landowner for milling.[33] Writing in the newspaper, *Gazeta da Tarde* in December 1880, Rebouças linked emancipation with the subdivision and sale of privately owned large landholdings.[34]

Rebouças and the abolitionist, Henrique de Beaurepaire Rohan, also linked the welfare of post-emancipation agrarian society to the provision of a resident and permanent local labour force.[35] Beaurepaire Rohan formulated his ideas in response to planters who began to consider possible alternatives to slave labour at the 1878 Agricultural Congress in Rio de Janeiro. Beaurepaire Rohan's proposals fell short of promoting the division and sale of large properties for the development of long-term agricultural foodstuffs-producing units. Instead, he proposed the simple conversion of large estates into agricultural colonies (*colônias agrícolas*). Under his plan, planters would settle former slaves and their families as *colonos* in a tenant farmer arrangement under which they would pay an annual quitrent and a fee to the landowner for processing crops in a central processing unit. Beaurepaire Rohan also considered perpetuating a rural labour force. The children of slaves who were legally free at birth under the 1871 Rio Branco Law would receive a primary-level education aimed at turning them into 'natural small-scale farmers' (*lavradroes naturais da pequena propriedade*).[36] Underlying Beaurepaire Rohan's aim to hold the adult slave population on the lands of their owners were two further objectives: to instil a work ethic into the children of slaves through 'the transforma-

---

32 See Graham, 'Free African Brazilians,' pp. 44–5, for details on other prominent African-Brazilian politicians, Francisco Salles Torres Homem and Francisco Otaviano de Almeida Rosa.

33 André Rebouças, *Agricultura nacional*, pp. 1–7, 111–12, 327–32 cited in Conrad *The Destruction of Brazilian Slavery* (Berkeley, 1975), p. 160.

34 *Ibid.*, p. 161 for his articles of 3, 4, 7, 8, 9, 10 and 11 December 1880.

35 Henrique de Beaurepaire Rohan, *O futuro da grande lavoura e da grande propriedade no Brasil: memória apresentada ao Ministério da Agricultura, Commércio e Obras Públicas* (Rio de Janeiro, 1878). Rebouças, *Agricultura*.

36 Beurepaire Rohan, *O futuro*, p. 12.

tion of the indolent classes into useful workers', and 'the promotion of the industrial and agricultural education of our young countrymen'.[37] As was already noted, such proposals aimed at optimal use of the labour force rather than the economic, technical, political, cultural or social incorporation of slaves and ex-slaves into society.

Two abolitionists who shared childhood experiences as slaves aimed their campaigns exclusively at emancipation. Luiz Gonzaga Pinto da Gama (1830–82) and José Carlos do Patrocínio were raised under the inequalities of slave-master relations. São Paulo's most prominent abolitionist spokesman, Luiz Gama, was born to a free African, Luiza Mahin, and a nobleman of Portuguese descent who sold him into slavery to pay off creditors. Gama was taken to Rio de Janeiro and then to São Paulo where he fled from his owner after learning to read and write. After successfully defending his claims to freedom he served in the *Força Pública* of São Paulo until his dismissal in 1869 and from there was employed as a civil servant. His public addresses, newspaper articles and collaboration with supportive masonic and/or republican backers, engaged public interest in abolitionism. The São Paulo *Correio Paulistano* reported Luiz Gama's robust courtroom defences of slaves in which he highlighted errors of misinterpretation on the part of acting judges and denounced police and local authorities for defiance of the law.[38]

Gama's participation in the organisation of the São Paulo Republican Party in 1872 did not deter him from his lifelong pursuit of the abolition of slavery, a fact that was publicly acknowledged at his premature death in 1882. His great personal anguish over white peoples' intolerance towards blacks emerges in his poetry as a reminder to historians of the racial dimension of attitudes towards slavery. For Gama, whom social mobility eluded, 'a black man faced insurmountable obstacles to recognition as a man of letters in Brazil's white society'.[39]

José Carlos do Patrocínio was born to Justina Maria do Espírito Santo, a slave of his Portuguese father, a Catholic priest-planter named João Carlos Monteiro, who never recognised Patrocínio as his son. José do Patrocínio spent his first 15 years in the rural Rio de Janeiro sugar-producing region of Campos before moving to the imperial court of Rio de Janeiro, where he trained as a pharmacist. Patrocínio gained notoriety from his first novel, a denunciation of a hanging of a white planter who was convicted and sentenced on the basis of incriminating testimony by his slaves.[40] The social

37 *Ibid.*, pp. 19–20.
38 Elciene Azevedo, *Orfeu de Carapinha. A trajetória de Luiz Gama na imperial cidade de São Paulo* (Campinas, 1999), pp. 245–64. Also, Graham, 'Free African Brazilians,' pp. 46–7.
39 Azevedo, *Orfeu*, p. 54.
40 On Patrocínio and the hanging, see my 'Fact, Fantasy, or Folklore? A novel case of retribution in nineteenth century Brazil,' *Luso-Brazilian Review*, vol. 43 no. 4 (1987), pp. 59–80.

dilemma facing drought-afflicted rural inhabitants in the north-east was the theme of his second novel whose publication coincided with his acceptance of an editorship of the abolitionist newspaper *Gazeta de Notícias* in 1877. Three years later, in collaboration with João Clapp, André Rebouças, Joaquim Nabuco and others, he founded the Brazilian Anti-Slavery Society (Sociedade Brasileira contra a Escravidão), and addressed abolitionist conferences in theatres, at banquets, at auctions and during political street rallies. Patrocínio, known more popularly as Zeca or Zé do Pato was also a regular contributor and featured columnist in 1881 in the abolitionist, Ferreira de Meneses's, *Gazeta da Tarde*, and a year after his election as a councilman *(vereador)* in 1886 he purchased the newspaper *Cidade do Rio*.

The approaching climax of the abolitionist campaign was given additional impetus and prominence by the public manifestations that accompanied the funeral of Luiz Gama in 1882. Yet three more years passed before the passage of the 28 September 1885 Saraiva Cotegipe Law that established a new emancipation fund and a new registry of slaves, while stipulating freedom to slaves over 60 years of age conditional upon an additional five years of service.[41] A year later, a law prohibited the whipping of slaves in punishment for crimes. The removal of this important deterrent to slave resistance proved to be a prime catalyst to slaves in São Paulo and Rio de Janeiro whose flight during the following two years destabilised the plantation complex and threatened to engage the country in civil strife.[42]

For Patrocínio the tensions between pro-slavery advocates and abolitionists, as well as the complicity of the monarchy and the conservative government fanned the spread of violence in the country. He warned: 'it is said that he (Dom Pedro II) calmed the country yet abolitionist propaganda was never so violent, the interests of slaveowners never so threatened; and for this reason, the government's only solution is the path to violence and this also leads to revolt, and what a revolt! That of those who have been raised beyond freedom's grasp.'[43]

In the face of massive civil disorder, Patrocínio reversed his position and on 19 March 1888 he urged Brazilians to unite in support of the sovereign's position in favour of emancipation: 'The idea of liberty from slavery is too powerful to be ensconced in the narrow moulds of the current Brazilian political parties, mere oligarchic conglomerations, organised to substitute the exploitation of the slave with the exploitation of the State.

---

41 Conrad, *The Destruction*, pp. 233–35.
42 *Ibid.*, pp. 238–41.
43 *Gazeta da Tarde*, 21 August 1886, cited in Conrad, *The Destruction*, p. 156. 'Dizem que le tranquilizou o país, porém nunca a propaganda abolicionista foi tão violenta, nunca os interesses dos proprietários de escravos estiveram tão ameaçados, por iso que só resta ao governo o caminho da violência e este é também o caminho da revolta, e que revolta! A das classes educadas fora da liberdade.'

It is necessary to look to a broader horizon. The extinction of slavery is a national idea [that] belongs to the Brazilian people, and every statesman is competent to bring that about.'[44]

Patrocínio's abolitionist objectives advanced after the passage of the 1871 Rio Branco Law. As the abolitionist movement radiated from urban centres into the hinterland, slaves actively engaged in the process of emancipation.

José do Patrocínio, Litografía de Antônio Pereira Neto, *Revista Illustrada*, no. 516 (1888).

44   Conrad, *The Destruction*, article of 19 March 1888, p. 207. 'A idea da libertação da escravatura é grande demais para se enquadrar nos estreitos moldes dos partidos atuais do Brasil, meros ajuntamentos oligárquicos, organizados para explorar o Estado em substituição da exploração do negro. É preciso ver mais longe e em horizonte mais largo. A extinção da escravidão é uma idéia nacional, pertence ao povo brasileiro, e todo estadista tem competência para realizá-la.'

Slave Actors: Slave Political Agency

The 1871 Rio Branco Law marked a watershed in the transition to free labour and engaged slaves of all ages, individually and collectively, willingly or unwillingly, in the emancipation process.[45] Portuguese-speaking Brazilian-born slaves and ex-slaves, including the children who were born to slave mothers after 1871, formed what has been termed a 'black wave' (*onda negra*).[46] According to Emília Viotti da Costa, 'in the coffee-growing regions Blacks moved from the level of cultural resistance to that of political resistance, from adherence to African religions to collaboration with the abolitionists.' Informal contacts of slaves with *caifazes*, as well as with ex-slaves and abolitionist traders, technicians and other sympathisers made many privy to abolitionist ideals and facilitated collaboration with secret protection and slave escape routes (a Brazilian variant of the North American 'underground railroad').[47] In 1873 slaves on an estate in the Rio de Janeiro provincial town of Sumidouro astounded the heirs to the property who had assured them that their customary rights to provision grounds and other arrangements with their former master would be respected. The slaves insisted that under the provisions of the 1871 Law, they were free and refused to serve the new owners.[48]

Solidarity among slaves took many forms. Kim Butler has addressed cultural ties during slavery that prevailed in post-slavery north-eastern Bahian brotherhoods, Afro-Brazilian religious centres (*terreiros*), practices such as *capoeira*, diet and extensive, often informal, family ties.[49] In the south-east, mainly in São Paulo, intellectual mobilisation through newspaper articles, public meetings and political associations carried on forms of mobilisation that, during slavery, were promoted by prominent Black thinkers and doers, like Luiz Gama, José do Patrocínio and André Rebouças.[50]

Less known, but recently emergent from court cases in Brazilian archives, are court cases involving slaves who engaged the public sphere in defence of their perceived customary rights, including emancipation. Joaquim Nabuco claimed that justice did not penetrate the feudal domain of the private sphere of the slaveowner and thought it useless for a slave to complain to

45   On slave agency, Emília Viotti da Costa, *Brazil. Myths and Histories* (Chicago, 1996), p. 302.

46   See Celia Marinho de Azevedo, *Onda negra, medo branco. O negro no imaginário das elites* (Rio de Janeiro, 1987); Flávio dos Santos Gomes, *Histórias de quilombolas: mocambos e comunidades de senzalas no Rio de Janeiro — século XIX* (Rio de Janeiro, 1993), p. 333.

47   *Caifazes* were activist followers of the revolutionary abolitionist, Antonio Bento, who succeeded Luiz Gama in the São Paulo abolitionist movement. The term is suggestive of a mystical association with Caiaphas, the high priest who delivered Jesus to Pontius Pilate. Conrad, *The Destruction*, p. 242.

48   Dos Santos Gomes, *Histórias de quilombolas*, pp. 349–50.

49   Kim Butler, *Freedoms Given, Freedoms Won* (Rutgers, 1999), chs. 4 and 6.

50   *Ibid.*

authorities. Many of the court cases and appeals that I examined from the *municípios* (towns and their surrounding areas) of Vassouras and Rio Bonito in the province of Rio de Janeiro concerned slave defendants who disputed slave ownership, use of slaves as collateral for loans and excessive cruelty to slaves by a slaveowner.[51] In the 1870s, in tandem with intensifying public and court attention to claims of arbitrary slave treatment, slaves whose most common form of resistance was escape confessed to acts of violence against masters, overseers and others. Removed from the private sphere of the master after confession and arrest by local authorities, they were confined to public jails to await trial.[52] Public defenders (*curadores*) were assigned to represent slave defendants, appeal local cases with unfavourable outcomes for slaves, engage in manumission procedures with owners, family members, other slaves and creditors who denied or imposed conditions on slaves who perceived themselves to be legally free.[53]

The cause of freedom for all slaves was spearheaded by the abolition of chattel slavery in the northern province of Amazonas and the north-eastern province of Ceará in 1884 and 1885, respectively. Yet, even in the face of victory for the abolitionist cause, there remained unresolved and unaddressed conflicts and grievances between masters and slaves. Two appeals cases to the Tribunal de Relação and the Corte de Apelação, the ultimate courts of appeal, document the limitations and sensitivities of the courts to the complexities and disappointments involved in slave-related issues. In 1882 the court-appointed public defender argued the case of four slaves: the *parda* (woman of colour) slave Rita and her two daughters and the *preta* (black) slave Mariana. Six years before, their owner had authorised and signed before two witnesses two letters that granted freedom to the two adult slave women. The public defender argued that the document represented a grant of freedom that, once agreed, could not be rescinded. The defendant challenged the claim, on the basis that the act was invalid since the letters had not been given to the plaintiffs. The judge who heard the case at the local level recognised the plaintiffs' claim to their freedom,

---

51   I have dealt in detail with cases involving slaves in *A Slave's Place, A Master's World. Fashioning Dependency in Rural Brazil* (London, 2000); also my 'Revision and Persistence: Recent Historiography on the Transition from Slave to Free Labour in Rural Brazil,' *Slavery and Abolition*, vol. 13, no. 2 (1992). Also, Sidney Chalhoub, *Visões de liberdade: uma história das últimas décadas da escravidão na corte* (São Paulo, 1990); Hebe Maria Mattos de Castro. *Das cores do silêncio: os significados da liberdade no sudeste escravista, Brasil, século XIX* (Rio de Janeiro, 1998); Robert W. Slenes, 'Senhores e subalternos no oeste paulista,' in A. Novais (ed.), *História da vida privada no Brasil* (São Paulo, 1998).

52   Azevedo, *Onda negra, medo branco;* Naro, *A Slave's Place*, ch. 5.

53   Richard Graham states that in the city of Rio de Janeiro between 1807 and 1831 two-thirds of the freed persons were women even among Africans where African-born men outnumbered women almost two to one. 'Free African Brazilians and the State in Slavery Times,' in Michael Hanchard (ed.), *Racial Politics in Contemporary Brazil* (Durham, NC, 1999), p. 32.

but ruled that freedom was conditional upon service to the defendant for the remainder of his life. The appeals court overturned this decision and ruled that the intention to grant freedom did not prove that there was, in fact, an effective grant of freedom. Some years later Rita and her daughters won their freedom but Mariana remained in service to her master.[54]

A different case illustrates one of many fine points of jurisprudence that the courts left unresolved. In 1869 the mistress of the slave Eloy willed him to the executor of her estate, providing that the latter met all of the provisions of her will within a year of her death. The executor initiated his duties in 1879 but took eight years to finalise the terms of the will. Eloy's court-appointed solicitor argued that the length of time made him ineligible to claim Eloy. Had the court ruled favourably Eloy would have passed to the State as public property, but in 1882 this was no longer legal. The appeals court refused to hear the claim.[55]

On 13 May 1888 the end of chattel slavery was decreed in the Golden Law (Lei Aurea) that Princess Isabel signed with immediate effect in a succinct text that José do Patrocínio had dictated years before. Approximately 700,000 slaves celebrated their transition from non-citizen to citizen and little else since the State had provided few tangible social and political benefits or civil protections under an effective rule of law to incorporate them into the republic that replaced the monarchy on 15 November 1889. The State did not indemnify slaveholders, but neither did it implement structural reforms of land ownership, alter the unequal social relations of the plantation complex, offer guarantees of civil rights or modify the rigid vertical social hierarchy, headed by planter class elites. Ex-slaves and, in broader terms, the poor non-white population and foreign immigrants were available to the free labour market but, as was the case in the post Civil War United States South, legal provisions and safeguards for education, technical training or a guaranteed salary (that the Cuban Patrocinato provided) were not officially forthcoming.[56]

54 Rio de Janeiro. Arquivo Nacional. Corte de Apelação, 1882. Juizo Municipal de Rio Bonito.
55 Arquivo Nacional. Corte de Apelação. Réu: Américo Brasileiro da Costa Moreira. Autor: o escravo Eloy, por seu procurador. No. 4226, Cx: m1745, Galeria C. Under the provisions of Decree 834 of 2 October 1851, the national treasury would receive unclaimable property from wills and testaments.
56 Barbara J. Fields argues that the Reconstruction amendments eliminated competing bases of sovereignty (such as master and slave) and established formal equality under the federal constitution for all citizens. However, she points out that it did not eliminate the inequality of human beings from the standpoint of social power. Supremacy and the social construction of race as an ideology to perpetuate inequality and limit the fulfillment of civil, political and social citizenship emerged in the United States in the post-emancipation years as did regional restrictions on physical mobility for ex-slaves. Barbara J. Fields, 'Ideology and Race in American History,' in James M. McPherson and J. Morgan Kousser (eds.), *Region, Race, and Reconstruction: Essays in Honor of C. Vann Woodward* (New Haven, 1982), p.163.

Legal impediments to physical mobility were absent in Brazil but in their place informal interpersonal ties operated as effective mechanisms to control labour movement and to maintain social exclusion. I would argue that the end of the monarchy did not prevent the passage of vagrancy clauses and exclusionist migration laws that complemented the previous exclusionist measures in the Land Law of 1850 and the literacy requirement to vote that was mandated by the Saraiva Law of 1881.[57] Such obstacles to poor peoples' full enjoyment of citizenship confirm a trajectory of consensus among political elites at the level of the State to 'regulate citizenship' through the creation of a 'desired type of citizen'.[58] For Celia Azevedo, 'at the root of Brazilian abolitionism one perceives an increasing desire for social balance which [would] be possible as long as the upper class [devised] appropriate rational policies for incorporating the lower classes into a hierarchical society, where each recognise[d] his place and [felt] himself part of a whole'.[59]

Otherness: Dealing with Difference in Comparative Perspective

Brazil's trajectory to abolition was different from the United States although the State played a defining role in both processes.[60] Brazil was not engulfed by regional divisions, civil war, the loss of 600,000 lives or military occupation of a vanquished region, as was the case of the United States. Rather, the perceptions of slaves as others cast a different tone to the exclusion process. Celia Azevedo argues that Brazilian slaves were viewed as domestic enemies, capable of destroying the moral integrity of family and household, evil and superstitious beings that were prone to communication with spirits and were perceived to be violent and rebel-

---

57   Murilo de Carvalho, *O teatro de sombras*, p. 160. The 1881 law eliminated elections in two rounds but prohibited votes by illiterates, made voting voluntary, introduced stringent measures to verify the income requirement and practically exluded wage earners who were not civil servants from the right to vote.

58   From its inception in 1854, the mid-century Land Law did not recognise claims to land ownership on the basis of the temporary shelters (*ranchos*) and sparsely cultivated short-term holdings that were common to squatters and slaves. The law's stipulation that public lands would henceforth pass to private ownership by means of purchase drastically compromised the ability of ex-slaves to own land. Under the 1881 Saraiva Law, literacy became a requirement for voting in place of former criteria of a stipulated income and property ownership. 'Regulated citizenship' is a term employed by Wanderley Guilherme dos Santos with reference to the Vargas era, and more latterly used by José Murilo de Carvalho, *El desenvolvimiento de la ciudadanía en el Brasil.* (Mexico, 1999).

59   Azevedo, *Abolitionism*, p. 14.

60   In contrast to Howard Winant, I argue that the Brazilian State played an active role in defining and carrying out the transition process. 'Racial Democracy and Racial Identity. Comparing the United States and Brazil,' in Michael Hanchard (ed.) *Racial Politics in Contemporary Brazil* (Durham, NC, 1999), p. 98.

lious.[61] Richard Graham implicates the State in 'preserving and building prejudice toward free African Brazilians'.[62]

The abolitionist movement in Brazil was secular. The Catholic Church condoned slavery, the Bible played no major role in Catholicism or in the politicisation of Brazilian blacks. Azevedo claims that American abolitionists politicised the concept of 'brother' in their regard for American blacks as human beings and brothers of one national family (despite the segregation of churches on the basis of race).[63] But an alternative interpretation suggests that American abolitionists saw themselves as active benefactors who were motivated in befriending slaves by self-aggrandising strategies that required passive victims.[64]

Brazilian perceptions of race and class also differed from the United States in the post-emancipation experience. In the United States, abolitionists targeted prejudice in the white majority and urged both the abolition of slavery and of racism in a society where population classifications based on race were bi-polar and linked to descendancy rule or heritage that aimed at segregation or exclusion. Racial classification in Brazil, on the other hand, was based on a continuum in which judgement was subjective and labels were based on a combination of phenotype — colour prejudice and social standing (label prejudice) that was assimilationist. Carlos Hasenbalg stresses the official non-discrimination position in Brazil that favoured a multi-racial democracy and the integration of blacks and mulattoes in the national culture and economy. Class was viewed as a definer of social mobility and preserved clearly defined class hierarchies that limited economic opportunities with more or less the same results, minus the glaring racial antagonisms that were witnessed in openly racist societies.[65] In other words, in contrast to the United States, the Brazilian State kept race relations out of the political arena, aided by successive censuses that, between 1890 and 1940, were devoid of the categories of colour, race or ethnicity.[66]

---

61 Azevedo, *Abolitionism*, p. xxiv.
62 Graham, 'Free African Brazilians, pp. 30–1.
63 Azevedo, *Abolitionism*, pp. xi, 65.
64 Cynthia Hamilton 'The Heroic Slave: Models of Agency,' paper presented at the International Centre for the History of Slavery Conference, University of Nottingham, 12 September 2000.
65 Carlos Hasenbalg, *Discriminação e desigualdades raciais no Brasil* (Rio de Janeiro, 1979), pp. 18–19.
66 Brazil's first official census of 1872 listed categories: white (*branco*), black (*preto*), brown (*pardo*) and mixed-indigenous (*caboclo*). In the 1940 census similar categories were listed under 'colour'. Only in 1950, in the PNAD studies and in the 1980 census was colour re-introduced resulting in more than 190 different self-definitions. See Jan Fiola, 'Race Relations in Brazil: A Reassessment of the "Racial Democracy" Thesis,' Occasional Papers no. 24, University of Massachusetts (Amherst, 1990), p. 19.

Identifying the National

Independent Brazil premised its blueprint of state formation on liberal, albeit truncated, principles. For Ada Ferrer a discourse of racial miscegenation valorised 'the physical, and the cultural, premised on the agency of the European and the passivity of the other', in Brazil. Yet, she adds, 'there remained a glaring disparity between the realisation of national unity and the concepts of national identity'.[67] As support for emancipation heightened political expectations of the emancipation decree that was signed on 13 May 1888, discontent with the institution of monarchy united advocates of a republic among sectors of the military, the Catholic Church and progressive planters.[68] Republicans held both slavery and the centralised and interventionist monarchy to be anachronistic to the advances of modernisation. Yet it had taken a strong and determined monarchical state to address and to bring to completion the transition to a free labour market. For Seymour Drescher the monarchy brought about its own demise with little provision for the consequences: 'without compensation for the slaveholders, welfare for the slaves and no planned transition to a new order.'[69]

José Murilo de Carvalho has observed that national identity in post-emancipation Brazil was forged on the basis of an 'inversion'.[70] During the twentieth century the realisation of political rights (participation in the exercise of power) and social rights (guarantees of the minimum levels of wellbeing and material security in accord with prevalent social standards) has taken precedence over civil rights (those basic civil protections that are necessary to assure individual liberty, such as the right of free movement, religious freedom, freedom of press, right to own property, right to justice) as identifiers of a national citizenship.[71] Whereas in post-emancipation Cuba, *cubanidad* signalled a revolutionary rhetoric of antiracism and a national identity based on the racial and social equality of all citizens during and after Cuba's independence struggles, an equivalent Brazilian term, *brasilidade*, still awaits legitimacy through a broad-based consensus over equal rights and the enjoyment of full citizenship by all citizens.

---

67   Ada Ferrer, *Insurgent Cuba. Race, Nation, and Revolution, 1868–1890* (Chapel Hill, 1999), p. 4.

68   On the fall of the monarchy, see Emilia Viotti da Costa, *The Brazilian Empire. Myths and Histories* (Chicago, 1985), ch. 9.

69   Seymour Drescher, 'Brazilian Abolition in Comparative Perspective,' *Hispanic American Historical Review*, vol. 68, no. 3 (1988), p. 459.

70   See Murilo de Carvalho, *El desenvolvimiento*, 3rd part, ch. X and Conclusion, pp. 146–68. For an updated and revised version in Portuguese of this text, see Murilo de Carvalho, *Cidadania no Brasil. O longo caminho* (Rio de Janeiro, 2001), pp. 219–20.

71   T.H. Marshall's forms of citizenship are summarised in Nancy P. Naro, *A formação dos Estados Unidos* (São Paulo, 1987), pp. 7 and 14. See also Silva, *Prince of the People.*, p. 118; Murilo de Carvalho, *Cidadania*, pp. 10–11.

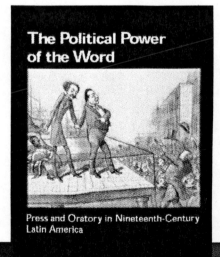

Printed in the United Kingdom
by Lightning Source UK Ltd.
93423